# The New Environmental Economics

For Sylvie, for Lila, for Jonas, with everlasting love

# The New Environmental Economics

## Sustainability and Justice

Éloi Laurent

polity

The right of Éloi Laurent to be identified as Author of this Work has been asserted in accordance with the UK Copyright, Designs and Patents Act 1988

First published in 2020 by Polity Press

Polity Press
65 Bridge Street
Cambridge CB2 1UR, UK

Polity Press
101 Station Landing
Suite 300
Medford, MA 02155, USA

ISBN-13: 978-1-5095-3380-0 (hardback)
ISBN-13: 978-1-5095-3381-7 (paperback)

A catalogue record for this book is available from the British Library

Library of Congress Cataloging-in-Publication Data
Names: Laurent, Eloi, author.
Title: The new environmental economics : sustainability and justice / Eloi
   Laurent.
Description: Cambridge, UK ; Medford, MA : Polity Press, 2019. | Includes
   bibliographical references and index.
Identifiers: LCCN 2019017448 (print) | LCCN 2019021750 (ebook) | ISBN
   9781509533831 (Epub) | ISBN 9781509533800 (hardback) | ISBN 9781509533817
   (pbk.)
Subjects: LCSH: Environmental economics. | Sustainable development.
Classification: LCC HD75.6 (ebook) | LCC HD75.6 .L3785 2019 (print) | DDC
   333.7–dc23
LC record available at https://lccn.loc.gov/2019017448

Typeset in 10.5 on 13pt Swift Neue
by Fakenham Prepress Solutions, Fakenham, Norfolk, NR21 8NL
Printed and bound in Great Britain by CPI Group (UK) Ltd, Croydon

# Contents

# Figures

## Figures

## Tables

# Introduction: Economics for the twenty-first century

Are we thriving or are we doomed? That is the question. In our early twenty-first century, two radically different views regarding the fate of humanity on Planet Earth co-exist.

The first one insists on the remarkable prowess of humankind: Once fearful creatures deprived of almost any significant natural advantages in a hostile environment, we have managed in a matter of a few thousand years – and even more in the last two centuries – to become Kings of Nature, Masters of the Biosphere, Rulers of Life. Driven by the power of social cooperation, humanity's journey toward prosperity in all corners of the world is truly impressive.

What is more, our collective success has allowed us to change for the better our biological and social self: We have become taller, stronger, healthier, smarter, freer, and, most probably, happier. To take just one striking example of our exponential progress, in the last fifty years alone, human health has been improved more than in the seven million years or so of human presence on Earth. Seen from this perspective, the future of humanity calls for reasonable optimism, if not outright cheerfulness. With the right combination of innovation and incentives, no insurmountable obstacle will stand in the way of our ingenuity.

The other view is decidedly grimmer. It argues that humanity is, to put it mildly, deeply disappointing: In a matter of a century, even more so since 1950, we have managed to substantially destroy our own habitat, the most hospitable planet for us in the Universe, harming our own well-being and that of our successors for shortsighted gains. To take just one illustration of how fast we are degrading the biosphere, cumulative man-made carbon dioxide emissions causing climate change in the last fifty years alone represent 70% of all recorded emissions (since 1750). *Homo sapiens sapiens*, the one who knows he knows, appears to be losing the great race between his intelligence and his avidity.

Even more frustratingly, our planet's riches have been squandered for the benefit of a handful among us: Our societies have become increasingly unequal, fragmented, and polarized in the last thirty years; all the while environmental degradations have accelerated. The planet and life on it will survive our inconsequence, as they have in their billions-year long history, but our near future is gloomy and we are to blame for it. We are right to be afraid of tomorrow. How do we make sense of these two competing narratives? Is one simply wrong while the other is right? Can they be reconciled at all?

The first possible bridging of these two accounts argues that both have their share of the truth; what really separates them is their time horizon: What was an undeniable success is turning before our eyes into an irrefutable failure. Yes, we were able to evolve toward prosperity but we are now destroying its very foundations, and we have to understand why. What kind of social dynamics are becoming dysfunctional to the point of threatening not just our well-being but our very existence?

Another way of doing justice to both arguments is to consider space rather than time: As far as we know, no human community can live outside of the biosphere, so that our exceptional well-being is conditional on our environment. While we have been made to believe that our welfare depends on extra-terrestrial systems powered by self-sufficient innovation, we are actually approaching the finite limits of our "Goldilocks" planet. Humanity's well-being has become detrimental to its sustainability: Our social systems have become self-destructive, a reality our economic systems and metrics obscure. This is why we have to find practical ways to value our environment and turn the vicious social-ecological spiral we are caught in into a virtuous circle. And we have to find them fast. These are the questions this book attempts to explore.

This is not, in fact, a standard economics textbook. The main reason why is because standard economics has evolved in the last decades of the twentieth century toward a much too narrow approach of social cooperation and human development, fixated on abstract obsessions like efficiency and growth. This book, instead, wants to equip readers with the data, analyses, and policy tools to understand and eventually face the complex social and ecological challenges of the twenty-first century. The positioning of this book, and therefore its purpose, is thus not dictated by ideological inclination but by a concern for relevance.

Yet, this is indeed an environmental economics textbook, which starting point should be the definition of the kind of environmental economics readers can expect to find in it. To put it simply, environmental economics today finds itself caught between physics and ethics, between the inescapable realities of the natural world and the justice imperative of human societies.

Economics entertains a special relation with physics. From the early days of the founding fathers of modern economics, Adam Smith, David Ricardo, and the whole Scottish and English classical school, economics has been fascinated by the quantitative precision and universality of physics laws. We now know that Adam Smith has been influenced by Newton. This fascination was on full display when economics attempted to break free from philosophy and political science, posturing as a science at the turn of the twentieth century. Then, economics started to dream of becoming the physics of the social world.[1]

And yet, economics has all but forgotten physics, inventing a closed-circuit world where the sun apparently does not shine, infinite growth is useful and desirable and all that exists and matters on the planet are households, firms, and governments. In the beginning of the twenty-first century, economics is in a sense caught up by physics and again dwarfed by it: Climate change has the power to destroy every single economy around the planet, including the best-managed, efficiency-driven, and most-developed ones. Economics today, very much like in the eighteenth century, is still dominated by physics: There is no economy possible outside of the biosphere and its biophysical laws. The large natural household that Ernst Haeckel had in mind when he coined the term "ecology" imposes its laws on the small human household to which Aristotle and Xenophon referred when they invented the word "economics." It will never be the other way around, whatever power humans may acquire on Earth.

The other glaring blind spot in today's mainstream economic analyses, models, and metrics is ethics and, more precisely, the analysis of distributional issues and the consideration for justice principles. And yet Arthur Cecil Pigou (1920) made it clear that injustice is in fact economists calling when he wrote: "Wonder, Carlyle declared, is the beginning of philosophy. It is not wonder, but rather the social enthusiasm which revolts from the sordidness of mean streets and the joylessness of withered lives, that is the beginning of economic science." David Ricardo or John Stuart Mill thought that inequality was the key issue of economic analysis. But at the end of the nineteenth century, political economy centered on justice gave way to an efficiency focused would-be "economic science" largely blind to inequality and fairness.

While inequality economics is making a much-needed comeback, environmental economics must embrace this revolution toward reality. Environmental economics is still too focused on mainstreaming environmental crises for decision-makers using standard economics frameworks and toolboxes: models, equilibrium, markets, prices. Because it is an attempt to speak the language of power, it might seem like a commendable effort, but it should mostly be looked at critically: The environment is not an economic issue among others. The current destruction of the biosphere, its social causes and consequences, actually offers a chance to go back to the key question of economic analysis: justice.

Linking physics and ethics through environmental economics is precisely what is needed to understand our world, a world where inequality and ecological crises feed one another. Sustainability is intertwined with justice: Human communities depend on natural ecosystems, environmental issues are social matters, planetary boundaries are human frontiers. This is a new day for environmental economics.

We have indeed lived through three ages of economics of the environment. In the first age – *resource economics* (which started roughly in the mid nineteenth century) – the central question was the efficient management of scarce natural resources, some renewable, some non-renewable. In the second age, *externality economics* took center stage (from the 1920s onward), with scholars seeking practical ways to lower degradations of the biosphere from economic activity by changing consumption and production behaviors through well-designed policy. Our time, since the early 1980s, has seen the emergence of *sustainability economics* as a potential answer to a hugely complex and daunting issue: Can we prevent the biosphere from collapsing under the weight of human domination? Can we maintain human well-being on Earth and if so, how, for whom, for how long?

Although each age saw progress, economics of the environment, like other disciplines, has very much been a process of cumulative knowledge. There is still much to learn from Pigou or Ronald Coase in order to design relevant climate mitigation policy, although they were unaware of climate change and their analyses were embedded in a now much discredited standard neo-classical vision of the economy. This is why this textbook is scientifically pluralist and does not exclude any insightful stream of knowledge on ideological grounds. But the following pages are guided by two strong imperatives: It is unreasonable (and empirically wrong) to dissociate humans from Nature and the economy from the biosphere that contains it (economics without the environment makes little sense in the twenty-first century); it is unconvincing and ethically dubious to reduce environmental economics to a science of efficiency that leaves aside distributional analysis and justice policy. In short, a fourth age of environmental economics is upon us and this textbook wants to introduce readers to it.

To put it simply, this textbook is different from existing ones because it attempts to bring together the insights of environmental economics (resource economics, externality economics) and ecological economics (sustainability economics) under the imperative of justice. Political economy of the environment is the disciplinary category that best fits this ambition. The two major crises of the early twenty-first century, the inequality crisis and ecological crises, demand to be studied jointly to be fully understood and possibly mitigated.

This academic line of work resonates with recent texts grounded in native culture (the "Cochabamba Declaration"),[2] religious ethics (the encyclical *Laudato Si*) and political thinking ("the Green New Deal" in the US or the promotion in the European Union of "sustainable equality"). In *Laudato Si*, published in June 2015, under the auspices of St. Francis of Assisi (friend of the poor and author of the Canticle of Brother Sun and Sister Moon, declared patron of ecologists by Pope John Paul II in 1979), Pope Francis writes: "We are faced not with two separate crises, one environmental and the other social, but rather with one complex crisis which is both social and environmental." In the "Green

New Deal" bill of February 2019,[3] US Democratic representative Ocasio-Cortez and her colleagues identify "systemic injustices" (social *and* ecological) as the root cause of US ill-being and intend conversely to implement a "fair and just transition" benefiting in priority "frontline and vulnerable communities."

Policy-makers in Europe are also advocating concrete proposals to advance the goals of "sustainable equality." A report from the Progressive Alliance of Socialists and Democrats in the European Parliament, for example, acknowledges that "inequality is an environmental issue just as environmental degradation is also a social issue."[4]

Finally, Greta Thunberg, a fifteen-year-old climate activist at the time, made the social-ecological connection explicit when she declared: "our biosphere is being sacrificed so that rich people in countries like mine can live in luxury. It is the suffering of the many which pays for the luxuries of the few."[5] "Our civilization is being sacrificed for the opportunity of a very small number of people to continue making enormous amounts of money."

By linking justice and sustainability in a "sustainability–justice nexus,"[6] a number of scholars echoes these concerns and argues that our societies will be more just if they are more sustainable and more sustainable if they are more just.[7] In the profound words of James Boyce: "economic activities that degrade the environment generally yield winners and losers. Without winners – people who derive net benefit from the activity, or at least think that they do – the environmentally degrading activities would not occur. Without losers – people who bear net costs – they would not matter in terms of human well-being."[8]

In the twenty-first century, it thus makes environmental sense to mitigate our social crisis and social sense to mitigate our environmental crises. We should worry about our fragile societies, weakened by inequality, facing unprecedented environmental shocks. We should be anxious about the potential explosion of injustice in the face of deteriorating ecological crises.[9] To give life to these concerns and translate them into meaningful policies, justice needs to take back its place as an input and outcome of environmental economics.

Consider the issue of climate change. A handful of countries, ten percent exactly (and a handful of people and industries[10] within these countries) are responsible for 80% of human greenhouse gas emissions, causing climate change that is increasingly destroying the well-being of a considerable part of humanity around the world, but mostly in poor and developing nations. On the other hand, the vast majority of the people most affected by climate change (in Africa and Asia), numbering in the billions, live in countries that represent almost nothing in terms of responsibility but are highly vulnerable to the disastrous consequences of climate change (heat waves, hurricanes, flooding) triggered by the lifestyle of others, thousands of miles away. Why is climate change still not mitigated and actually worsening before our eyes, while we have, as we will see in detail in this book, all the science, technology, economics, and policy tools we need to fix it? Largely because the most responsible are not the most vulnerable, and vice-versa. Climate justice is the key to understanding and eventually solving the urgent climate crisis. Climate justice is the solution to climate change.

What is true in space among countries is also true in time, between generations. Climate strikes and marches have taken place and grown in momentum in a number of countries around the globe in 2019 (on March 15, 2019, in 120 countries and 2,000 cities, hundreds of thousands of students strike to call on global leaders to act against climate change). Part of the new generation is now aware of the grave injustice it will suffer as a result of choices over which it has yet no power. But the recognition of this inter-generational inequality comes up against the wall of intra-generational inequality: The implementation of a true ecological transition cannot escape the social challenges of here and now; in particular the imperative of inequality reduction. The ecological transition will be social-ecological or it will not be. It will be just or just not be. This is why, to take just one example, when this book will explore the necessity of carbon taxation, it will also highlight the need for social compensation of the poorest households who are the hardest hit by energy price increases.

There are indeed two possible ways to connect the current inequality crisis with ecological crises. The first arrow of causality, which runs from inequality to environmental degradation, can be labelled "integrative social-ecology," as it shows that the gap between the rich and the poor and the interaction of the two groups leads to the worsening of environmental degradations and ecological crises that affect every member of a given community (for example, greater international income inequality leads to more waste and pollutions being outsourced to poorer countries).

The reciprocal arrow of causality that goes from ecological crises to social injustice can be labelled "differential social-ecology," as it shows that the social impact of ecological crises is not the same for different individuals and groups, given their socio-economic status (the most vulnerable socially are "ecological sentinels" in the sense that they are first and foremost affected by current ecological crises: the poor generally suffer the most from environmental degradations). In the words of the Brundtland Report: "As a system approaches ecological limits, inequalities sharpen. Thus, when a watershed deteriorates, poor farmers suffer more because they cannot afford the same anti-erosion measures as richer farmers. When urban air quality deteriorates, the poor, in their more vulnerable areas, suffer more health damage than the rich, who usually live in more pristine neighborhoods. When mineral resources become depleted, late-comers to the industrialization process lose the benefits of low-cost supplies."[11]

The main goal of this book is to show how social dynamics, such as inequality, cause environmental degradations and, reciprocally, how environmental conditions such as climate change impact social dynamics. It is aimed at considering the reciprocal relationship between social and environmental issues, demonstrating how social logics determine environmental damage and crises and exploring the reciprocal relation, that is, the consequences of these damages on social inequality. Environmental risk is certainly a collective and global horizon but humans are socially differentiated actors of their living conditions. In this spirit, at every turn, this textbook will articulate social and natural systems, highlighting social and political causes and consequences of environmental issues. Who is responsible for what and with what consequences for whom? Such is the central question on which the following pages will shed light.

Far from a survey of authors, schools, and controversies, I will first attempt to define a consistent social-ecological framework and then apply it to the real-life ecological challenges of the twenty-first century, focusing on biodiversity and ecosystems, pollution and waste, energy and climate change, well-being and the environment, and urban sustainability.

The book is divided into two parts, Part I providing ideas and tools, Part II applying them to the major social-ecological challenges of the twenty-first century. Chapter 1 intends both to familiarize the reader with big ideas and notions important to the book (the purpose of economic analysis and policy, the imperative of justice, the challenge of sustainability) and to show her/him why and how history of thoughts up until the twentieth century (very often forgotten in existing textbooks) matters when revisiting our own ecological challenges in the light of classical ideas and intuitions. Chapter 2 will lead readers toward understanding how humans became the dominant force in the biosphere and *de facto* stewards of the Earth's ecosystems. But it will also show that domination does not imply autonomy: The economy is not a separated system from the biosphere; quite the contrary, and the principle of interdependence of species fully apply to humans. Hence the paradox of domination and dependence that defines the Anthropocene, the age where humans rule the Earth.

Chapter 3 will start by illustrating the co-dependence of natural and social systems through environmental history classic studies (such as the US "Dust Bowl" of the 1930s), to introduce readers to the ways economics can be useful in governing natural resources in a sustainable and fair way. It will then contrast Garrett Hardin's social pessimism with the empirical evidence and theoretical breakthroughs of Elinor Ostrom in understanding how "commons" can be successfully and sustainably governed. In this perspective, the notion of environmental justice is essential to map and grasp. It has been defined by the US Environmental Protection Agency as "the fair treatment and meaningful involvement of all people regardless of race, color, national origin, or income with respect to the development, implementation and enforcement of environmental laws, regulations, and policies." But there is no universal approach to it. Chapter 4 thus aims at equipping readers with analytical tools to understand the plurality of its approaches. Finally, to conclude Part I, Chapter 5 will assemble a "critical environmental economics toolbox," putting inequality and justice back at the center of analysis and policy.

Part II opens with biodiversity and ecosystems challenges, which are daunting. For each of the Earth systems studied in this chapter, a brief review of its importance and role in the biosphere and current and future state will be presented. The chapter will also focus for each system on political dynamics and social issues, such as inequality in access to food and energy or the role of poverty in biodiversity destruction. In Chapter 7, two models of economic system are being contrasted: The current economy in which massive resource extraction leads to pollution and waste and a twenty-first century economy that genuinely minimizes the use of natural resources and toxic materials as well as the emissions of waste and pollutants over the life cycle of the service or product. This chapter will explore how to shift economic systems from one to the other, discussing the meaning and possibility of "decoupling."

In Chapter 8, the much-documented nexus between fossil fuel consumption and climate change will be detailed as well as the policy needed to accelerate the on-going but painfully slow low carbon transition. This low carbon transition must be a "just transition" that gives its full place to climate justice. On this path, it is decisive to demonstrate that environmental sustainability is not incompatible with well-being; quite the contrary. Energy transition can lead to massive job creation and mitigation of ecological crises can provide crucial health co-benefits, while new indicators of well-being, resilience and sustainability can reform policy for the better. This is what Chapter 9 intends to show.

Social-ecology analysis and policy are the topics of Chapter 10. The gap between the rich and the poor and the interaction of the two groups leads to the worsening of environmental degradations and ecological crises that affect everyone, but not the same way. The current global effort to avoid the worst of these consequences and shift social and natural systems toward a more sustainable path does not take place in a vacuum but in a specific institutional context where capitalism, globalization, and digitalization all impact the social-ecological transition. Chapter 11 will thus explore their complementarities but also many contradictions. Finally, Chapter 12 focuses on urban sustainability and polycentric transition. Under the combined influence of globalization and urbanization, cities (and metropolitan areas) have become key players alongside nation-states in our world. They matter greatly in the opportunities given to people (geography influences history) but also have a critical impact on sustainability (cities account for 75% of global $CO_2$ emissions). As Elinor Ostrom rightly pointed out, "polycentric transition" toward sustainability is happening, with each level of government seizing the opportunity of the well-being and sustainability transition to reinvent prosperity and policy without waiting for the impetus to come from above. But cities and localities, like nation-states, regional organizations, and international institutions, have to articulate the challenge of sustainability with the imperative of justice.

# Part I
## Ideas and tools

# 1

# What the classics know about our world; what twentieth-century economics forgot

History of thoughts, too often forgotten in existing conventional economics textbooks, is not just about remembering past insights and forgotten intuitions. It is mostly about confronting older thinking to current challenges to understand how problems, and more importantly solutions, can look alike or differ from one era to the next. In this respect, contrary to a common belief, the twin concern for sustainability and justice has been around for quite some time in economic analysis.

## The physiocrats: Natural resources as political power

The physiocrats, a group of philosophers and policy-makers in eighteenth-century France,[1] can claim two important firsts regarding economics: They were the first to build a consistent model of the economy where natural resources played the central role; they were also the first to pretend, falsely, that economics was a science, the physics of the social world, based on universal and robust laws. François Quesnay and Anne-Robert-Jacques Turgot were towering figures of the movement, with Pierre de Samuel Du Pont de Nemours and Marquis de Mirabeau as important secondary characters.

François Quesnay (1694–1774), the founder of physiocracy from an intellectual standpoint, was a physician by training and saw the economy as a human body, where blood circulation amounted to trade and social classes mirrored vital organs. Quesnay's *Tableau économique* (Economic Table), first published in 1758, embodies the underpinnings of physiocracy. For the physiocrats (*physis* is Greek for Nature and *kratein* means governing), the economy should be understood as a "government of Nature" based on two principles, corresponding to their two-sided approach: The first holds that the economy is governed by natural laws; the second that wealth and, in the end, political power belongs to those who control natural resources.

In the *Tableau*, farmers produced wealth, transformed by landowners into capital, while workers and artisans are just "sterile" groups. "The productive class" according to Quesnay is the one responsible for bringing to life the annual wealth of the nation through the "culture of the territory." "The class of proprietors" (that includes the landowners) subsists, thanks to the income or net product of the crop, which is paid to them annually by the productive class. The "sterile class" is made up of all citizens engaged in other services and work other than those of agriculture, and whose expenses are paid by the productive class and the class of proprietors, who themselves derive their income from the productive class.[2] The distribution of natural resources benefits and organizes society and determines its hierarchy.

Physiocrats were fierce liberals,[3] who thought that government's intervention was unwarranted in an economy efficiently governed by natural laws. The root of their anti-interventionist creed was their belief in the universal laws of economics, close to the laws prevailing in physics. In that, they strongly opposed the "Colbertist doctrine," named after Louis XIV's influential Minister Jean-Baptiste Colbert.[4] They also resented the then dominant mercantilist doctrine, which viewed international trade as a zero-sum game and recommended protectionism and imperial conquest to increase national wealth.[5]

Physiocrats believed that a "natural order" founded economics as a "science": In *De l'origine et des progrès d'une science nouvelle* (1768), Dupont de Nemours affirms: "Economic science being nothing other than the application of the natural order to the government of societies, is as constant in its principles and as demonstrable as the most certain physical sciences."

Among the most brilliant minds of their time, physiocrats also exerted influence on economic policy. Quesnay became known in policy circles as the leader of *les économistes* (the economists), a group of advisers omnipresent in economic debates at the royal court dedicated to early industrial modernization of France and agricultural reforms. This is probably the start of the influence of economists on public discourse and ultimately public policy, that extends until now, of which Turgot was the embodiment and the founding figure.

Jacques Turgot (1727–1781) was appointed Controller General of France by the new King Louis XVI. True to its liberal principles, Turgot introduced freedom of circulation and pricing of grains. But poor harvests lead to higher prices for bread and violent riots erupted in the provinces and the Paris region. In 1776, the minister doubled down by decreeing freedom of enterprise and competition in the agricultural sector. The unpopularity of his economic remedies among the people suffering from the price increase as well as the opposition from privileged classes controlling powerful corporations weakened his position and doomed him politically. Under the impetus of the Queen and Minister Maurepas, he resigned on May 12, 1776.

His most famous measure, the promulgation of the Edict of July 19, 1764, is true to physiocratic principles and policy recommendations: It officially liberalized grain and flour trade entirely in all the kingdom of France except for Paris and its surroundings (the Edict states that "the culture of land" is "the surest source of wealth for a State").

The physiocrats fought for their ideas and briefly governed by them in a country where agriculture accounted for the vast majority of national wealth. But their insights and prescriptions can be adapted to today's context of geopolitical struggles over rare earths, minerals, and fossil fuels. Even more fundamentally, natural resources command civil conflicts, with environmental wars fought from Palestine to Lake Chad (both over water access). As a matter of fact, the French Revolution can be seen as the first social-ecological revolt of moden history: Scholars[6] have shown that the climatic context that preceded 1789 (a hot spring and summer followed by bad autumnal weather turning into a harsh winter) played a key role in fostering social unrest due to the impact of climate on crops and bread production.

Physiocrats therefore help us to understand the essential link between natural resources and political power. Malthus held an extreme view of this link when he assessed that, given the scarcity of subsistence, only some humans should have the privilege to survive.

## Malthus and sustainability analysis

In 1798, in his brief and lugubrious essay on the principle of population, where cynicism quarrels with fatalism, Reverend Thomas Robert Malthus states what he believes to be the iron law of human tragedy. We are, says Malthus, caught between production and reproduction: Our incontinent desire to procreate violently comes up against the limits of our ability to feed our offspring. The tragic is mathematical: If the food subsistence grows at an arithmetical rhythm (1, 2, 3, 4 ...), the population grows in turn at a geometric rhythm (1, 2, 4, 8 ...). So, while only resources only add up, humans are multiplying. Humanity is running to ruin, and of its own doing. The reasoning seems irresistible: "At the end of two centuries, population and means of subsistence will be in the ratio of 256 to 9, after three centuries, 4096 to 13." If they want to prosper, humans must learn to control their own growth.

Nearly two and a half centuries later, Malthus' mistake is glaring: "Human population and well-being have grown together, exponentially. The great desynchronization promised by the pessimist pastor has turned into an abundance of prosperity absolutely new in the long history of human history. To put it simply, there are seven times more people on the planet than in Malthus' days and their life expectancy is twice as high as when he made his gloomy prediction. The irony is that Malthus was pretty good at describing the situation that prevailed over the seven million years of human presence on the planet before he took the pen. But, at the precise moment when he states his theory, it became empirically false. The first industrial revolution (of which Malthus did not see the premises around him), the successive agricultural revolutions, the progress of medicine, the emergence and development of the welfare state (which he could not imagine and would most certainly have resented), will prove him more and more wrong over the decades, until today.

But, if Malthus was wrong on substance, he was not mistaken about the form: A great desynchronization, potentially more destructive than the one he had imagined, did indeed start on his watch. Consider, to measure it as precisely as possible, five fundamental indicators of human development for about a century: population, human development (income, health, education), gross domestic product (GDP), carbon dioxide emissions, and extraction of natural resources (Graph 1.1).

What can we discern? There are clearly three periods, three ages of human development whose characteristics differ quite sharply: In the first age, the first half of the twentieth century, population increases and human development grows even faster. Malthusian pessimism is spectacularly invalidated: "More people on average experience greater well-being. $CO_2$ emissions are

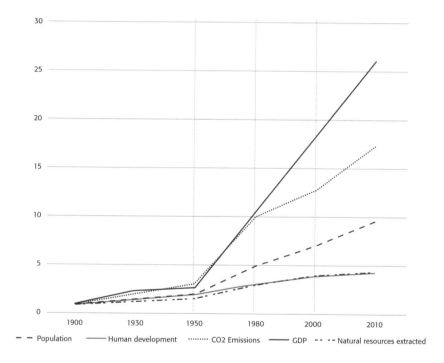

Graph 1.1   Three ages of human development* (factor of increase: 1900 = 1)

*   The historical human development index aggregates, on an equal weighted basis, an income indicator, an education indicator and a health indicator.

*Source:* Human Development Report database, Global Carbon Project. Leandro Prados de la Escosura, World Human Development, 1870–2007, *Review of Income and Wealth*, 61 (2), June 2015: 220–247 and Maddison Project Database and Krausmann Fridolin, Simone Gingrich, Nina Eisenmenger, Karl-Heinz Erb, Helmut Haberl, and Marina Fischer-Kowalski, 2009. "Growth in global materials use, GDP and population during the twentieth century." *Ecological Economics*, 68 (10), 2696–2705

growing a little faster than human development, but at a slow pace, extraction of natural resources grows at the pace of human development and Gross Domestic Product (GDP) reflects, exaggerating a little, a new prosperity of the human species, seemingly compatible with the preservation of its habitat, the biosphere."

During the second period, between 1950 and 1980, the great desynchronization begins: While the growth of human development slows down and is gradually caught up by that of the population, $CO_2$ emissions and GDP are racing and natural resources extraction is multiplied by 2.5. At the end of the period, in 1980, $CO_2$ emissions and GDP grew by a factor of ten compared with the beginning of the twentieth century, tripling the pace of population growth and human development.

The third age of human development is the time of illusion: While population and human development are stabilizing at the same rate of growth, $CO_2$ emissions continue to grow much faster than both, and natural resources extraction doubles again, while GDP, completely disconnected from human reality, masks the gravity of the ecological crisis (in that period, biodiversity declines substantially).

The increase in human development in the second half of the twentieth century has been achieved at the cost of environmental degradation (in the form of $CO_2$ emissions) four times higher than in the first half of the century, even though the population increased only slightly more than in the years between 1900 and 1950 (2.4 against 1.6). It is therefore mostly the qualitative means of human development that are in question – and not just the quantitative demographic pressure – in the explosion of post-Second World War environmental degradation. The beginning of the twenty-first century is even more "inefficient" when we relate human well-being to its ecological cost. Emissions growth increases at its highest rate ever (almost 75%), contrasting with the growth of human well-being and population (only 10%) and up to 1 million species are threatened with annihilation because of human activity.

To sum up: Between 1900 and 1950, it was necessary to triple $CO_2$ emissions to obtain a doubling of human development. Between 1950 and 2000, this same doubling required more than a quadrupling of $CO_2$ emissions. At the beginning of the twenty-first century, a doubling of human well-being would be achieved at the cost of a multiplication by almost eight of the $CO_2$ emissions responsible for climate change. In other words, Malthus has his accounting revenge and we are faced with a new crisis of paces: To the now synchronized arithmetic growth of the population and well-being responds the geometric progression of environmental degradation that will eventually overcome human recent and fragile prosperity.

How do we get out of this trap? Faithful to the idea that there is no problem whose absence of solution cannot be exhausted, we can think first of all that this great desynchronization will be solved by itself, in the fashion of Malthus, by amputation of human well-being and disappearance of the least resilient part of the population. The health consequences of climate change are, in fact, becoming better known and more and more tangible (see Chapter 9). Climate change and the ecological crises it will aggravate have, no doubt, the power to destroy in a few decades the human progress of the last two centuries. The Malthusian stagnation was explained precisely by famine crises, which "naturally" regulated the level of the population. Malthus himself was in favor of abandoning the poorest part of the population to its fate by suppressing the laws that could support it.

This Malthusian method is the implicit choice made by human societies at the beginning of the twenty-first century: About 90% of the so-called natural catastrophes of the last twenty years are linked to climatic phenomena, and they have affected the existence of 2.3 billion people, who live for the most part in the poorest countries on the planet. The current rate of degradation of the biosphere promises the world's most vulnerable hell on Earth.

Malthus leaves us with a haunting intuition of our sustainability crisis and a dismal response to it. David Ricardo, over whom Malthus exerted a strong intellectual influence, offered more humane responses in dealing with the inescapable limits of human development on a finite planet.

## David Ricardo and planetary boundaries

"Planetary boundaries" are quantitative thresholds "within which humanity can continue to develop and thrive for generations to come." Crossing these boundaries entails the risk of generating large-scale abrupt or irreversible environmental changes. Scientists warned us recently that "Four of nine planetary boundaries have now been crossed as a result of human activity: Climate change, loss of biosphere integrity, land-system change, altered biogeochemical cycles (phosphorus and nitrogen)." Two of these, climate change and biosphere integrity, are "core boundaries." Significantly altering either of these would "drive the Earth System into a new state."[7] This is certainly breakthrough science, yet the classical economists from the eighteenth and nineteenth centuries had the intuition that human development was in fact constrained by the scarcity of Nature.

What has been referred to as the "grandiose dynamic" of the English classical school (whose major triad includes Adam Smith, David Ricardo, and John Stuart Mill) is based on the assumption of the domination of Man by Nature. In the view of the authors, Man does not (cannot) destroy Nature: He takes advantage of his fertility but, in return, Nature imposes on him his rhythm of exploitation and his finitude, and promises him a stationary state as an horizon. According to the classics, economic growth is only possible as long as all available land is not exploited, agricultural productivity being a gift that cannot be manipulated by technological progress.

It is not the prospect of the deterioration of natural resources, let alone the depletion of natural stocks, that leads to the melancholic conclusion of the classics, but the comparison between what the Earth can offer and what it takes for humans to subsist. The analysis of Malthus was the most accomplished expression of this disillusioned comparison before David Ricardo developed his idea of "diminishing returns" and John Stuart Mill his vision of the "stationary state."

The work of David Ricardo (1817) is indeed profoundly marked by Malthus' (wrong and not so wrong) reasoning. But Ricardo refined it considerably by formulating his theory of agricultural rent. In his analysis, the scarce resource is, quite naturally, agricultural land whose limited availability in the United Kingdom was glaring, while the industry just began its take off. Ricardo framed his famous reasoning in terms of "differential rent": The most fertile lands are the first to be cultivated, but, as the pressure of demand increases because of the increase of the population, less fertile land must be exploited. Because these new lands are less productive, their unit cost of production is higher, so the selling price required for production on these new lands is also higher. But the market price being unique, the owners of the most fertile land benefit from a "differential" rent. "Diminishing returns" occur because of the lower productivity of the lands gradually being cultivated under the pressure of the consumption of their yields by a growing population.

Ricardo saw globalization and technological progress as solutions to the law of diminishing returns. But he had more confidence in trade than in technology. Considerably refining and extending the "absolute advantages" of Adam Smith,[8] he greatly enlarged the circle of countries that could beneficially take part in globalization (potential partners of his home country). He also thought that if agricultural innovations would accelerate (as will be the case throughout the twentieth century), then diminishing returns could be overcome. But Ricardo envisioned a "steady state" of the economy, at the very end of Chapter V of the Principles of Political Economy, where neither globalization nor progress in techniques operate any longer. John Stuart Mill will push the idea much further in the middle of the nineteenth century, all the while the first industrial revolution was booming all around him.

## John Stuart Mill and the steady state

In Chapter VI of Book IV of his *Principles of Political Economy*, published in 1848, John Stuart Mill devotes key developments to what he calls "the Stationary State."[9] The question asked by Mill is that of the fundamental purpose of economic activity: "To what goal? Toward what ultimate point is society tending by its industrial progress?"

Although he believes in wealth creation through the application of liberal economics principles, Mill writes that "the increase of wealth is not boundless: At the end of what they term the progressive state lies the stationary state." The revolutionary nature of Mill's questioning of the very finalities of the liberal economy lies in his understanding of the profound impact human societies are already having on the biosphere. "If the Earth must lose that great portion of its pleasantness which it owes to things that the unlimited increase of wealth and population would extirpate from it," he writes, "for the mere purpose of enabling it to support a larger, but not a better or a happier population, I sincerely hope, for the sake of posterity, that they will be content to be stationary, long before necessity compel them to it."

But if Mill is pessimistic on the finality and purpose of what we would now call economic growth, he is optimistic on the ability of humans to find a new path to development and believes that "a stationary condition of capital and population implies no stationary state of human improvement."

It is in the building of fair and shared prosperity that humans will find this new meaning, according to Mill: "Only when, in addition to just institutions, the increase of mankind shall be under the deliberate guidance of judicious foresight, can the conquests made from the powers of nature by the intellect and energy of scientific discoverers, become the common property of the species, and the means of improving and elevating the universal lot."

Hence, in the middle of the nineteenth century, Mill discovers the sustainability–justice nexus. While a number of scholars today advocate "de-growth" in order to avoid the worst of ecological crises, it was John Stuart Mill, a founding father of the neo-classical school, who first envisioned, at the peak of the first industrial revolution, the transition to a "stationary state" where social and environmental concerns would be addressed jointly.

## What twentieth-century economics forgot

For Rodrik (2016),[10] modern economics would be different from (and allegedly superior to) other social sciences by its mastery of formal models. Twentieth-century economics would be remarkable for the gradual improvement of its quantitative techniques, building on the invention of the social statistics (by Quetelet) and mathematical formalization (by Cournot), to develop econometrics (Cowles commission), game theory (von Neumann) up to computational and big data economics today. In reality, the question of instruments appears secondary in the constitution of twentieth-century economics. The real rupture is not formal but substantial: it is the break with philosophy, ethics, and justice.

While, as we have just seen, issues of distribution and principles of justice were at the heart of the work of the founding fathers of what has long been called for a good reason "political economy," they have been marginalized and in the end almost forgotten in the course of the last century. This move away from justice by neo-classical economics was compounded by a focus on short-term policy by its most formidable opponent: Keynesian economics. Let us study these two counter-revolutions in turn.

To begin with, twentieth-century neo-classical economics forgot about inequality. Three key moments marked that reversal. First, it was the admission in 1887 of Charles Dunbar, who viewed economics as a science that should stay clear of ethical considerations, into the American Economic Association (founded in 1885). Dunbar would become AEA's second President, taking over Richard T. Ely, a progressive who lamented the "contradiction between things as they are and our social ideal." Second, the development of welfare theorems by Léon Walras in 1920 and the definition of optimality by Vilfredo Pareto in 1930 ended up conflating productive and distributional issues, abandoning inter-personal comparisons and limiting justice policy to the hypothetical possibility – but seldom the reality – of compensation of the "losers" by the "winners" on the market. Finally, the "great dilemma" posited by Arthur Okun between equity and efficiency in the 1970s – the former being assimilated as a loss in terms of the latter – separated even more mainstream economics from distributional concerns.

Hence, in the course of a century, neo-classical economics offered three possible options for considering justice: to deny it, to assume it, and finally to trade it off. In his Richard T. Ely lecture, labor economist Finis Welch went as far as to engage in a reasoned and passionate "defense of inequality," arguing that: "All economic science proceeds from inequalities."[11]

This defense of inequality in the name of efficiency is, simply put, a serious mistake. Fundamentally, inequality is not just unfair: it is both inefficient and unsustainable. Numerous scholars have been working in the last two decades to demonstrate that the current income inequality crisis (a detailed picture of which can be found in the recently released World Inequality Report 2018)[12] hinders progress in key dimensions of human well-being and economic dynamism. Wilkinson and Pickett[13] have shown that higher income inequality translates into lower physical and health attainments for US states and comparable countries at the international level (income inequality increasing the prevalence of obesity, drug abuse, stress, mental illness).[14] Stiglitz[15] has extended the logic of the argument to show how income inequality favors rents to the detriment of innovation and gradually plagues economic development.

Inequality is not just detrimental to current well-being but affects both resilience (collective resistance to shocks) and sustainability (understood as the long-term horizon of human well-being, that must be compatible with the limits of the biosphere). The seminal work of the late Elinor Ostrom[16] can be understood as drawing a connection between equality and the ability of communities around the world to organize efficiently in order to exploit natural resources sustainably and to resist ecological shocks such as climate change. This line of analysis has been extended to show that, through several other channels, inequality harms sustainability[17] (an issue we will explore in detail in Chapter 10).

Finally, the idea that self-interest and efficiency are the key incentives of human behaviors is deeply unconvincing. Amartya Sen showed that humans look much more like "rational fools" than *Homo œconomicus* while the quest for fairness appears to be a much more powerful incentive than the pursuit of efficiency. Justice is neither a by-product, a collateral benefit, nor an instrument of efficiency: It is the core demand of humans everywhere on the planet.

In fact, inequality economics has made a noted comeback in the last fifteen years, contrasting with its eclipse from academic and policy debates between the late 1970s and early 2000s (the critical and popular global success of Thomas Piketty's *Capital in the 21st Century*, that documents the contemporary rise in income and wealth inequality, being the most visible sign of this renewed interest). Two scholars have been trailblazers in this renewal: Amartya Sen, who has renewed theories of justice, and Anthony Atkinson, who has revisited the empirical measurement of inequality, both lines of work putting back distributional issues at the center of economics, where they were in the eighteenth and nineteenth centuries before their recent eclipse.

But neo-classical economics' turn away from distributional issues and justice concerns was not the only blind spot in twentieth-century economics. Keynesian economics, while arguing for justice, largely forgot about the long run. In his *General Theory* (1936), a book that laid the foundations of modern macroeconomic analysis, Keynes made no mystery of his commitment to equality: "The outstanding faults of the economic society in which we live are its failure to provide for full employment and its arbitrary and inequitable distribution of wealth and incomes." But, in an earlier text, *A Tract on Monetary Reform* (1923), he was equally clear about his focus on short-term economic analysis: "The long run is a misleading guide to current affairs. In the long run we are all dead." In this implicit attack on Ricardo, Keynes wanted to direct policy-makers' attention to here and now social predicament and imbalances rather than the long-run equilibrium posited by neo-classical models. But in doing so, he also laid the ground for a disregard of environmental concerns in the name of short-term job creation and purchasing power increase, pitting prosperity against posterity. This alleged trade-off between social and environmental goals remains to this day one of the most solid obstacles to ambitious environmental policy. And yet, as the impact of climate change on human health around the world makes clear, in the age of ecological crises of which Keynes had no conscience or intuition, it is the short term that has become, in truth, a bad compass of current affairs.

In all fairness, Keynes did try to grasp long-run issues, most notably in his "Economic possibilities for our grandchildren" essay (1930). In this visionary text, Keynes predicts the spectacular increase of living standards in the twentieth century and equates it with the fact that, as he put it, "mankind" would be "solving its economic problem." But he was, here again, deeply mistaken in arguing that "for the first time since his creation man will be faced with his real, his permanent problem – how to use his freedom from pressing economic cares, how to occupy the leisure, which science and compound interest will have won for him, to live wisely and agreeably and well." Alas, the "real and permanent" problem of humankind – to take good care of its habitat – is only getting worse. Actually, humankind has *not* solved its economic problem because it has *not* solved its ecological problem.

# 2

# Humans within the biosphere: The paradox of domination and dependence

Over the last two centuries, humans have become the dominant force of the biosphere and *de facto* stewards of the Earth's ecosystems. But biospheric principle of interdependence and collaboration of species fully applies to humans: There is no economy outside of our habitat. Hence the paradox of domination and dependence that defines our geological time, the Anthropocene, as literally an age where humans rule the Earth.[1]

As I have already pointed out in the Introduction of this book, economics and ecology share common roots. Economics is etymologically more than two millennia older than ecology: Aristotle and Xenophon coined the phrase using *oikos* and *nomos* to refer to the rules of management of the household, what we would now call microeconomics. When the German biologist Ernst Hæckel coined the word "ecology," he did so using the same radical, *oikos* but pairing it with *logos* or science.[2] Economics and ecology are thus, at their roots, compatible, provided that one understands that the rules of the small human household cannot be imposed on the science of the great natural household. The general framework of this chapter (and this book) is not the relationship between humans and Nature but between humans and the rest of Nature. What's fundamentally new in this relation is the fact that today, after billions of years of evolution, the natural world depends on us as much as we depend on it. In other words, our time is marked by an aberration: Apparently, the human household has come to dominate the natural household, a reality illustrated by the growing pressure the human population is putting on ecosystems (Box 2.1).

## Box 2.1 The population (on-going) problem

The fear of overpopulation occupied the heart of environmental conscience of the 1960s and 1970s, as evidenced by the reverberation of Paul Ehrlich's (1969) book announcing the imminent explosion of the "population bomb." As the author acknowledges today, the "bomb" has been partly defused by the decline in fertility rates in the developing world, a drop in which the education of women was the most powerful driver. The annual growth rate of the world's population reached its peak (about 2%) in the mid 1960s, when Ehrlich's book appeared, to be divided by almost two (about 1.1%) since then (see table below).

| Population growth rate, 1950–2050 in % over 5-year intervals | | | |
|---|---|---|---|
| | World | More developed regions | Less developed regions |
| 1950–1955 | 1.78 | 1.20 | 2.05 |
| 1955–1960 | 1.80 | 1.17 | 2.08 |
| 1965–1970 | 2.05 | 0.84 | 2.52 |
| 1970–1975 | 1.95 | 0.78 | 2.37 |
| 1980–1985 | 1.78 | 0.58 | 2.15 |
| 1990–1995 | 1.52 | 0.42 | 1.81 |
| 2000–2005 | 1.25 | 0.33 | 1.47 |
| 2010–2015 | 1.18 | 0.29 | 1.37 |
| 2015–2020 | 1.09 | 0.26 | 1.25 |
| 2050–2055 | 0.48 | -0.02 | 0.56 |

Source: United Nations. Department of Economic and Social Affairs, Population Division (2017). World Population Prospects: 2017 Revision, custom data acquired via website

Yet, the population problem is not behind us: According to the latest data revision by the UN Population Division, the global population is still expected to grow substantially: from 7.5 billion in 2017 (6.25 in the developing world and 1.25 in the developed world) to 8.1 billion in 2030 (6.9 in the developing world, 1.2 in the developed world) and then 9.5 billion in 2050 (8.25 in the developing world, 1.25 in the developed world). Hence, the absolute increase of human population in the next decades, and the related pressure on the biosphere, is an inescapable reality driven by the increase of about two billion people in the developing world, especially the fifty countries where demography remains extremely dynamic.

## Human evolution toward planetary dominance: The small household and the bigger one

In his *Mediterranean and the Mediterranean World in the Age of Philip II*, French historian Fernand Braudel makes the hypothesis that the long geographical duration, which captures an almost immobile history (that of humans in their relations with the environment which surrounds them), can be set apart from the social time (economic and social cycles) and individual time (personal history). Because human development has accelerated so much during the twentieth century, we distinguish less and less clearly these three time horizons (geographical, social, and individual). We must now understand their contiguity, their correspondences, their interweaving. The story of humanity's relationship with its environment has turned from a quiet lake into a tumultuous waterfall.

John Muir, who was instrumental in the creation of the first national parks in the United States in the 1870s and 1880s, said that when he wanted to know the news, he would go to the mountains. He meant to signify to his contemporaries that nothing was really new in their modernity and that only the contemplation of Nature brought to his soul a real regeneration. Today, our news is actually in the mountains: It is on the skin of sorrows of glaciers that we can read our future (in the Alps, the glacier surfaces have shrunk by half between 1900 and 2012).

Let us take stock of this acceleration of ecological time and the confusion of human and natural history. Earth was created 4.5 billion years ago. Life on Earth appeared 3.5 billion years ago. Manlike creatures first walked the face of the Earth seven million years ago. *Homo sapiens sapiens* emerged in 200,000 BCE. Already, we can see how late humans arrive in the biosphere picture. But then things start to really accelerate: Agriculture is developed around 10,000 BCE, industrial revolution is, so to speak, in full steam around 1850 CE, industrial growth kicks in 1950 CE and becomes global in 1990 (with the development of China and India). To put things in perspective, in a mere one hundred years, humans have become completely dominant on a planet that started its own evolution several billions of years before them.

Hence we get the idea of the Anthropocene, combining humanity and geology, a time when "the global effects of human activities have become clearly noticeable" (Crutzen and Stoermer, 2000).[3] In the social-ecological approach of this book, we can more precisely define the Anthropocene as an age where social systems rule natural systems and are affected back by the dynamics they set in motion. To put it differently, the domination of human societies of the biosphere has not ended their dependence on the biosphere. This is what Vitousek and his colleagues meant when they wrote more than twenty years ago with profound wisdom supported by groundbreaking data: "It is clear that we control much of Earth, and that our activities affect the rest. In a very real sense, the world is in our hands – and how we handle it will determine its composition and dynamics, and our fate."[4]

## The biosphere: Interdependence and collaboration

The general mistake so often made in studying human environment is to set apart humans and the natural world. Humankind depends on the natural world (climate, biodiversity, ecosystems) and the natural world now depends on humankind because of human domination ("wild" species for instance must be preserved by human ingenuity in order for them to survive human expansion). Strictly defined, humans are organisms within ecosystems (an ecosystem[5] is a community of animals and plants interacting with one another and with their physical environment, echoing the definition of ecology coined by E. Haeckel in 1866 as the "relation of the animal both to its organic as well as its inorganic environment").

The biosphere is the ecosystem of ecosystems: It is composed of biomes (different types of ecosystems with certain climate, fauna and flora such as tropical rainforests or deserts), which themselves contain smaller ecosystems (like rivers, lakes) in which live natural creatures, among them human beings (who are ecosystems themselves, home to thousands of bacteria). Because humans have literally colonized the biosphere (see Chapter 6), they have formed "Anthromes" (or Anthropogenic Biomes)[6] on the surface of the planet such as cities, villages, croplands, and pastures. But because humans remain part of Nature, they can learn a great deal from other natural beings in order to improve their own well-being.[7] Natural beings are connected to their environment by energy and nutrient flow. Among them, humans interact with their physical environment, for example by extracting oxygen from the atmosphere and returning carbon dioxide (in too large amounts, as Chapter 8 will make clear), and have collaborated with other organisms in many ways for a very long time (the companionship between humans and dogs is at least 30,000 years old).

The idea of laws of evolution reduced to mechanisms of fierce competition between individuals for transmission of the best gene is indeed much too reductive. It has already been discredited a long time ago. The division of work exists in many species: Just observe the inside of an anthill or a hive, to be convinced. The British evolutionary biologist William Donald Hamilton even showed, fifty years ago, that individuals of certain species help members of their first circle to reproduce, which ensures an indirect form of gene transmission to the next generation. Research recently highlighted the ability of some insects not only to sacrifice themselves but to sacrifice their reproductive capacity, so that other individuals can perpetuate themselves. This is the case of "workers" among bees, ants, or termites.[8] Collaboration among individuals of the same species is in fact a necessity for survival and reproduction: Some dolphins who know how to hunt alone decide nevertheless to associate with congeners to implement a sophisticated technique aimed at locking their prey in concentric circles in order to maximize the volume of the catch.

Where humans and other animals part ways is in the unique ability of humans not only to collaborate (for survival and reproduction) but also to cooperate in building, sharing, and passing on to future generations common knowledge.[9] Yet this unique cooperation occurs in social systems embedded in and dependent on the biosphere.

## Thermodynamics and material flow analysis: A wider economics

In the Court devoted to his work in the Detroit Institute of Arts lies a magnificent fresco by Mexican painter Diego Rivera. Commissioned by Henry Ford to glorify entrepreneurs and painted between 1932 and 1933, it exalts instead, in its lower panel, workers. But its upper panel reveals a striking truth: Labor and capital are only possible because of a third and sustaining production factor: The extraction of natural resources (represented in the fresco by mountain gods who allow a flow of energy to descend toward the car assembly line pictured in the lower panel). Human production depends on the biosphere, which provides energy and materials without which all economic models would remain purely theoretical.

The amount of energy human societies receive from the sun is astounding: 8,000 times what they need to power the global economy. Energy that drives ecosystems comes almost entirely from the sun, a fraction of its rays (about 7%) being captured by green plants for growth via the process of photosynthesis and sustaining human life. But ecosystems' energy is governed by a law of entropia: It can neither be created or destroyed (first law of thermodynamics) and its usage produces waste heat that humans cannot use again (second law of thermodynamics).

Economies are exactly like organisms: They need not only energy but nutrients to function.[10] Material resources abundant on Earth and useful for humans are comprised of the biomass (wood and crops for food, energy, and plant-based materials), fossil fuels (coal, gas, and oil), metals (such as iron, aluminum, and copper) and non-metallic minerals (including sand, gravel, and limestone), all of which feed the economy. In fact, at a time when the digital revolution is supposed to make economies immaterial, humans today extract close to 90 billion tonnes of material resources; more than three times the amount they needed fifty years ago.[11]

## Social and natural systems, standing and collapsing together

Since its emergence in the 1980s, ecological economics has focused on the joint study of natural and human systems. It goes beyond both conventional environmental economics, which reduces the application of the standard neo-classical model to ecological issues, and ecology, narrowly understood as the science of the natural world. The causes and consequences of climate change render obvious this need to think in social-ecological terms. The difficulty is to think about these issues in a truly integrated way, not by juxtaposing natural sciences (physical and natural) and social sciences, but by intermingling them, combining them, articulating them. What is more, this joint study should be dynamic, since on both sides systems evolve and even co-evolve; that is to say, evolve together dynamically.

In its broadest sense, the theory of co-evolution postulates that ecosystems reflect the characteristics of social systems (state of knowledge and techniques, values, social organization) and that social systems in return reflect the characteristics of natural systems (species, productivity, temporal and spatial differentiation, resilience). An essential assumption here is therefore the notion of co-dependence, biological and dynamic, between human systems and natural systems in a "socio-ecological system," or "social-ecological system," or "coupled human-environment system."

Another important concept in this respect is that of resilience. The notion of resilience, nowadays widespread in many disciplines, was born in the field of psychology. It was introduced by Holling in 1978 in the ecological literature and broadly defined as the ability of a system to tolerate shocks without changing its nature (i.e. retaining core ecological functionings). It is clear that ecological resilience should be combined with social resilience in the event of an ecological shock. We can illustrate this point with the role played by mangroves in Asian coastal areas.

Mangroves are aquatic forests that provide coastal human communities with forest and fisheries resources. They also protect shorelines from erosion and ocean hazards such as tsunamis (they also have the ability to store carbon). The destruction of mangroves to develop shrimp fishing along the Asian coasts has significantly increased the vulnerability of coastal populations that were severely hit by the Asian tsunami of December 2004. A 2005 study showed both that human activities reduced the area of mangroves by 26% in the five countries most affected by the tsunami, and that remaining mangroves had significantly reduced the destruction caused by the tsunami.[12]

Elinor Ostrom (2009) has sought to systematically understand what she calls "complex social-ecological systems" such as those. Such systems do not lend themselves to simplistic typologies and indeed suppose a certain complexity of analysis. They can be broken down into four essential elements: resource systems, resource units, users, and governance systems. Ostrom takes the example of a protected park where there are forests, animal and plant species, and water resources. These include: resource systems (the park contains wooded areas, fauna and flora, water systems); resource units (for example, trees, shrubs, plants in the park, different types of wildlife, volume and flow of water), users (who use park resources for recreational purposes, subsistence, or commercial); and finally governance systems (a national government, NGOs involved in park management, rules of use and exploitation of resources).

Each of these four subsystems is itself composed of several second-level variables (for example, the size of a resource system, the growth of a resource unit, the degree of user cooperation, or the level of governance). Ostrom then defines two additional notions: Interactions between users (information sharing, deliberation process, and so on) and their results (economic and ecological outcomes). This complex social-ecological analysis must also take into account the social, economic and political context upstream and the effect on other social-ecological systems, in other words add to the four internal systems already described two external systems. From this dynamic and complex framework, Ostrom has managed to derive novel ways to govern the commons.

# 3

# Governing the commons fairly

Deprived of the rich diversity of life, which is as much a source of material well-being as a reservoir of knowledge, we would become biologically impoverished but we would also erode intellectually. Our dependence on the natural world is therefore very real and it is because we do not understand it that we are blindly attacking ourselves when we brutalize it. We thus have to find ways to govern the world of which we have become the stewards. This starts by understanding the long perspective of the mutual history of social and natural systems and then moving to the practical ways to build robust human institutions to enjoy natural resources in a sustainable way.

## Environmental history: Social and natural systems in perspective

Environmental history, that can be traced back to the early 1970s, offers a bilateral approach, shedding light on how humans have been affected by their natural environment and how reciprocally they have affected their environment. The birth of environmental history is generally located in August 1972, with the publication of a special issue of the *Pacific Historical Review* and more specifically a seminal article by Roderick Nash.[1] In it, Nash writes: "I never intended to teach the history of the land in the manner of geologists. I would, rather, attempt a history of attitude and action toward the land. This would involve a description of environmental change, but my interest in it would be as evidence of man's values, ideals, ambitions, and fear." Donald Worster was a pioneer in this historical field. In his masterpiece,[2] he explores the interrelation between the Great Depression and over-exploitation of land in the Great Plains. The key insight of Worster's work is that the same society has produced both events under the influence of the same system: unfettered capitalism. "It cannot be blamed on illiteracy or overpopulation or social disorder. It came about because the culture was operating in precisely the way it was supposed to ... The Dust Bowl ... was the inevitable outcome of a culture that deliberately, self-consciously, set itself

[the] task of dominating and exploiting the land for all it was worth," writes Worster.

Commenting on the work of Worster, one of the leading contemporary figures of environmental history, William Cronon (1992),[3] explains that "Our histories of the Great Plains environment remain fixed on people because what we most care about in nature is its meaning for human beings. We care about the dust storms because they stand as a symbol of human endurance in the face of natural adversity – or as a symbol of human irresponsibility in the face of natural fragility. Human interests and conflicts create values in nature that in turn provide the moral center for our stories." He adds "I would urge upon environmental historians the task of telling not just stories about nature, but stories about stories about nature."

Cronon's book on the development of the mid-West region[4] expands on the idea that the social system imposes itself in some way on the natural world. Women and men are able to build cities in which fundamental assets are themselves. This is the case of the city of Chicago, devoid of almost any environmental asset at the time of its founding but which was able to take advantage of its social assets to become the urban center of the industrial development of the United States.

The history of the environment thus sheds light, beyond the moral apprehension of Nature, on the social and political dimension of the human relationship to the natural world. These issues were present at the very beginning of environmental governance, in the early nineteenth century.

## The early beginnings of environmental governance: Preservation and conservation

In the contemporary period, the environmental preoccupation went through a mystical age, from the publication of *Nature* in 1836 by Ralph Waldo Emerson to the fight of John Muir, eventually supported by Theodore Roosevelt, for the creation of the first national parks in the United States. Muir (1838–1914) is certainly the most famous figure of the preservation movement. An ardent defender of the Yosemite Valley in the United States and founder of the environmental NGO Sierra Club (1892), his advocacy of Nature as a healing place for humans overwhelmed by the industrial world finds strong echoes today (see Box 3.1). It should not, however, be forgotten or overlooked that he held racist views over Native Americans living in Yosemite and supported their removal and even extermination.

## Box 3.1 John Muir: Preservation and healing

The tendency nowadays to wander in wildernesses is delightful to see. Thousands of tired, nerve-shaken, over-civilized people are beginning to find out that going to the mountains is going home; that wildness is a necessity; and that mountain parks and reservations are useful not only as fountains of timber and irrigating rivers, but as fountains of life. Awakening from the stupefying effects of the vice of over-industry and the deadly apathy of luxury, they are trying as best they can to mix and enrich their own little ongoings with those of Nature, and to get rid of rust and disease. Briskly venturing and roaming, some are washing off sins and cobweb cares of the devil's spinning in all-day storms on mountains; sauntering in rosiny pinewoods or in gentian meadows, brushing through chaparral, bending down and parting sweet, flowery sprays; tracing rivers to their sources, getting in touch with the nerves of Mother Earth; jumping from rock to rock, feeling the life of them, learning the songs of them, panting in whole-souled exercise, and rejoicing in deep, long-drawn breaths of pure wildness. This is fine and natural and full of promise. So also is the growing interest in the care and preservation of forests and wild places in general, and in the half-wild parks and gardens of towns. Even the scenery habit in its most artificial forms, mixed with spectacles, silliness, and kodaks; its devotees arrayed more gorgeously than scarlet tanagers, frightening the wild game with red umbrellas – even this is encouraging, and may well be regarded as a hopeful sign of the times.

John Muir, Our National Parks, 1901. Accessible at https://vault.sierraclub.org/john_muir_exhibit/writings/our_national_parks/chapter_1.aspx

Muir passionately promoted "preservationism," a radical approach to protection, in which nature acquires an intrinsic value: It is worthy of being protected for itself, against the harmful effects of societies, according to a principle of separation of the natural and social world. The notion of wilderness is central to the movement (Muir would write that "the clearest way into the Universe is through a forest wilderness").[5]

But the political dimension of the preservation movement also needs to be highlighted. In a speech delivered at the cornerstone ceremony for the Roosevelt Arch[6] in Yellowstone National Park in 1903, Theodore Roosevelt (October 27, 1858 to January 6, 1919), the 26th President of the United States, insisted that national parks were created "for the benefit and enjoyment of the people" and that "the park idea is noteworthy in its essential democracy." Environmental resources are thus part of human justice (we will come back to this in detail in Chapter 4). To make these resources freely available to the greatest possible number, regardless of money or power, must be part of the democratic project (legally transposing natural resources in the public domain, as for instance the National Trust[7] does in the UK, is part of this "essential democracy" process). From a policy perspective, preservation, as implemented by Theodore Roosevelt, with the creation of national parks, has put justice, both intra-generational and inter-generational, at the forefront.

In contrast to preservationism, "conservationism" has instead proposed a reasoned management of natural resources exploited for human well-being. The movement's momentum has greatly benefited from the publication of a major book, *Man and Nature* by George Perkins Marsh (1801–1882). In it, the ideal of harmony between the natural world and humanity is contested (Marsh writes about "the hostile influence of man," the true "disturbing agent" of the biosphere) and the picture of a "second Nature" close to what Cicero has envisioned[8] emerges. Celebrated as soon as it was published in 1864, the book was republished with an even more explicit title: *The Earth as Modified by Human Action* in 1874. Lewis Mumford[9] claimed in 1924 that *Man and Nature* was the source of the entire conservation movement.

Gifford Pinchot (1865–1946), the most important figure of the conservationist movement that sought to bring balance back in the relation between "Man and Nature," promoted the notion of "wise use" of resources and will later become the first head of the US federal forest service, one of the first sectors where the concept of sustainability emerged. This sustainable use of natural resources (to be achieved through government regulation) is not the same as *laissez-faire* "green" capitalism. The goal of conservationism is not to make money but to ensure that natural resources continue to be available for human enjoyment in the future. Yet, conservationism understood as natural utilitarianism brings about the issue of inter-generational inequality, as this statement of Pinchot in 1909 makes clear: "The first principle of conservation is development, the use of the natural resources now existing on this continent for the benefit of the people who live here now."[10]

The very real opposition between preservation and conservation, that has inspired many environmental debates such as the choice between "strong" and "weak" sustainability,[11] has been mythologized over time. Preservationism is as political as it is mystical and conservationism is not as market-oriented as it seems. The truth remains that while Muir and Pinchot were originally friends and allies, they became increasingly alienated until their different philosophies led them to bitterly oppose one another in the battle over the damming of Hetch-Hetchy in Yosemite,[12] a fight lost by Muir. It is nevertheless equally true that both movements have insisted on the necessity for environmental governance that Elinor Ostrom was able to document and conceptualize through her re-discovery of the "commons."

## Governing the commons, from Garrett Hardin to Elinor Ostrom

Biologist Garrett Hardin deserves credit for opening the way to the commons framework, showing that not only human arrangements could end up promoting secession and defection but that, moreover, they could lead to collective ruin. In 1968, Hardin published a resounding article in which he deplored the "tragedy of the commons" at work in the world. His reasoning is apparently convincing: The "invisible hand" imagined by Adam Smith[13] – according to which, in a market economy, individuals must be concerned only about their personal interests without ever worrying about the fate of others

– leads in environmental matters not to the "wealth of nations" promised by Smith but to the ruin of citizens.

The allegory chosen by Hardin is that of shepherds exhausting the pasture they share without owning it, for lack of distributing its use effectively. The logic of Hardin's demonstration resembles Mancur Olson's "free rider" problem: If each farmer intends to privatize his gains (the sale of well-fed cows on the market) while socializing its costs (grass consumption), the pasture will be rapidly exhausted (the "invisible hand" ransacking the common resource). Breeders, along with their animals, will soon wither away. Since "injustice is preferable to total ruin" it is wise, according to Hardin, to institute a "mutual coercion, mutually agreed upon." In other words, to resort to a central authority able to impose its choices on individuals for their own good.

The revolution of the commons, that will give back hope in self-organized efficient cooperation, was born out of a major flaw in the reasoning of Hardin. Hardin evokes a tragedy of the commons, but the illustration he gives rather evokes what we would now call "open access resources." Common resources, or commons, are resources held under the regime of common property by a human group (a category distinct from both private and public property), while free access resources are non-exclusive, meaning that no one can be stopped from consuming them (see Chapter 6). For example, access to the open sea is free, as too are the fishing areas that are there. This explains why fish stocks are subject to a "tragedy of free access" or even a "tragedy of self-service": In the last twenty-five years, while ships became increasingly powerful (their fishing capacity increasing considerably), they have returned to their nets fewer and fewer fish simply because stocks are running out (90% of commercial fish stocks are already fully exploited or over-exploited). Like in a Greek tragedy, even though this situation is known to all, fish and fishermen disappear inexorably, year after year.

Hardin's pasture is thus not a common, and if it were one, it would probably not be over-exploited. It is what Elinor Ostrom has attempted to demonstrate throughout her academic career, which started with the study of water management in California. This inaugural work echoes that of another famous economist among the too-rare women of this discipline, Katharine Coman, published in the first issue of the *American Economic Review*, in 1911. (Coman highlighted the economic problems posed by irrigation systems, that can be solved by resorting to commons.)

Ostrom will gradually expand her topic to systematically analyze the institutions that allow (or do not allow) sustainable exploitation of natural resources. How do Maine lobster fishermen in the United States distribute fishing rights equitably while taking care of their resource, which is also the source of their sustained livelihood? That's what Ostrom's work seems to clarify.

Hardin predicted that individuals' pursuit of their personal interest would lead to collective impoverishment and that only an outside authority was able to produce and impose standards to bend these behaviors and rescue collective prosperity from individual greed. Ostrom's masterpiece (1990)[14] will demonstrate, conversely, that institutions invented by human communities can themselves foster preservation through cooperation. It is therefore a double invalidation of Hardin's hypothesis: Efficient cooperation is possible and it is self-determined.

Ostrom starts from a fundamental discovery: In the so-called "public goods" game, individuals cooperate much more than what by standard theory assumes, especially if they have the opportunity to punish free riders. This game is based on a somewhat complex setting. The organizers explain to the participants that, during several consecutive rounds, they will be associated with other players anonymously, each being endowed with a starting bet, say twenty euros. In each round, all players are confronted with two options: either to put their money in a common account or deposit it in a personal account, knowing that the gains of the common account are repaid on each individual count at the end of each round in proportion to the contributions. However, the common account yield is lower than that of personal accounts, so that its profitability depends on the cooperative goodwill of the players (the higher the contributions to the joint account are, the more it will bring back to each player). The profitability results of the common account are announced at the end of each round of play, which allows each player to guess the decisions of others and to adapt his own accordingly for the following turn.

In such a game, the logic of individual interest and uncertainty about the cooperative ability of other players should induce individuals not to cooperate, that is never to contribute to the common account. Reality is strikingly different: Players start by investing on average half of their endowment on the common account. The willingness to cooperate is thus much stronger than expected, especially if players are given the means to punish the non-cooperators (for instance through financial fines imposed on those who never contribute to the common account).

Ostrom will go on to verify this theoretical intuition throughout the world and will make an even bigger discovery: In hundreds of meticulously documented cases, humans are able to avoid the "tragedy of the commons" by building collective rules whose pillars are reciprocity and trust. The "public good" is no longer an abstract common account, but, very concretely, rivers that should be preserved from pollution, forests that must be reasonably exploited, fish that must be harvested with moderation to allow them to reproduce. From Swiss forests to Japanese pastures, irrigation systems in Spain to irrigation systems in Nepal, Ostrom shows that humans are able to cooperate for preserve, conserve, and prosper.

From her field observations, Ostrom will draw core principles for a sustainable management of common resources. These principles, eleven of them, can be simply understood as the rules of the game of human environmental cooperation (see Box 3.2).

## Box 3.2 the rules of the game of environmental cooperation

1A. User boundaries: Clear and locally understood boundaries between legitimate users and nonusers are present.

1B. Resource boundaries: Clear boundaries that separate a specific common-pool resource from a larger social-ecological system are present.

2A. Congruence with local conditions: Appropriation and provision rules are congruent with local social and environmental conditions.

2B. Appropriation and provision: Appropriation rules are congruent with provision rules; the distribution of costs is proportional to the distribution of benefits.

3. Collective choice arrangements: Most individuals affected by a resource regime are authorized to participate in making and modifying its rules.

4A. Monitoring users: Individuals who are accountable to or are the users monitor the appropriation and provision levels of the users.

4B. Monitoring the resource: Individuals who are accountable to or are the users monitor the condition of the resource.

5. Graduated sanctions: Sanctions for rule violations start very low but become stronger if a user repeatedly violates a rule.

6. Conflict resolution mechanisms: Rapid, low cost, local arenas exist for resolving conflicts among users or with officials.

7. Minimal recognition of rights: The rights of local users to make their own rules are recognized by the government.

8. Nested enterprises: When a common-pool resource is closely connected to a larger social-ecological system, governance activities are organized in multiple nested layers.

*Source:* Elinor Ostrom "Beyond markets and states: Polycentric governance of complex economic systems," Prize Lecture, 2009 ©The Nobel Foundation

These principles have emerged from the communities studied themselves. By contrast, rules imposed by authority upon local groups by distant governments often are counterproductive because the authorities in question do not have sufficient information or legitimacy (the privatization of natural resources also suffer from many limitations, to begin with their injustice).

In the Ostromian framework of analysis, we clearly see the importance of the relationship – fundamental, but often neglected – between resources and trust, or natural and social capital. Economist Partha Dasgupta has also insisted on the importance of institutional trust in the management of natural resources exploited in common. In environmental governance systems, it is critical that participants are properly informed on future gains from social cooperation.[15] Mechanisms of trust and mistrust are also at the heart of international environmental governance, starting with climate negotiations (see on this point, Finus 2008).[16] The governance of the commons can be sustainable only if it acknowledges distributional issues and justice principles. We now turn to their study.

# 4

# Spheres of environmental justice

The notion of environmental justice embodies the sustainability–justice nexus. It has been defined by the US Environmental Protection Agency (EPA) as "the fair treatment and meaningful involvement of all people regardless of race, colour, national origin, or income with respect to the development, implementation, and enforcement of environmental laws, regulations, and policies." But this is only one approach to environmental justice and there is no universal approach to what is fair. In *Spheres of Justice: A Defense of Pluralism and Equality*, philosopher Michael Walzer defines a "complex equality," built on the principles of pluralism in the distribution of social goods. In this spirit, this chapter aims at equipping readers with analytical tools to grasp the plurality of approaches to environmental justice.

The concern about "environmental justice" was born in the United States at the end of the 1970s in the context of racial progress and civic activism. Agyeman, Bullard, and Evans define the situation of environmental injustice that was then underlined as one where "people of colour are forced, through their lack of access to decision-making and policy-making processes, to live with a disproportionate share of environmental 'bads' – and thus to suffer the related public health problems and quality-of-life burdens."[1] The defining episode of the environmental justice movement took place in Warren County in 1982, when African-American residents of this North Carolina district opposed the building of a toxic waste landfill nearby.

This inaugural struggle led to the drafting and publication of the first comprehensive report on environmental justice in 1987 (*Toxic Wastes and Race* by the United Church of Christ, covering the US). Delegates to the First National People of Color Environmental Leadership Summit (held on October 24–27, 1991, in Washington DC) subsequently drafted and adopted seventeen principles of environmental justice. Among them: "the sacredness of Mother Earth, ecological unity and the interdependence of all species, and the right to be free from ecological destruction" and "public policy [...] based on mutual respect and justice for all peoples, free from any form of discrimination or bias." These concerns are not abstract demands: In the US, minorities and poor communities are indeed overwhelmingly exposed to pollution and its detrimental effects on health and human well-being (see Box 4.1).

## Box 4.1 The top 20 of the "Toxic 100"

The annual "Toxic 100" reports are the work of economists Michael Ash and James Boyce at the Political Economy Research Institute (University of Massachusetts Amherst). The "Toxic 100 Air" ranks companies by comparative chronic human health risk from air pollutants directly released or transferred to incinerators (and not destroyed) from large facilities in the US in 2015. It also calculates shares of the total population health risk borne by people living below the poverty line or by people in minority racial/ethnic groups (table). As the data clearly show, the burden of pollution falls disproportionately on poor people and non-whites in the US.

| Toxic 100 Air Rank | Corporation | Toxic score (pounds released) | Poor Share % | Minority Share % |
|---|---|---|---|---|
| 1 | DowDuPont | 6,021,585 | 22 | 51 |
| 2 | Berkshire Hathaway | 5,587,777 | 20 | 34 |
| 3 | General Electric | 4,813,749 | 25 | 55 |
| 4 | Royal Dutch Shell | 4,666,378 | 20 | 67 |
| 5 | TMS International Corp | 3,172,269 | 33 | 72 |
| 6 | Arconic | 2,671,242 | 24 | 58 |
| 7 | LyondellBasell Industries | 2,431,292 | 20 | 70 |
| 8 | Freeport-McMoRan | 1,925,413 | 27 | 48 |
| 9 | Exxon Mobil | 1,919,199 | 24 | 69 |
| 10 | United Technologies | 1,839,298 | 18 | 49 |
| 11 | BASF | 1,795,499 | 26 | 44 |
| 12 | Schlumberger | 1,613,639 | 23 | 70 |
| 13 | Koch Industries | 1,440,316 | 19 | 44 |
| 14 | BP | 1,401,273 | 19 | 35 |
| 15 | Nucor | 1,272,847 | 34 | 67 |
| 16 | Huntsman | 1,166,673 | 18 | 41 |
| 17 | Valero Energy | 1,145,710 | 20 | 65 |
| 18 | Eastman Chemical | 1,083,117 | 22 | 24 |
| 19 | Phillips 66 | 1,041,909 | 19 | 57 |
| 20 | Occidental Petroleum | 1,037,515 | 20 | 66 |

*Note:* The official poverty rate in 2015 was 13.5%; non-Hispanic whites made up 63% of the country's population in 2015, minorities thus representing 37%.

Environmental justice, in the US, then moved from activism to policy and became part of the US EPA agenda in 1994, following an executive order from the Clinton Administration.[2] It has developed in many parts of the world since then. In Scotland for instance, where the "Choosing our future" strategy was adopted in 2005, policy-makers acknowledged that "Scotland's most deprived communities may also be most vulnerable to the pressures of poor local environments. Environmental justice is focused upon addressing this inequity. When we talk about environmental justice we are talking not only about addressing the unfair burden carried by communities who live in the most degraded environments but also about fairness in providing the information and opportunities for people to participate in decisions affecting their local environments."[3] They added: "Environmental justice is both an urban and a rural issue. It is concerned just as much with local street-level environmental problems as with larger-scale sources of pollution and the built environment is as significant as green places and biodiversity."

One can highlight the similarities and differences between the US and European approaches: While the procedural and distributive aspects of justice are well distinguished in both cases, Europeans emphasize the social conditions that produce environmental injustices, whereas Americans insist on the racial dimension of discrimination and exclusion from the decision-making process of ethnic minorities.[4]

But environmental justice is both older in time and broader in space: At least four different streams of environmental justice can be identified, starting with the Marxist approach.

## The Marxist approach

For Karl Marx, "Labour is, in the first place, a process in which both man and Nature participate, and in which man of his own accord starts, regulates, and controls the material re-actions between himself and Nature." There is thus a close relation between what Marx refers to in the chapter "Machinery and large-scale industry" in the first volume of the *Capital* as "robbing the worker" and "robbing the soil." In other words, there is a direct connection from the alienation of labor to the alienation of Nature. It was only in the 1980s that Marxist studies once again took a serious interest in the ecological question, under the impulse of work conducted by John Bellamy Foster, James O'Connor, or Paul Burkett.

Three major related ideas emerged or re-emerged from the Marxist conceptual matrix: the rupture of social metabolism as a cause of ecological crisis; the predatory nature of capitalism on ecosystems; and finally "social ecology" as a general framework to understand how environmental degradations can stem from social predicaments.

The process of rupture of social metabolism ("a metabolism prescribed by the natural laws of life itself" according to Marx) is detailed in the first volume of the

Capital: "Capitalist production ... disturbs the metabolic interaction between man and the Earth, i.e. it prevents the return to the soil of its constituent elements consumed by man in the form of food and clothing; hence it hinders the operation of the eternal natural condition for the lasting fertility of the soil."[5] This idea came to be known as the "metabolic rift" (an expression introduced by John Bellamy Foster to refer to Karl Marx's notion of the "irreparable rift in the interdependent process of social metabolism"). The notion of metabolism (Stoffwechsel in German or "material exchange") refers to the fact that the labor process is understood as a mediation in a larger system of physical exchanges, which imposes limits on him, and to which he remains inevitably united.

According to this perspective, the ecological crisis would be the consequence of a disruption in the exchange of materials between societies and their environment, a disturbance that can occur in different historical conditions, but that the capitalist mode of production greatly accelerated. Moore[6] has indeed shown how capitalism has brought about a way of organizing collective relations with nature, and of organizing them in the perspective of an ever wider and more intense exploitation (fossil fuels being a case in point as they feed the intensification and expansion of capitalist exploitation).

Murray Bookchin represents a different stream of eco-marxism. In a series of books and articles, the first of which was "Ecology and revolutionary thought" (1964), the American thinker and activist emphatically asserted the central thesis of what he called "social ecology." Informed by the belief that "all ecological problems have their roots in social problems,"[7] social ecology, defined by Bookchin, does not incriminate individual human motivations, the greed to consume or to enjoy. His concern is the social system, not the individual. Because of this focus on institutions rather than individuals, Bookchin sought new forms of human cooperation, offering to build "communalism" at the local level, against the false alternative of centralized power and laissez-faire (the importance of local social-ecological transitions, especially at the cities level, will be explored in Chapter 12).

## Eco-feminism

Eco-feminism is an activist movement and academic discipline that posits a fundamental connection between the exploitation of nature and the exploitation of women and finds the same oppressive ideology to be at the root of the domination of both women and the biosphere. As an academic discipline, eco-feminism was christened by Françoise D'Eaubonne in Feminism or Death (1974). It was Carolyn Merchant's The Death of Nature (1980) that deepened the critique of the double patriarchal exploitation.

The founding moment of the activist movement was probably the "Women and Life on Earth: Ecofeminism in the Eighties" conference held at Amherst

(March 1980). The conference's speakers explored the connections between feminism, militarism, health, and ecology. The event was followed by the formation of the Women's Pentagon Action, a feminist, anti-militarist, anti-nuclear war weapons group. The movement then grew in the 1980s and 1990s, bringing together members of the feminist and green movements.

One of the 1980 conference organizers, Ynestra King, explained in clear terms the common belief that drove participants: "Ecofeminism is about connectedness and wholeness of theory and practice. It asserts the special strength and integrity of every living thing. For us the snail darter is to be considered side by side with a community's need for water, the porpoise side by side with appetite for tuna, and the creatures it may fall on with Skylab. We are a woman-identified movement and we believe we have a special work to do in these imperilled times. We see the devastation of the Earth and her beings by the corporate warriors, and the threat of nuclear annihilation by the military warriors, as feminist concerns. It is the masculinist mentality which would deny us our right to our own bodies and our own sexuality, and which depends on multiple systems of dominance and state power to have its way."[8]

Because concepts of nature and gender are socially constructed, they vary across cultures. Hence the need for eco-feminism to integrate a plurality of cultural perspectives. In *Staying Alive* (1988),[9] Vandana Shiva extends eco-feminism to developing countries and non-Western cultures (in her case India) to find out how ecological destruction and marginalization of women are connected and, more precisely, how rural Indian women feel and perceive ecological destruction and how they have designed and implemented processes to end the destruction of nature and begin its regeneration. The path-breaking work of Bina Agarwal[10] on gender inequality as a cause of environmental dysfunction is a fundamental reference of contemporary eco-feminism.

## Indigenous environmentalism

Indigenous environmentalism can probably claim to be the oldest of environmental justice traditions but it is also one that was not explicit in the very communities where it was practiced. Rather, indigenous environmentalism has been re-discovered by environmentalist thinkers who have looked to indigenous peoples for inspiration and guidance in order to reinvent a more balanced relationship between contemporary societies and billion years old ecosystems. Yet, the assumption that indigenous people were the "original ecologists" or "original conservationists," living in perfect harmony with the environment, is doubly wrong: It caricatures the natural world as harmonious and indigenous people as "noble savage."

Still, indigenous environmentalism stems from the undeniable fact that native people (approximately 370 million persons occupying 20% of the Earth's territory, from as many as 5,000 different cultures) are more exposed to environmental degradations because of their proximity to natural systems and their social vulnerability. Juan Martinez-Alier[11] makes a fundamental case in this respect: A case that shows the cost of extracting, transport, and consumption of natural resources, which are intensifying on the surface of the planet and which result in considerable amounts of pollution and waste, is first and foremost endured by the poorest and most vulnerable, a number of whom are indigenous.

In this respect, there is a deep injustice between developed and developing nations that the complex notion of ecological debt tries to capture and measure (Box 4. 2).

## Box 4.2 The ecological debt

At least two definitions of the concept of ecological debt co-exist. The first is the debt that we have collectively contracted toward the biosphere (in the form, for example, of the destruction of certain species for which humankind is responsible), toward our fellow human beings (in the form, for example, of harmful consequences of extreme events caused by climate change of human origin), and toward future generations (for instance with respect to the scarcity of water resources as a result of their over-exploitation). This definition of ecological debt is both the most accurate and the most difficult to measure. But it is not the one that is generally used in international forums.

Since the beginning of the 1990s, the idea has prevailed that rich countries, because they have transferred part of the ecological cost of their development to the poor countries, have been guilty of a misconduct that calls for compensation. But this ecological debt as a debt of rich countries suffers from a paradox: It claims justice and reparation but generally refuses to quantify the damages suffered in the name of the moral impossibility of monetizing natural resources.

The most interesting quantitative exercise related to this definition of the ecological debt was carried out by a team led by Thara Srinivasan (University of Berkeley) and published in 2008.[12] Researchers involved in this publication endeavored to evaluate the distribution of environmental costs (resulting from deforestation, climate change, or over-fishing) by distinguishing three types of countries according to their level of development. Their calculation, which is based on many debatable assumptions, nevertheless leads to a very interesting result. It shows that poor countries bear the same "gross" share of global environmental costs as rich countries (20%), while middle-income countries bear 60% of costs. But once these costs are weighted by the level of development of the countries that assume them (what could be called the "net cost"), the distribution is radically transformed: 45% for poor countries, 52% for intermediate countries, and only three percent for rich countries.

Another interesting result of the study is to show that more than half of these environmental costs for poor countries come from the activity of two other categories of countries, not just the rich ones but also the emerging economies. This empirical finding reflects the complex and changing reality of our rapidly changing world, where the category "developing countries" is too general and can hardly accurately encompass

China or India. More than any other phenomenon, it is this dynamic that today completely blurs the notion of ecological debt.

This empirical assessment also leads to allocating more than 95% of the ecological debt owed by rich and intermediate countries to poor countries to climate change. If there is ecological debt, it is therefore primarily a climate debt. This notion of climate debt was only seriously debated in 1997 when the Kyoto Protocol was drafted (following a proposal from Brazil) and was then rejected.

From this fact results a counter-intuitive truth: Ecology is not a luxury but a necessity; it is not the prerogative of a wealthy class who would have sublimated its material needs but the condition of survival for disadvantaged people on all continents. The poor are anxious for their environment because they are the first victims of its degradation. As "ecological sentinels," they alert us to the reality of crises in progress that they are the first to feel because of their social vulnerability, just as the inhabitants of the islands of the Pacific alert us to the speed of the rise of the seas and oceans under the effect of climate change. As Schlosberg and Carruthers (2010) argue: "Threats to indigenous peoples – their rights, lands, and cultures – have been a powerful catalyst to mobilization, as native communities fight against the companies, governments, policies, and other forces that threaten to fragment, displace, assimilate, or drive them toward cultural disintegration."[13] Moreover, members of indigenous communities (and more broadly local communities) are critical actors in the preservation of biodiversity and ecosystems they depend on and other humans benefit from (IPBES, 2019). Actually, a larger community has gathered over the years around the idea of indigenous environmentalism, as witnessed by the two Cochabamba Declarations in 2000 and 2010 (Box 4.3).

It was in Cochabamba, in the year 2000, that a whole constellation of social movements – ecologists, peasants, inhabitants of urban peripheries, indigenous people – was formed against the privatization of water. This "water war" led, for the first time, to the expulsion of a multinational that had just won the concession of the water market. This is a proof of the importance of what Martinez-Alier has called "ecological distribution conflicts" to highlight environmental justice issues all over the world.

In 2010, after the failure of the Copenhagen summit on climate change (2009), Cochabamba was again the place where the environmental indigenous movement rallied and gathered other groups. From April 19 to 22, nearly 35,000 activists and intellectuals from 142 countries responded to the invitation of Bolivian President Evo Morales and gathered for the People's Summit on Climate Change and the Rights of Mother Earth.

## Box 4.3 The Cochabamba Declarations

### The Cochabamba Declaration of December 8, 2000

We, citizens of Bolivia, Canada, United States, India, Brazil:

Farmers, workers, indigenous people, students, professionals, environmentalists, educators, nongovernmental organizations, retired people, gather together today in solidarity to combine forces in the defense of the vital right to water.

Here, in this city, which has been an inspiration to the world for its retaking of that right through civil action, courage, and sacrifice, standing as heroes and heroines against corporate, institutional, and governmental abuse, and trade agreements which destroy that right, in use of our freedom and dignity, we declare the following:

For the right to life, for the respect of nature and the uses and traditions of our ancestors and our peoples, for all time the following shall be declared as inviolable rights with regard to the uses of water given us by the Earth:

Water belongs to the Earth and all species and is sacred to life, therefore, the world's water must be conserved, reclaimed, and protected for all future generations and its natural patterns respected.

Water is a fundamental human right and a public trust to be guarded by all levels of government, therefore it should not be commodified, privatized, or traded for commercial purposes. These rights must be enshrined at all levels of government. In particular, an international treaty must ensure that these principles are noncontrovertable.

Water is best protected by local communities and citizens who must be respected as equal partners with governments in the protection and regulation of water. Peoples of the Earth are the only vehicle to promote democracy and save water.

### World People's Conference on Climate Change and the Rights of Mother Earth April 22, 2010

Today, our Mother Earth is wounded and the future of humanity is in danger. Under capitalism, Mother Earth is converted into a source of raw materials, and human beings into consumers and a means of production, into people that are seen as valuable only for what they own, and not for what they are.

It is imperative that we forge a new system that restores harmony with nature and among human beings. And, in order for there to be balance with nature, there must first be equity among human beings.  We propose to the peoples of the world the recovery, revalorization, and strengthening of the knowledge, wisdom, and ancestral practices of Indigenous Peoples, which are affirmed in the thought and practices of "Living Well," recognizing Mother Earth as a living being with which we have an indivisible, interdependent, complementary, and spiritual relationship. To face climate change, we must recognize Mother Earth as the source of life and forge a new system based on the principles of:

- harmony and balance among all and with all things; complementarity, solidarity, and equality;

- collective well-being and the satisfaction of the basic necessities of all; people in harmony with nature;

- recognition of human beings for what they are, not what they own;

- elimination of all forms of colonialism, imperialism and interventionism; peace among the peoples and with Mother Earth.

## The capabilities approach

To understand why environmental inequalities may be unjust, one must adopt an explicit theory of justice. As we have seen, many conceptions of justice co-exist and determine different streams of environmental justice. One of them consists in embracing the capability-building and human development framework developed by Amartya Sen. In essence, the capability approach recommends that well-being be assessed beyond material conditions and also reflect the quality of life of a given person. Among the determinants of quality of life, environmental conditions appear as of great and growing importance.[14]

Based on Sen's analytical framework, we can define an environmental inequality: A situation that results in an injustice or is unjust if the well-being and capabilities of a particular population are disproportionately affected by its environmental conditions of existence.[15] The environmental conditions of existence consist of, negatively, exposure to pollution and risks, and, positively, access to amenities and natural resources (water, air, food). The particular character of the population in question can be defined according to different criteria: social, demographic, spatial.

Environmental justice, therefore, can be said to aim at identifying, measuring, and correcting environmental inequalities that result in social injustice. It implies the adoption of an effective arsenal of public policies grounded on scientific research. Yet, one should be clear that environmental justice does not imply that environmental conditions must be equal for all citizens or groups, but that they should not disproportionately affect their well-being and capabilities with respect to the rest of the population.

A striking example of injustice has been provided by Janet Currie in her study of the lasting effect of pollution on socio-economic fate: "Individuals may start with very different endowments at birth because of events that happened to them during a critical period: the nine months that they were in utero. In turn, endowments at birth have been shown to be predictive of adult outcomes and of the outcomes of the next generation." She adds that "Mechanisms underlying the perpetuation of lower socio-economic status: Poor and minority children are more likely to be in poor health at birth, partly because their mothers are less able to provide a healthy fetal environment. Poor health at birth is associated with poorer adult outcomes, which in turn provide less than optimal conditions for the children of the poor."[16] Toxicologists refer to the first 1,000 days in the life of a child (gestation and the first two years of life) as the period when he or she is critically exposed to or protected from environmental nuisances and pollutions that can impact her or his life for decades.

Different categories of environmental inequality[17] exist and they must be broken down to be properly mitigated.

- Environmental inequality in exposure and access, resulting from the unequal distribution of environmental quality between individuals and groups. Exposure to environmental nuisances, risks, and hazard, on one hand (Box 4.4), are different from inequality in access to environmental amenities, such as green spaces but also energy. Fuel poverty, which is the outcome of unequal social access to energy, is becoming a considerable social problem in a number of European countries like the UK (Box 7.1);
- Environmental inequality regarding the effects of public policy arises when the impact of environmental policies are unevenly distributed among individuals and social groups. For instance, energy and carbon taxation could end up disproportionately burdening those on the lower side of the income spectrum (this kind of injustice triggered the "yellow vests" revolt in France at the end of 2018);
- Environmental inequality with respect to involvement in policy-making means that individuals and groups with more resources have more access to environmental policy-making on a local, national, or global level (simply because, for instance, they are informed of hearings at townhalls and can afford to attend and participate);
- Finally, the lifestyles of different individuals and social groups have unequal environmental impacts (households in the top 10% in the US have a carbon footprint three times higher than households in the bottom 10%).

## Box 4.4 Air (ine)quality

Studies on the health effects of outdoor (ambient) and indoor (household) air pollution, especially particulate matters pollution, nitrogen dioxide, and ozone, have made important progress in recent years. In early 2014, the WHO doubled the figure previously admitted for the number of premature deaths linked to air pollution (to seven million deaths for 2012, or one in eight of total global deaths), a figure confirmed in May 2018. The conclusion of the experts from WHO is unequivocal: "Few risks have a greater impact on global health today than air pollution." A study[18] published in March 2019 estimated that outdoor pollution alone caused 8.8 million extra deaths globally, rather than the previously projected 4.5 million (because of the health damages due to fine and even nano-particulates). This is a major health problem for developing and developed countries.

Inequality is obvious at the international level: 97% of cities in low and middle-income countries with more than 100,000 inhabitants do not meet WHO air quality guidelines, while in high-income countries that percentage decreases to 49%. Yet, within rich regions, while air quality has increased, air inequality remains strong.

It has been estimated that about 19% of Europeans are exposed to dangerous particles in the air they breathe (referred to as PM10) above the EU daily limit and about 30% of Europeans are exposed to bad ozone ($O_3$). Furthermore, about nine percent are exposed to nitrogen dioxide ($NO_2$) concentrations above the annual threshold. Air pollution is the single largest environmental health risk in Europe: The aforementioned 2019 study estimates that the annual excess mortality rate from ambient air pollution in Europe is 790,000 and 659,000 in the EU-28 (air pollution reducing life expectancy in Europe by about 2.2 years). About 80% of cases of heart diseases and strokes, as well as a similar percentage of lung cancers, are linked to air pollution. Health pollution is also associated with health impacts on fertility, pregnancy, new-borns, and children (Eurostat, 2017 data).

A comprehensive European study[19] recently evaluated the health impact of particulate matters of pollution in France. The results, on average, reflect the extent of the health problem: If the WHO standards were met, life expectancy at age thirty could increase by 3.6 to 7.5 months depending on the French city studied.

But the study also reveals spatial or "territorial" inequality attached to this exposure: The health impact varies considerably across urban areas (by a factor 2 between Toulouse, the least polluted city studied, and Marseille, the most polluted one) and even within urban areas themselves. Living close to road traffic significantly increases morbidity due to air pollution (near roads carrying heavy car traffic, the study found an increase of 15 to 30% of new cases of asthma in children and chronic respiratory and cardiovascular pathologies prevalent among adults aged 65).

From the overall impact of the environment on health, one can work one's way down to territorial inequality and finally to the impact on most vulnerable social groups living in urban areas. At the bottom of this chain, injustice is compounded, as air pollution can have long-lasting effects on children's capabilities throughout their lives. Similarly, modern research in toxicology emphasizes the impact of prenatal and perinatal environment on the biological and social development of children.

Some studies in France have assessed this inequality issue systematically, like the Equit'Area project,[20] which carefully measured the differential exposure to air pollution of socially disadvantaged people in French cities. The results are particularly conclusive for exposure to nitrogen dioxide in the cities of Lille and Marseille. In practical terms, a child born today in a district of Marseille in close proximity to a transportation corridor is the victim of socially unjust environmental inequality (in the sense of our definition above) due to particulate matters that can affect health, development, and status throughout life.

Three criteria of environmental inequality can thus be analyzed: The first according to the generating fact of inequality (e.g. exposure or sensitivity), the second according to the inequality vector (e.g. air pollution) and finally the third according to the criterion of inequality (in this latter category, we can find age: exposure to heat waves of the elderly; socio-economic position in a building: living on the ground floor in case of flood or under the roofs in case of heat wave; neighborhood: the children of modest families in French cities of Marseille or Lille are more exposed to fine particle pollution and therefore to its lasting social consequences; geographical position: the coastal areas for storms, urban areas deprived of vegetation for heat waves).

By combining these elements, we can assess that the environmental inequality experienced by a Parisian child living near dense traffic during a spike of pollution due to 2.5 PM particulate matters is an inequality of exposure whose vector is air pollution, and the criteria are age, neighborhood, and locality (at play, with possible others such as race and income level). When it comes to measuring environmental inequality, multiple measures rather than single indicators are needed.[21]

All these injustices regarding the environment are not only topics for research and concern for policy but also legal cases to be examined by courts. Environmental justice is in fact currently making progress in tribunals around the world (see Box 4.5).

## Box 4.5 Environmental justice before the law

There are today dozens of legal actions intended by citizens across the world against states and corporations to denounce their perceived inaction or wrongdoings whereby they delay or block adequate action in mitigating climate change and therefore endanger human well-being.

In Urgenda Foundation v. The State of the Netherlands, C/09/456689/HA ZA 13–1396 (June 24, 2015), The Hague District Court determined the Dutch government must reduce $CO_2$ emissions by a minimum of 25% (compared to 1990) by 2020 to fulfil its obligation to protect and improve the living environment against the imminent danger caused by climate change, introducing the notion of "duty of care" in acting against climate change. On October 9, 2018, The Hague Court of Appeal upheld the lower court decision finding that the Netherlands is breaching its duty of care by "failing to pursue a more ambitious reduction" of greenhouse gas emissions, and confirmed the obligation made to the Dutch government to reduce its emissions by at least 25% by the end of 2020.

On similar grounds, the case known as People's Climate Case was introduced on May 23, 2018 before the Court of the European Union, when a dozen families from Europe and beyond (Portugal, Germany, France, Italy, as well as from Romania, Kenya, Sweden, and Fiji) complained that the 2030 climate objective of the European Union was inadequate, invoking a violation of their human rights. On August 13, 2018, the European Court of Justice ruled that the families' complaint against the European Parliament and the Council of the European Union was legally acceptable.

Finally, in 2015 and 2016, attorneys general in New York, the Virgin Islands and Massachusetts launched investigations to determine whether Exxon Mobil had lied to the general public about climate change risks and its investors. The cases are still pending.

# 5

# Natural resources, externalities, and sustainability: A critical toolbox

Conventional economics tends to view the environment as a field for problem-solving: Where issues exist, economists, like social engineers, offer practical and efficient tools to solve them. This is the reason why most environmental economics textbooks start directly with the economist's toolbox. While indeed potentially and conditionally useful, those tools have little relevance if they are not embedded in the sustainability–justice nexus, and are not informed by the current co-dynamic of social and natural systems. This is why they appear only now in this book. They should also be put in their historical context, hence the need to retrace the different streams of literature from where they have originated. Above all, it is essential to outline their limitations, weaknesses, and even failures.

Economics of the environment, whose premises, as we have seen, go back to the English liberal school, was born with Harold Hotelling as a science of the management of scarcity and efficient allocation of natural resources.[1] Interestingly enough, Hotelling's major paper was an attack on the philosophy of the American conservationist movement, which advocated a slowdown or even a halt in the extraction of natural resources by means of an increase in their prices, including through taxes imposed by the state.

Hotelling essentially argues that public instruments are not warranted to solve extraction issues: The market can help producers find the optimal management rule of goods that are storable, but not reproducible, referred to as "exhaustible resources" (e.g. coal, oil, gas, ores). Optimally managing the stock of these resources is a matter of determining which resource flow will bring the most revenue over the entire extraction operating period. The equilibrium condition, later called "Hotelling's rule," stipulates that the price of the natural resource and therefore the rent attached to it must grow at a rate equal to that of the interest rate. This relation between the rate of extraction and the interest rate is the foundation of discounting analysis.

With Arthur Cecil Pigou,[2] externalities became the heart of environmental economics focused on pollution management. The general problem of environmental economics is the underestimation by the economic system of the real cost of extraction and consumption of natural resources. Two key tools make their appearance with Pigou: the social cost and externalities. The cost to society of environmental damage or natural resource consumption as a whole (the social cost) is generally higher than their cost for individuals (the private cost). When an individual fills a tank with gas, she only pays for the market price of the energy, not for the local and global pollutions resulting from the combustion of fossil fuels. This disconnection is called an externality (negative in this case) and it gives rise to a "market failure": The market fails in pricing environmental damage correctly, leaving a gap between the private and the social cost. The seminal work by Pigou led to the definition of an externality as a positive or negative interaction between two economic agents (producers, consumers, public authority) that is not mediated by the market and thus not priced. Environmental economics is still defined today by the idea of pollution as an externality. To "internalize" an externality is to give it a price, to bring the externality back into the market, so that it is accounted for by economic agents in their behaviors.

Pigou takes the example of the sparks created by railway engines that can set surrounding cultivated fields on fire: Pieces of glowing charcoal sometimes escape from chimneys and trigger forest or field fires near railroad tracks. Pigou considers that a tax on the damage inflicted by the railway company would encourage the installation of devices preventing the accident from happening and would limit the damage. This reasoning laid the groundwork for the "polluter-payer" principle (those who create environmental damage should bear the costs of mitigating it).

The challenge of sustainability, which emerged in the 1970s in the academic and public debate – especially with the work of the Meadows team at the Massachusetts Institute of Technology (MIT) and their report for the Club of Rome "The Limits to Growth" – led to a re-foundation of environmental economics. Simply put, sustainability analysis' core question is the possibility of maintaining human well-being at an at least constant level for future periods and future generations. The point is no longer to exploit natural resources profitably or to measure the ecological damage of economic activity and devise practical tools for remedying it, but to analyze whether the economic system itself will stand the test of time, given current patterns of consumption and production. As a sub-discipline of sustainable economics, "ecological macro-economics" has developed a lot in recent years.[3] This concern for sustainable development made a remarkable breakthrough on the international scene with the publication of the Brundtland Report in 1987 "Our Common Future" – roughly three decades ago.

In parallel, the concern for sustainability has crystallized a disciplinary evolution, from the economy of the environment (or environmental economics) to ecological economics. This shift was spearheaded by the members of the Resources for the Future Association, founded in 1952 by William Paley (Columbia University), the first think-tank devoted exclusively to environmental issues, and some vagabond and free spirits, standing in between disciplines rather than barricaded in one, such as Nicholas Georgescu-Roegen, Kenneth Boulding (Box 5.1), and Herman Daly.

---

### Box 5.1 Kenneth Boulding

"Anyone who believes that exponential growth can go on forever in a finite world is either a madman or an economist": With that sentence, Kenneth Boulding became one of the most widely quoted economists of all times. Boulding was a British economist who has worked throughout a rich intellectual life and academic career marked by the spirit of independence to enrich economic theory and analysis by building bridges with other social disciplines as well as with natural sciences.

In 1968, he presented his most emblematic article, "Economics as a Moral Science" (Boulding, 1969), when he was elected to the influential presidency of the American Economic Association. In it, he expresses his profound aversion to what he facetiously calls "the Immaculate Conception of the indifference curve" according to which the preferences of individuals are supposed to be known without it being necessary to understand how they become. According to Boulding, no science, not even the most obscure, can claim to divest from ethical considerations. Economics is thus a moral science, a truth re-asserted later with force by Amartya Sen and Anthony Atkinson.

For Boulding, just as the economy is not an autonomous system with respect to ethical considerations, it is not an extra-terrestrial system either: It is included in a physical and natural environment from which it cannot be abstracted. To his ethical criticism that brings into play the idea of well-being (largely neglected by orthodox economics), Boulding adds an ecological criticism, in which the issue of sustainability takes center stage. In "A Reconstruction of Economics" (1950), Boulding had already begun to develop a model of relationships between material flows and behaviors of economic agents.

In what is certainly his best-known contribution to the general public, "The Economics of the Coming Spaceship Earth" (1966), Boulding uses the metaphor of the spaceship to describe planet Earth (spaceship Earth) and its physical limits. He then opposes the ethos of the cowboy (conquest, spirit of the frontier, unlimited consumption) to that of the astronaut, who must adjust his behavior to limited natural resources (and must therefore place recycling at the center of its ethos).

Because of his concern both for inter-disciplinarity and well-being, Boulding is obviously one of the spiritual fathers of ecological economics.

---

Their shared belief was that nature should be brought back in economic reasoning in a mode other than instrumental. The environment changes the nature of the economy. Ecological economics[4] is simply defined as the joint study of natural systems and human systems that aims at overcoming both environmental economics understood in the narrow sense of applying neo-classical analysis to environmental issues and ecology understood in the narrow sense of the science of the natural world. Ecological economics focuses on revaluing natural resources in relation to human well-being, rethinking how economic wealth is being assessed.

The new environmental economics this book puts forward builds on these different streams of analysis and policy but adds to them by concentrating on a key interconnection of our time: the sustainability–justice nexus. This central concern is a serious challenge to the neo-classical version of environmental economics.

In a remarkable series of videos echoing his far-reaching work,[5] which can serve as an ideal complement to this textbook, James Boyce distinguishes two types of efficiency: cost-effectiveness and cost-benefit analysis. The former, says Boyce, is about optimizing means: how to reach a goal using the least possible necessary resources. The latter is about defining ends: What goals should be pursued? What goals can be neglected? As we have seen in Chapter 1, this distinction is decisive from the perspective of the new environmental economics because neo-classical (as well as Keynesian) economics has pursued efficiency to the detriment of sustainability and justice. But one needs to be as clear and precise as possible when using terms as complex as "justice" and "inequality."

Let us start with simple definitions of a difference, an inequality, an inequity, and an injustice. The existence of a difference stems from the mere observation of a disparity leading to a positive rather than normative judgment (a person is richer or healthier than another regardless of any fairness assessment). An inequality can be defined as a systematic difference, which systematic character has been inferred from an empirical framework; it also leads to a positive judgment (descendants of immigrants in France exhibit higher unemployment rates than descendants of natives). The existence of an inequity supposes a normative approach: For instance, the World Health Organization (WHO) defines health inequities as "avoidable inequalities" arising from social and economic rather than biological conditions (this definition entails a certain view of what is avoidable or not and how it can be avoided via appropriate policy actions). Finally, an injustice (or unfairness) is a fully normative view and can only be defined by resorting to a theory of justice. One of them, as we have seen in Chapter 4, is Amartya Sen's capabilities approach (which differs from the injustices resulting from other ethical and/or philosophical conceptions). Dynamic justice is the most demanding form of justice, as it seeks equity among current generations but also between current and future generations.

At least three types of inequality can stand in the way of neo-classical efficiency: inequality among living beings (humans and non-humans), inequality among humans today (synchronic or intra-generational inequality) and finally inequality among humans today and humans tomorrow (diachronic or inter-generational inequality). Intra and inter-generational inequality can be domestic (inequality within individuals and groups within the US) or international (inequality between the US and Senegal). Finally, these inequalities can be of income or power. As was shown in Chapter 1, inequality (especially high and growing inequality of the type we have seen emerging in the last thirty years) derails economic efficiency from a number of standpoints (Chapter 10 will provide further analytical and empirical evidence of this derailment).

This is because neo-classical economics rests on the identification of social welfare with maximization of net present value measured by cost-benefit analysis. When justice (including dynamic, i.e. inter-generational justice) is introduced as an input (in the form of inequality derailing efficiency) the edifice of neo-classical economics sways. When justice is introduced as an outcome (as an equal or more desirable goal than efficiency), it collapses altogether.

If dynamic justice is considered as a new objective for environmental economics (as the new environmental economics does), then the neo-classical model becomes irrelevant because it was never designed to pursue justice, provided that justice is neither denied, assumed, nor traded off (Chapter 1).

Let us illustrate this statement. In 1991, in an infamous memo to the World Bank, then chief economist Larry Summers argued that: "the economic logic behind dumping a load of toxic waste in the lowest wage country is impeccable." The logic in question was textbook cost-benefit analysis: Given the lower wages of workers in developing economies, the cost of harming their health and possibly taking their lives with pollution outsourcing appeared inferior to the cost of keeping polluting industries within developed nations. When justice rather than efficiency is considered as a goal, this "logic" vanishes: Human beings have an equal right to be healthy regardless of their nationality and socio-economic conditions. When dynamic justice (inter-generational justice) is considered, this "logic" becomes counter-productive: Allowing for the outsourcing of dirty industries from rich to poor countries means that pollution is never reduced but merely transferred, as we will see in Chapter 8 with the case of climate change, resulting in the increase of global emissions, which eventually will harm the health of workers in developed nations.

There are many types[6] and schools of justice and environmental justice (see Chapter 4) and choosing among their criteria and demands is no easy task. But there is no doubt that they require a whole new set of assumptions, methods, instruments, and policy standards than environmental neo-classical economics. Let us be more specific in our critical approach to the environmental economics' toolbox and start reviewing its core instruments.

## The economic nature of environmental goods

Paul Samuelson, the founding father of public economics, proposed in 1954 to classify goods (in the broad sense of what may be useful to humans) according to two simple criteria: exclusivity and rivalry. A good is "rivalrous" if one person's consumption reduces the consumption of another one. A good is "excludable" if it is possible to prevent somebody from consuming it.

The complexity of the current and future climate crisis is that climate is both non-exclusive (it is not technically possible to prevent anyone from benefiting from it) and non-rival (its use by an individual does not prevent others from enjoying it).[7] Because climate is a non-exclusive good, all countries, especially the top emitters (starting with China), have to be included in any meaningful international climate agreement (see Chapter 7). But, because climate is a non-rival good, strong constraints are needed to support this universal partici-pation, to ensure that fully sovereign nations cooperate effectively within the framework of the United Nations and do not continue to behave as if the atmosphere could store infinite amounts of $CO_2$ without serious consequences. Many natural resources, which seem to be abundant or even unlimited, are similar in nature to climate. They are what Samuelson called "pure public goods."

Two types of goods are thus easily identifiable: Pure private goods (such as fossil fuels and mineral ores that belong to private individuals and organiza-tions or state companies) and pure public goods (such as climate or pure air).

James Buchanan (1965) characterized a third type of good, which he labelled "club goods." Groups of individuals can indeed create private associations (or clubs) to provide themselves with non-rivalrous but small-scale goods and services that they can enjoy while excluding non-members (a municipal pond fits this description, as well as Gramercy Park in Manhattan, accessible only to residents of the surrounding 39 buildings that hold the 383 keys to its gates). A fourth category of environmental goods, that are non-excludable but rival, include so-called open-access resources such as ocean fishing.

The whole point of this matrix is to characterize the specific institu-tional constraints attached to each environmental resource, and thus the distinct challenges that environmental policy faces for each of them. Defining adequate property rights is viewed in this respect as the key measure leading to sustainable exploitation of natural resources. But this characteristically neo-classical approach is too narrow.

In fact, Elinor Ostrom challenged this neat typology, introducing social justice considerations into Samuelson's criteria: Many open-access goods are actually common-pool resources or commons, meaning that they are not just goods but a set of social relations based on justice principles (see Chapter 3). In line with this idea, Ostrom suggested replacing the notion of "rivalry of consumption" with that of "subtractability of use," characterizing commons as goods sharing the attribute of subtractability with private goods and the difficulty of exclusion with public goods. If these goods are to be managed sustainably, justice rather than efficiency will have to take center stage (again, see Chapter 3). These equity considerations are also central for natural resources valuation.

## The many values of natural resources

The general framework for analyzing the economic valuation of natural resources is an analytical chain: Biodiversity determines the vitality and resilience of ecosystems (i.e. ecosystems functions); these functions in turn determine their ability to render "services" to humans which finally support human well-being (recently, the broader notion of Nature's "contributions" to humans has been introduced).

In other words, the ecosystem services sustained by biological diversity freely provide goods and services to humans that should be valued in order to be protected. The Millennium Ecosystem Assessment (2005) defined Ecosystem Services as "the benefits people derive from ecosystems." Besides provisioning services or goods like food, wood, and other raw materials, plants, animals, fungi, and micro-organisms provide essential regulating services such as pollination of crops, prevention of soil erosion and water purification, and a vast array of cultural services, like recreation and spirituality.

These different services in turn determine our capabilities (in the sense of Sen): Our health (ability to access adequate nutrition, to escape preventable diseases, to drinking water, to a healthy atmosphere, access to sources of energy protecting from heat and cold), our security (ability to live in a clean and healthy environment, to mitigate vulnerability to ecological shocks and stress), the essential elements for a pleasant life (ability to access resources providing income and leading to well-being), and finally, good social relations.

Pollination (transferring pollen grains from the male anther of a flower to the female stigma) is one example of such ecosystem service. The IPBES (The Intergovernmental Science-Policy Platform on Biodiversity and Ecosystem Services) has recently estimated that 75% of the world's food crops depend at least in part on pollination while the annual value of global crops directly affected by pollinators could be assessed as being between US$235 billion and US$577 billion. Yet, 40% of invertebrate pollinator species – particularly bees and butterflies – are facing extinction.[8] One of the key insights of natural resources valuation is that replacing natural ecosystem services with a humanly engineered one is extremely costly and time-consuming. Such is obviously the case when humans must hand-pollinate fruit trees because natural pollinators have been decimated by chemicals-intensive agriculture.

Although some estimates exist about the actual economic value of ecosystem services such as the one provided by the IPBES, comprehensive and accurate economic valuation of natural resources is so complex that it is seldom robust and convincing. An animal or plant species has indeed many possible values. The easiest to grasp are of course the ones related to utility and efficiency: Natural resources have a value of use, direct (food, contemplation), or indirect (pollination, climate regulation). But they also have a value of non-use (the "existence value"), an option value (the possibility of using the resource in the future), a quasi-option value (an unknown value may be in the future), and even a legacy value (passing the resource to others). Properly estimated, the "economic value" of natural resources goes well beyond their immediate utility for current generations: It is the complex product of all these values (see Figure 5.1).

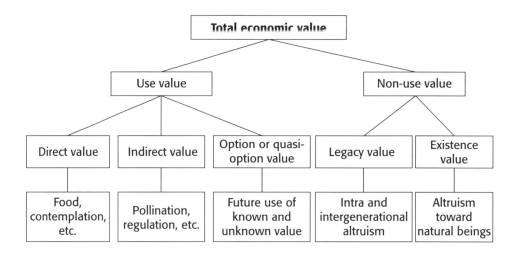

Figure 5.1   The many values of natural resources

Existing valuation methods, which are the building blocks of cost-benefit analysis, overlook both this complexity and the equity issues attached to giving a price to natural resources. The "revealed preference" method relies on behaviors and experiments to estimate the demand function of agents for an environmental good (economists generally believe that, in the words of Fuchs 1983, "what people do is more relevant than what they say").

The most obvious case is when a market exists for natural resources and can be used to evaluate the value of an environmental good or service. This will be the case, for example, with fossil fuels or minerals: The resource will be monetized at the market price. One can also directly evaluate the costs of the use of the resource from, for example, its distribution (it is then the distribution of the resource which is monetarized). This is true of water: Its value is represented by the benefits it provides to users, but its price is that of the market. It includes the costs of water supply (capital and operating costs of extraction, treatment, and transportation of water to the point of use). These costs will be recovered by the distributor from the user: The users must pay all the costs related to the extraction, collection, processing, and distribution of water, but also the collection, treatment, and discharge of waste water. The final price of the water finally corresponds to the pre-raised charges from the consumers.

Yet, markets are hardly efficient guides for environmental policy. Energy markets for instance depend on economic and geopolitical issues completely disconnected from climate change, such as, for the oil market, the rivalry between Saudi Arabia and Iran, that weight on supply, and the fluctuations of the Chinese economy, that weight on demand. In the last decade alone, oil prices went from $95 to $60 then up to $110 and down to $40 and back up to $70 (Graph 5.1), as if on a roller coaster.

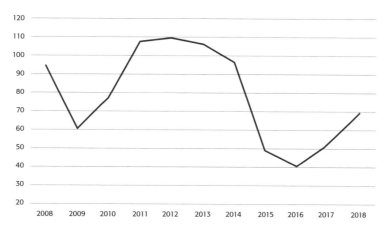

Graph 5.1  Oil prices, 2008–2018 in $

*Source:* Average annual OPEC crude oil price from 2008 to 2018 (in US dollars per barrel)

The belief or hope that energy markets will drive economic behaviors rationally in directions favorable to human well-being is simply misplaced and not backed by empirical evidence. But researchers and policy-makers encounter cases where such markets simply do not exist. They then often turn to instances where people have faced exogenous changes in the price and quantity of goods available and infer from the observed behavior (whereby individuals reveal their otherwise hidden preference) the relationship between price and quantity, and therefore their demand. The two main revealed preference methods are the transport cost method (what agents are willing to pay for accessing a natural amenity, for instance the cost of driving to a park or a beach) and the hedonic price method (which derives from preferences expressed for goods, mainly places of residence which have environmental attributes, for instance the price people are willing to pay to live near Central Park in New York).

These methods are very limited in and of themselves. Both methods suppose that markets operate in accordance with the ideal-type of the competitive market, and that the players in these markets are able to anticipate costs and future benefits perfectly. More importantly, these valuation techniques do not take into account power and income inequality.

The "stated preference" methods are, instead, based on individuals' opinions and consist, as shown by surveys, in assessing their willingness to pay for environmental goods and services. When environmental services are not traded on a market (such as fossil fuels), and there is no immediate indirect way of valuing them, it is indeed possible to value their cost and benefit as perceived by the people whose well-being they will affect (the residents of a housing complex where a park will be built, or inhabitants of a village where it is planned to operate an incinerator). This method – also called "contingent valuation" – also obviously assumes that users are reasonably informed about the benefits and costs of the project to be evaluated, which is not the case in reality. It also neglects the distributive dimensions of the evaluated projects.

Yet, it is possible to imagine and design valuation methods that are closer to political science than economics by organizing a collective evaluation of the value of natural resources, leading, after a political deliberation, to determining the economic value of the resource in question not only for individuals but also for the community to which they belong.

Such is the case when "citizens' conferences" are convened to evaluate the relevance of projects that affect their neighborhoods and lives. Such conferences should be organized and moderated so that every voice is being heard in the deliberation and counted in the decision (a city like Paris has a significant part of its budget allocated via such a collective decision process).

Using "revealed preferences" and "declared preferences" techniques, cost-benefit analysis (CBA) is the central method of conventional environmental economics. It aims both at determining the economic value of natural resources and the public policy that should result from this valuation. Cost-benefit analysis can be defined as the assessment of a public investment or a policy change that takes into account all the costs and benefits incurred (the beneficial and harmful effects of projects or policies), expressed in monetary terms. It is a public decision support tool routinely used by authorities all over the world, at the national level (when the Obama administration decided to move away from coal and develop new sources of energy with the American Clean Energy and Security Act of 2009) and local level (when the city of London decided to implement, starting in April 2019, an "Ultra Low Emission Zone" in the same area as the Congestion Charge[9] it introduced in 2003). Because the techniques sustaining cost-benefit analysis based on monetary valuation omit distributional issues, they can lead to unfair policy and outright counter-productive calculations, as in the case of the economic cost of air pollution illustrates (Box 5.2).

## Box 5.2 The monetary cost of air pollution

In order to alert governments to the importance of environmental regulation, the OECD regularly calculates and publishes estimates of the economic cost of ambient air pollution. In one of its recent reports,[10] the organization provided such estimates for its countries' members, relying on the method of "value of statistical life" (VSL), which aggregates individuals' willingness to pay for fatal-risk reduction. One way to calculate VSL is to aggregate the loss of income (and thus consumption) induced by premature death. This indicator, widely used to design regulation policy (on pollution but also on road accidents) is, by construction, higher for rich countries than for poorer ones.

So, it is no surprise to see that, according to this method, the loss of a Turkish life has 40% less value than the loss of a British life (see table), an ethically dubious outcome (as if economic valuation had erased human values). But cost-benefit analysis is not just unfair in this case, it is also counter-productive. More people in Turkey die of air pollution than in the UK and yet the overall economic cost appears to be much higher in the UK compared to the cost in Turkey. According to this calculation, it thus makes more sense economically to reduce pollution in countries where fewer people die of it.

| | 2010 | | |
|---|---|---|---|
| | No. of deaths (n) | VSL 2010 in USD millions | n x VSL, 2010 USD millions |
| Turkey | 28,924 | 2,024 | 58,548 |
| United Kingdom | 24,064 | 3,554 | 85,524 |

And, what if certain values cannot be expressed in monetary terms or there is a conflict between values? The case of the US Endangered Species Act (ESA) provides a good illustration of the limits of cost-benefit analysis.

The Endangered Species Act (ESA) is a US legislation explicitly grounded in the preservation of natural value. Passed in 1973, it recognized that natural heritage is of "esthetic, ecological, educational, recreational, and scientific value to our nation and its people." It aims at maintaining this plural value of natural resources, even in the face of important monetary cost: Indeed, a 1978 Supreme Court decision allowed for the preservation of a small fish to hold up the construction of a Tennessee Valley Authority damming project (the ESA prohibited the endangerment of the listed species, regardless of how much money had been spent on the dam). While it is estimated that the ESA has successfully saved more than 99% of species listed, in 2018, US federal lawmakers considered a "Modernized Endangered Species Act" that would transfer the authority of the Endangered Species Act (ESA) to local governments and private interests and in reality introduce CBA as the main tool for deciding on species preservation. While the law was not passed, it is symptomatic of the temptation of current US policy-makers to give priority to private (often business sector) interests over general interest.

Economic valuation is indeed fundamentally linked to distributional issues. It can in fact be shown that more equal societies have a higher valuation for environmental public goods and that non-market benefits of environmental policy accrue over-proportionally to poorer households.[11]

## The problem of social cost and its imperfect solutions

As we have seen, the economic analysis of environmental issues is based on the fundamental idea of an under-valuation by the price system of the use of natural resources and the environmental damage attached to it: The social cost of consuming these resources is usually higher than its private cost. A full tank of diesel actually costs much more than a few tens of euros: Rightly priced, the fuel consumed should cost several hundred euros.

There are theoretically three possible causes for this undervaluation: Poorly defined property rights (leading to the tragedy of open access), poorly under-stood externalities, and poorly targeted public subsidies and taxes. The question then is how to restore the "ecological truth" of the prices of goods that depend directly or indirectly on the use of natural resources. How, in the case of climate change mitigation, can the price system reflect the social cost of intensive use of carbon in contemporary societies?

This question refers to two dimensions of public action: The target (the "social" price, which must reflect the "social" cost of carbon and be deter-mined by the public authorities), and the instruments mobilized to achieving it. A "right price" can have two meanings: exact and fair. In other words, instruments and targets must be efficient, that is, tailored to address the problem they intend to mitigate. But they should also be fair: They must lead to a necessary change in behaviors at the lowest possible economic cost, while not harming certain groups of current and future generations.

The gap between a price system that would reflect the growing climate crisis and actual price systems is quite large: A recent OECD report covering energy use in 42 OECD and G20 countries, amounting to 80% of world $CO_2$ emissions, estimates that the carbon-pricing gap – which compares actual carbon prices and real climate costs, resulting in a theoretical 30 euros fee per ton of carbon – was 76.5% in 2018. The vast majority of emissions in industry and in the residential and commercial sector is entirely unpriced, the report finds. The carbon pricing gap is lowest for road transport (21% against the 30 euros benchmark) and highest for industry (91%). The gap is over 80% in the electricity and the residential and commercial sectors. Country analysis on 2015 carbon prices shows large variations, with carbon pricing gaps ranging from as low as 27% in Switzerland to above 90% in some emerging economies. France, India, Korea, Mexico, and the United Kingdom substantially reduced their carbon pricing gaps between 2012 and 2015. Yet, still only twelve of the 42 countries studied had pricing gaps of below 50% in 2015.[12] Yet efficient and fair carbon pricing is analytically conceivable and feasible from a policy perspective (Boyce, 2018).[13]

If price systems must be altered to equalize social cost and private cost, two questions must be distinguished: What features should economic instruments used have, and how should we determine a "social" value (or "social cost") of carbon that is efficient[14] and fair? If the answer to the first question deals with the short-term horizon of public policy, there is no way of avoiding long-term considerations to attempt to answer the second question. Again, distributional issues take center stage in both time horizons.

Let us first consider the relatively simpler question of environmental policy economic instruments. Apart from education and information,[15] there are three major short-term economic tools that can be used to reach a socially designed environmental goal such as social carbon price in order to mitigate climate change (but any environmental policy can be considered: controlling urban pollution, preserving tropical forests).

The first instrument is often referred to as "command and control": It consists of norms and standards of production and consumption determined by the public authority using its regulation power and imposed, under the sanction of financial penalty, to manufacturers and households (public authorities determine the minimum desired level of air or water quality, or the maximum level of a pollutant, that must be maintained).

Such policy can produce rapid and significant change. In the US, new norms on lightbulbs introduced in 2012 have led to the development of LED, compact fluorescent and halogen incandescent lightbulbs that have taken over older types of incandescent light bulbs in a mere few years (the latter now represent a meager 6% of the market, while their share was 68% in 2010). As a result, and because new generation lightbulbs consume around 30% less energy than previous ones, electricity use by American households has declined over the past eight years.[16]

When it comes to biodiversity and ecosystems management, the command and control approach takes the form of conservation areas. The Natura 2000 network in the European Union, that extends over all 27 EU countries, contains over 26,000 sites and covers around 18% of the EU land and sea, has allowed a number of threatened species to come back to life. At the global level, the Nagoya Agreement (2010) aims to protect 17% of the planet's land and inland waters, and ten percent of coastal and marine waters by 2020 (up from 13% of land and one percent of marine areas).[17]

The second instrument, "cap-and-trade," stems from the work of British economist Ronald Coase, although Coase himself was wary of the idea (Coase 1960). It is a market mechanism that relies on the theory that the market-place, provided it exists, can allocate pollution efficiently and determine its right price. The role of the public authority is limited here to determining a maximum volume of pollution (a "cap") that will, for instance, decrease every few years, defining property rights (allocating permits of pollutions to the firms involved in the market) and let actors on the market, through their supply and demand, determine the price of pollution (via the possibility of "trade"). Firms are inclined to reduce their pollution to find themselves in a selling position on the market (having more permits than they actually need), if the price of permits is high enough.

Finally, drawing on the work of Pigou, "Pigovian taxation" relies on the fact that taxes frame behaviors and that tax systems have grown a lot in contemporary economies: Government should thus use them to deter harmful social behaviors (and favor collectively desired ones). Public authorities should thus engage in changing behaviors for the better (for instance in terms of health) through taxation, by developing new economic incentives (creating a tax on plastic bags to limit their use, creating a tax on carbon to mitigate climate change). In this case, the public authority will determine the price and leave it to the market to determine the volume.[18]

Each of these three theoretical tools can be further understood using real-life examples. They are, in fact, being used in the European Union (EU) to mitigate climate change, the EU being the region of the world most advanced in setting and using climate change mitigation instruments, albeit with too limited results.

Since 2005, and following the requirement of the Kyoto Protocol (1997) to establish "flexibility mechanisms," the European Union's climate strategy has been essentially based on a "cap and trade" system. On the one hand, member states and the European Commission have determined a gradually declining ceiling of pollution (first fixed at 2,375 megatonnes (Mt) of $CO_2$e, to be cut by 43% by 2030). On the other hand, they have allocated exchangeable permits among the 11,000 participating companies to be traded for a price. The greenhouse gas emissions covered by this European carbon market (whose technical name is EU ETS), about 55% of all member states emissions, dropped by 26% from 2005 to 2016, but the price signal issued on this market is about three times lower than it should be according to existing estimates of carbon social price in the EU (around 10 euros a ton against the 30 euros calculated by the aforementioned study by the OECD). Environmental taxation, the second economic instrument used by Europeans, is more developed in Europe than elsewhere in the world[19] but still too little: It represents on average in 2016 a little more than six percent of total tax revenue (five percent in France), this proportion declining since 2002 when it stood at almost seven percent. At this level, incentives to pursue low-carbon strategies are too limited. Yet, most Nordic countries (especially Denmark and Sweden) that have implemented environmental taxation as early as 1991, and have today higher levels of green taxes than anywhere else in the world, have been successful economically, socially, and environmentally. The example of Sweden speaks for itself: From 1996 to 2006, while the weight of taxation decreased by eight points on work and increased by twelve points on energy, energy intensity has fallen by thirty points, greenhouse gas emissions have been reduced by 15%, all the while the unemployment decreased from nine to six percent. Today, carbon taxation in Sweden stands at 120 euros for a ton of $CO_2$.

Finally, the policy of norms and standards ("command and control") by which the public authorities determine standards of emissions of $CO_2$ ("command") for certain products, starting with motor vehicles, then make sure they are respected by car-makers ("control"), suffers from the cynicism of some European manufacturers who have invested in the innovation of test fraud rather than in low-carbon innovation.

The European Union must therefore seriously reform the instruments of its climate strategy if it wants to achieve the emission reduction targets it has set for itself in 2030 (-40% of emissions compared to the level of 1990) and 2050 (-80%). This does not mean that economic instruments are doomed to fail but that they must be carefully designed and adequately reformed over time if they are to remain relevant. As Boyce (2018) puts it: "A cap-and-permit system, or alternatively a carbon tax indexed to a fixed emission-reduction trajectory, not only can spur cost-effective mitigation and cost-reducing innovation but also, crucially, can ensure that emissions are held to the target level."

This brings us to two important considerations with respect to environmental policy's instruments: their respective merits and their distributional impact.

There are three major debates concerning the comparative advantage of "command and control," "cap and trade," and environmental taxation. The first one is that most economists prefer "market instruments" (cap and trade and taxation) over "authoritarian" solutions (command and control) on the grounds that the former will be more cost-effective than the latter (producers know better than the government what they can achieve and at what cost). But the so-called "Porter hypothesis" asserts that firms can actually benefit from such environmental regulations. A recent survey of existing studies points to two important conclusions: On balance, studies examining the link between environmental regulation (oftentimes measured as compliance costs) and innovation (measured as either R&D expenditures or patents) conclude that there is a positive link between the two, although the strength of the link varies. Environmental regulation appears to spur innovation (Ambec et al., 2013; Esty and Porter, 2005).

The second debate stems from the seminal work of Weitzman (1974) on the respective merit of taxation and pollution markets under uncertainty. Uncertain about the exact cost for a firm of reducing its pollution levels[20] (as is the case for instance with $CO_2$ emissions reduction), the public authority might impose too high a cost on firms using a tax rather than a cap and trade system. What is more, taxation does not ensure that the volume of pollution is effectively reduced at the level of the pre-determined goal.[21]

The third debate is related to the political economy of each instrument. On this ground, cap and trade might also be preferred to environmental taxation: Introducing pollution permits given or sold to firms is supposed to be more socially acceptable and thus politically feasible than introducing new taxes paid directly or indirectly by consumers.

While those arguments all have value, they can also be misleading. In their light, one could assume that those policy instruments are substitutes for one another (some being simply better than others, given the context). They are actually complements: Environmental policy is more effective when its instruments are used in combination rather than in isolation. This is obvious for education and awareness policy: it enhances all economic instruments. But let us be more specific and go back to our EU example. There are two types of greenhouse gas emissions in the EU: diffuse emissions (decentralized emissions coming from households heating their homes and driving their cars) and centralized emissions (coming from power plants or energy-intensive industries such as cement). It makes good economic sense to combine a "cap and trade" system for centralized emissions and to develop carbon taxation for diffuse emissions – because a pollution market for 500 million actors is hardly manageable, and yet diffuse emissions are very dynamic in the EU and should be controlled. But, command and control alone is not efficient enough to do the trick.

According to the European Environment Agency (2009), road vehicles used for passenger transport have seen the combustion intensity of fossil fuels they use decline by more than 40% between 1990 and 2005, and their carbon intensity decline in the order of two percent. On the other hand, the number of kilometers travelled has literally exploded over the same period, progressing by more than 100%, as well as an increase in the number of private cars in the total fleet (by almost ten percent). Freight transport is evolving in a similar way, with more than 80% increase in mileage, 40% increase in the number of trucks in the total vehicle fleet, while their carbon intensity is two percent and their burning intensity nearly 30%. In other words, technological innovations (driven by public authorities) are not enough to offset the volume effect of road transport since 1990. In total, greenhouse gas (GHG) emissions related to transport, attributable to 90% of road transport, have increased by more than 16% in the European Union between 1990 and 2015. This is a classic case of "rebound effect" (see Box 5.2) that should be addressed both by taxation and regulation.

Finally, the distributional impact of instruments available in the environmental economist's toolbox should not be overlooked. Carbon taxes are in reality energy taxes that hurt the poor much more than the rich (the share of energy budget in a country like France is 2.5 times higher for the bottom 10% than for the top 10%). Social compensations should be introduced to insure that environmental policy is fair and that the low-carbon transition is a just transition (see Chapter 10). This was the implicit concern behind the recent proposal, initially outlined by James Boyce in 2013,[22] to introduce "carbon dividends" in the US, an option supported by thousands of economists in a statement published in the *Wall Street Journal* in February 2019. The proposal stated: "To maximize the fairness and political viability of a rising carbon tax, all the revenue should be returned directly to US citizens through equal lump-sum rebates. The majority of American families, including the most vulnerable, will benefit financially by receiving more in 'carbon dividends' than they pay in increased energy prices."[23]

Distributional issues are also important in cap-and trade systems: The choice of the EU not to auction permits has resulted in windfall profit for companies initially involved in the EU ETS in 2005. The design of these policy instruments should thus be done with attention to both efficiency and fairness. Such should also be the case when determining the "social price" that they should, in combination, aim at. Our ecological crises are indeed long-term and even very long-term problems. This is why we cannot escape inter-temporal considerations when considering them. To introduce time is to introduce future generations and the value we place on their well-being.

At first glance, everything seems simple for the public decision-maker: The choice of an environmental policy (aimed for example at reducing greenhouse gas emissions) will depend on the comparison between its social cost and its social benefit. If the benefit exceeds the cost, the policy will be implemented by the political authority in the name of the common good. But, since this comparison covers several successive generations (we set climate objectives for the horizon of 2050 or 2100), without projection over time, such policy is meaningless. This projection in time supposes a discounting calculation, that is to say a translation into the language of the present of future events and their consequences. Discounting calculation, which is commonly used to assess the profitability of private investments, should also be used to analyze and quantify the consequences of climate change, but also biodiversity loss or depletion of ecosystem services.

If the interest rate is the price of time, then the social discount rate is the value of the well-being of future generations. Applied to environmental issues, it can be understood as the metric that will determine the efforts to be made today to avoid imposing future problems on future generations for which they are not responsible. Justice thus lies at the heart of discounting.

The technique of social discounting supposes indeed a calculation of appreciation or depreciation of future costs and benefits in relation to the present. Its rate depends fundamentally on two sets of variables: On the one hand, the preference for the present; on the other hand, the degree of inequality and risk aversion (these two dimensions being represented by the elasticity of the marginal utility of consumption) multiplied by the future growth rate.

Ramsey (1928)[24]: $R = p + e^*g$;

Where $R$ is the social discount rate (aka social rate of time preference), $p$ is the pure rate of time preference, $e$ is the elasticity of the marginal utility of consumption, and $g$ is the growth rate of per capita consumption.

This deceivingly simple equation implies three nested ethical calculations. Let us start with the most symbolic: The choice of the rate of preference for the present (also called "pure rate of time preference"). It represents the fact that the value of a present consumption is always greater than that of the same consumption in the future (faced with simple choices between present and future gains, we "edit" information, exhibit risk aversion and bias for the present).[25] How do we apply this idea to a human community? Convinced that it could not be a reliable compass, the economist Frank Ramsey described this preference, that discounts "later enjoyments in comparison with earlier ones" as "a practice which is ethically indefensible and arises merely from the weakness of the imagination." This is indeed a rate of social impatience to consume and that is why Ramsey thought it should be the lowest possible, the closest to zero. If, like Ramsey, one refuses for moral reasons to grant the preference for the present generations, one will normalize this first variable to zero, which will mean that future generations are on an equal footing with the generations. Any other value of this parameter should be justified on ethical grounds.

There remain two other variables: the inequality and risk aversion and the future growth rate of consumption. This latter value is generally considered positive: We are richer than past generations, so future generations will probably be richer than us. We must therefore depreciate the costs they will have to incur. But, by refining the definition of wealth to include the inter-generational value of natural capital, this statement may no longer be obvious. A number of key ecosystems has already disappeared, dilapidated by earlier generations, so that we cannot enjoy their benefits, however rich we are in monetary terms (such as in the case of the Aral Sea or Lake Chad). When it is understood as comprehensive wealth (see Chapter 9) and assessed over time, future consumption might well be negative.

This doubt about the wealth of future generations appears clearly if we consider the contemporary phenomenon of accelerated destruction of global biodiversity. Biodiversity is a reservoir of knowledge about life, its destruction is thus a net loss of intelligence that affects human health and well-being in addition to depleting the services provided by ecosystems whose vitality depends on biological diversity. Researchers have shown that the disap-pearance of the polar bear and the brown bear would, in particular, deprive us of valuable knowledge that could help cure type 2 diabetes and osteoporosis.[26] The destruction of biodiversity is therefore both a direct biological threat to humans and the loss of an intellectual opportunity, a potential for knowledge. Its preservation, which presupposes efforts and sacrifices for the present generations, must obviously proceed from an ethical calculation.

Hence, we should not commit to fewer efforts and even sacrifices now to preserve environmental resources because we think that our descendants will on average be richer than us but, on the contrary, we should do more (for example by extending the perimeter of protected areas), in the name of inter-generational equity, to preserve the resources that our descendants can only enjoy if we do not destroy them. The choice to include future generations, "awaiting members of our moral community," as political scientist Terence Ball puts it, is therefore an ethical choice revealed by dynamic economic analysis. The economist Partha Dasgupta suggests in this respect that we should use negative discount rates to take into account the impoverishment of future generations in natural capital.[27]

The last ethical bet, and not the least, involves the calculation of aversion to inequality and risk. Indeed, the elasticity of the marginal utility of consumption can be interpreted as a measure of inequality aversion, on the assumption that an additional consumption unit will provide more utility to a poor person than to a rich person (therefore, in order to take into account inequalities, the elasticity parameter must be different from 1, a value that would assume either income equality in society or the linear evolution of marginal utility with the level of income). To assume that the marginal utility does not decrease with the level of consumption is therefore to imagine a world without inequalities. The spatial dimension is combined here with the temporal dimension: To the concern of inter-generational equity is added the concern for intra-generational equity.

Inequalities in the face of ecological conditions count indeed in the space of our generation (that is to say, between rich and poor countries and rich and poor individuals in each country today), because the poorest countries and individuals are already the most affected by ecological crises. But they also count in time, as these individuals and countries will be even more affected in the future when those crises worsen (multiplication of heat waves, storms, fires, floods). However, the efforts that are required in the present to counter ecological crises (for example, paying a carbon tax to reduce our polluting emissions) are much more painful for the poor than for the rich.

Climate change will hit poor countries much more severely than rich countries and vulnerable individuals than resilient individuals, which must be taken into account when calculating costs; hence the efforts to be made today. If island states, like Tuvalu, which asked at the Paris conference that the increase in the tolerable global maximum temperature be lowered to 1.5 degrees, it is because with two degrees of increase by 2100, their well-being and indeed their very existence are threatened. This is not the case for the richest countries, which can to some extent support an increase of two degrees. In estimating the cost of climate change and the related efforts and sacrifices that current generations are willing to make today to avoid its worse consequences, one must imperatively take into account the inequalities in space and time between countries and between individuals.

The social discount rate is therefore fundamentally based on ethical choices (sometimes referred to as "preferences") rooted in more or less explicit justice principles and not on objective or technical parameters. It is essential to understand this because social discount rates are the central variables of climate change models. The Stern report (2008) for instance was based on a discount rate of 1.4%, when the US economist Bill Nordhaus (who used the simulation model DICE, "Dynamic Integrated Model of Climate and the Economy") promoted a discount rate of around 5% in various works (see Table 5.1).

Because social discounting is applied over a long period of time, it results in very important differences of valuation (a social discount rate of 2% applied to one million euros in economic cost results comes to 552,000 euros after 30 years and 138,000 after a century, a rate twice that high at 4% results in the same amount being reduced to 308,000 after 30 years and a mere 20,000 after a century). Thus discounting can and, in fact, often does result in the misleading compression of time into "present value." The illusion is obvious: Whenever one looks at costs occurring at dates far enough apart in time, choosing a positive social discount rate value, even a very low one, minimizes the costs of our decisions for future generations and maximizes benefits closer in time. Discounting collapses time but also our responsibility.

Because we choose social discount rates that are too low on dubious ethical grounds, we end up minimizing the efforts that are needed of us in the short-run. The two following tables (5.1 and 5.2) respectively display the different options for the social discount rate (and its components) and the corresponding options for carbon taxation. In Table 5.1, we see that the most significantly different parameter is also the most subjective one (the rate of pure preference for present), while in Table 5.2, we see that using a 2.5 percent discount rate rather than a five percent one (a factor 2 difference) results in carbon taxation five times higher for 2020.

| Table 5.1 Social discount rate options | | | | |
|---|---|---|---|---|
| Author | % Rate of pure preference for present | Inequality aversion | % Anticipated Growth rate | % Implied social discount rate |
| Stern (2008) | 0.1 | 1 | 1.3 | 1.4 |
| Cline (1992) | 0 | 1.5 | 1 | 1.5 |
| IPCC (1996) | 0 | 1.5–2 | 1.6 – 8 | 2.4 – 16 |
| UK: Green Book (HM Treasury, 2003) | 1.5 | 1 | 2 | 3.5* |
| Arrow (1999) | 0 | 2 | 2 | 4 |
| France: Rapport Lebègue (2005) | 0 | 2 | 2 | 4* |
| Nordhaus (2008) | 1 | 2 | 2 | 5 |

*Decreasing with the time horizon. *Source:* Adapted from IPCC (2015)

| Table 5.2 Social cost of $CO_2$, 2010–2050 (in 2007 dollars per metric ton of $CO_2$) with three different social discount rates | | | |
|---|---|---|---|
| | 5% | 3% | 2.5% |
| 2010 | 10 | 31 | 50 |
| 2020 | 12 | 42 | 62 |
| 2030 | 16 | 50 | 73 |
| 2040 | 21 | 60 | 84 |
| 2050 | 26 | 69 | 95 |

*Source:* Adapted from EPA

One point is clear: The determining factor in the collective choices we make today about the future of the biosphere is not our perception of uncertainty, but our conception of equality.

Let us consider one final example of how carbon price calculation reflects justice considerations. In an attempt in 2018 to reverse his predecessor climate policy, the Trump administration directed the EPA to recalculate the "social cost of carbon" used by federal agencies when they attempt to assess the costs and benefits of climate regulations.

The EPA Report[28] argues that each ton of carbon dioxide emitted by a car or a coal plant in 2020 would only cause around $1 to $7 in economic damages, much lower than the roughly $50 in total damages estimated previously. This is because the EPA focused solely on damages from climate change that would occur within the borders of the United States rather than across the entire globe and then discounted the harm climate change could inflict on future generations. By refusing to take into account intra and inter-generational justice, the EPA's report shows how much it really matters in social discounting calculation.

# Part II
## Twenty-first-century social-ecological challenges

# 6

# Biodiversity and ecosystems under growing and unequal pressure

Biodiversity and ecosystems, where vitality and resilience are intertwined in the biosphere, matter for two simple reasons. First because they underpin societies and economies, forming the life-support system of humans and determining their well-being today and in the long run. Second, because their contemporary degradation – and even destruction – is related to social dynamics, both from the standpoint of causes and consequences.

## Plants and animals

Biodiversity (biological diversity), a term coined in the 1980s by the biologist Edward Wilson, denotes the wealth and variety of all living things, the total variability of life. Biodiversity is typically considered at three levels: species diversity, genetic diversity, and ecosystem diversity. The first category is the most widely used and refers to the variety and abundance of species in a given geographical area, the number of species in a certain location at a certain point in time being the most commonly used measure of biodiversity.

But life on Earth, 3.5 billion years old, can be estimated in a number of different ways. One of them is to assess the current respective biomass of its components.[1] It then appears that the sum of the biomass on the planet is roughly 550 Gt C (giga tonne of carbon), of which 450 Gt C (or 80%) are plants, 70 Gt C (or 15%) are bacteria and only 0.3% are animals. In this latter category, humans represent a mere 0.06 Gt C. Yet, it appears that the biomass of humanity and the livestock it maintains for its use weigh much more than wild mammals. In fact, it has been estimated that the 7.6 billion people on the planet, representing just 0.01% of all living things in terms of weight, have caused the loss of 83% of all wild mammals and half of plants.

This crisis of biodiversity caused by humanity, of growing proportion and tremendous consequence, is being documented in study after study (Ceballos et al., 2017). While close to 2.5 million species (1.9m animals and 400,000 plants) have been identified and named, recent work suggests extinction rates at present are up to 100–1,000 extinctions per 10,000 species per century, a rate 100 to 1,000 times higher than the pace experienced on Earth over the last 500 million years, suggesting that biodiversity, because of human expansion, finds itself on the edge of a sixth mass extinction.[2]

More than 26,000 of the world's monitored species (27% of 93,577 monitored species in total) are now threatened with extinction (classified as vulnerable, critical, or endangered), according to the latest "red list" assessment of the natural world published by the IUCN. The Living Planet Index,[3] a time series metric compiled since 1970 by the World Wide Fund for Nature (WWF), shows that between 1970 and 2014, vertebrate animal populations (mammals, birds, fish, reptiles, and amphibians) dropped by 60%. The extinction rate is on average 23% and 31% in the Nearctic (North America) and Palearctic (Europe, North Africa, North Asia, and the Middle East). It reaches 56% in the Afrotropical region (sub-Saharan Africa) and skyrockets to 64% in the Indo-Pacific basin (India, Indonesia, and Australia), and even 89% in the neo-tropical area (South America and Central America).

This accelerated loss of biodiversity is extremely costly for human development: Biodiversity sustains ecosystem functions that themselves sustain ecosystem services that sustain human well-being. But this crisis is not caused mainly, as was the case in the past, by natural phenomena but by anthropogenic factors; that is to say that it results from human action (in order of importance, the destruction of the habitat of the species, the introduction of foreign species, the over-exploitation of resources, various pollutions, and finally climate change).

A human-driven phenomenon, biodiversity erosion reciprocally has some far-reaching human impact. As documented by the IPBES in its latest regional assessments published in 2018 and first global assessment (2019), this impact can be felt in all corners of the world. For instance, Africa's rich and diverse ecosystems are under severe threat, although they generate flows of goods and services that are essential in providing for the continent's food, water, energy, health, and secure livelihood needs. More than 62% of the population for instance depend directly on these services in rural areas, while the urban and peri-urban population supplement their incomes, as well as their energy, medicine, and other essentials, from ecosystem-based resources.

In this regard, as argued by Sukhdev (2011), "there is an inextricable link between persistent poverty and the loss of ecosystems and biodiversity" (see also Holland et al., 2010).[4] The relationship between poverty and environmental degradation is grounded on an objective reality: People in poor countries are much more dependent on natural resources than people in rich countries, natural resources representing a much larger share of their income and employment opportunities (employment in agriculture represents two-thirds in developing countries but only five percent in OECD countries). Natural resources are, in fact, the real wealth of the majority of people in poor countries.[5] To put it in ecological economics language, if ecosystem services stemming from agriculture, forestry, and fisheries account for between six and 17% of national income in Indonesia, India, and Brazil, they account for between 47 and 89% of the income of the poor in those same countries. Because of this dependence, there appears to be a vicious social-ecological spiral in many developing countries.

Conde and Christensen[6] illustrate this idea with the case of Haiti, one of the poorest countries in the world, where 65% of the population lives with less than a dollar a day. The country has suffered massive deforestation (97% of the forest cover is now gone), which has exacerbated the erosion of soil and in several places reduced rainfall by 40%, limiting irrigation possibilities. Even when it is possible, given the magnitude of soil erosion, it causes flooding. As a result, drinking water is seriously polluted and 90% of Haitian children suffer from intestinal parasites due to this pollution. In this context, the exploitation of what remains of Haitian natural resources is one of the few means of survival for a population that, in doing so, destroys what remains of its quality of life. Haiti, a country rich in biodiversity and poor in human development is not an isolated case (see Box 6.1).

## Box 6.1 Biodiversity, human development, and political freedom

According to the NGO Conservation International, 35 areas in the world qualify as hotspots. Representing 2.5% of Earth's land surface, they harbor more than half of the world's plant species as endemics – i.e. species not found anywhere else – and nearly 43% of bird, mammal, reptile, and amphibian species as endemics. Two criteria are used to define biodiversity hotspots: 1,500 vascular plants must be endemic and the area must have 30% or less of its original natural vegetation. Biodiversity hotspots are thus both of key importance for global biodiversity and threatened.

A review of the list of those 35 hotspots reveals that, aside from New Zealand, Japan, or California, a majority of these areas is both poorly developed and plunged into serious civil and political difficulties. For instance, by cross-referencing data from the United Nations Development Indicator and those of the Freedom House Institute (which measure civil liberties and political rights), it can be shown that the "Mesoamerica," "Caribbean," "Andean" tropical, "West African Guinea Forests," or "Horn of Africa" areas have both a low level of human and democratic development (see table). There is indeed a worrisome two-way social-ecological link between biodiversity degradation, human underdevelopment, and poor governance.

Reading: The Human Development Index (HDI) is a summary measure of average achievement in key dimensions of human development: A long and healthy life, being knowledgeable, and having a decent standard of living, it ranges from 0 to 1. Freedom House scores range from 1 to 7, with 1 representing the greatest degree of freedom and 7 the smallest degree of freedom; they are based on measures of political rights (Electoral Process, Political Pluralism, and Participation and Functioning of Government) and civil liberties (Freedom of Expression and Belief, Associational and Organizational Rights, Rule of Law, and Personal Autonomy and Individual Rights).

|  | Human development index, value, and rank (on 187) | Political rights | Civil liberties | Political situation |
|---|---|---|---|---|
| **Caribbean** | | | | |
| Haïti | 0.498 (168) | 5 | 5 | Partially free |
| **Mesoamerica** | | | | |
| Honduras | 0.617 (133) | 4 | 4 | Partially free |
| Nicaragua | 0.658 (124) | 5 | 4 | Partially free |
| Madagascar | 0.519 (161) | 3 | 4 | Partially free |
| **Horn of Africa** | | | | |
| Somalia | No data | 7 | 7 | Not free |
| Djibouti | 0.476 (172) | 6 | 5 | Partially free |
| Sri Lanka | 0.770 (76) | 3 | 4 | Partially free |
| **South East Asia and Asia-Pacific** | | | | |
| Philippines | 0.699 (113) | 3 | 3 | Partially free |
| Burma | 0.578 (148) | 5 | 5 | Partially free |

*Source:* UN and Freedom House

By the same token, more than one-third of the world's population depends on biomass (plants and animal excrement) for cooking. Between 1.6 million and 1.8 million children and women die each year due to domestic pollution from the use of household hazardous ovens, which also contribute to deforestation and climate change through "black carbon" (soot). According to the United Nations, these furnaces produce 25% of black carbon in the world, which contributes ten to 40% of global greenhouse gas emissions.

Poverty is thus the cause of domestic, external, and even global pollution, of which the poor are the first victims.[7]

## Seas and oceans

Oceans and seas cover over 70% of the Earth's surface and represent 90% of the volume of the biosphere. They play a critical role in key ecosystem services to humanity: climate regulation, provisioning of food, livelihoods, cultural uses.

As an illustration, 3.5 billion people depend on oceans as a source of food (20% of their average per capita intake of animal protein), more than one billion people depend on fish for 100% of their daily protein intake and 350 million jobs worldwide depend on the marine sector.[8]

However, oceans and seas are being degraded in many ways. Plastic pollution is out of control. Three-quarters of marine litter is now composed of plastic. According to the latest estimates, between 4.8 million tonnes and 12.7 million tonnes of plastic waste enter the ocean every year, due to inadequate waste management.

Because 26% of carbon dioxide emissions are absorbed by seas and oceans, they become more and more acid, threatening their resident living creatures (surface ocean acidity has already increased by 30% since pre-industrial times). One striking example of this degradation is the destruction of coral reefs that nurture thousands of marine animals (while reefs cover less than 0.1% of the total area of the world's ocean, they support over 25% of all marine fish species). Three-quarters of the world's coral reefs are now threatened with extinction. (The Great Barrier Reef, the world's largest reef system composed of close to 3,000 individual reefs is threatened by warmer ocean temperatures, which put stress on coral and lead to coral bleaching.)

| Table 6.1 World fisheries and aquaculture (million metric tons) | | |
|---|---|---|
| Category | 2011 | 2016 |
| **Production** | | |
| Capture | | |
| Inland | 10.7 | 11.6 |
| Marine | 81.5 | 79.3 |
| Total capture | 92.2 | 90.9 |
| Aquaculture | | |
| Inland | 38.6 | 51.4 |
| Marine | 23.2 | 28.7 |
| Total aquaculture | 61.8 | 80 |
| Total world fisheries and aquaculture | 154 | 170.9 |
| **Utilization** | | |
| Human consumption | 130 | 151.2 |
| Non-food uses | 24 | 19.7 |
| Population (billions) | 7 | 7.4 |
| Per capita apparent consumption (kg) | 18.5 | 20.3 |

*Source:* FAO

The importance of fish stocks for human well-being cannot be overstated. In 2015, fish accounted for about 17% of animal protein consumed by the global population. Between 1961 and 2016, the average annual increase in global food fish consumption (3.2%) outpaced population growth (1.6%) and exceeded that of meat from all terrestrial animals combined (2.8%). In per capita terms, food fish consumption grew from 9.0 kg in 1961 to 20.2 kg in 2015, at an average rate of about 1.5% per year. Preliminary estimates for 2016 and 2017 point to further growth to about 20.3 and 20.5 kg, respectively (Table 6.1).

## Fresh water

Virtually all fresh water potentially available for human usage is stored in the ground as ground water. According to the FAO (United Nations), the total volume of water on Earth is about 1.4 billion km3 but the volume of fresh-water resources is only 35 million km3, or about 2.5% of the total volume (the rest being oceans and other saline water). Moreover, of these fresh-water resources, about 24 million km3, or 70% of the total, are in the form of ice and permafrost in mountainous regions, in the Antarctic and Arctic regions.

The FAO keeps close track of fresh-water use and its data point very clearly to a global water crisis. Globally, the annual precipitation on land is about 110,000 km3, of which 56% is evapotranspired by forests and other natural landscapes and five percent by rain-fed agriculture. The remaining 39% (or 42,920 km3) are the worldwide theoretically available annual renewable fresh water (surface water and ground water) resources for human uses and the environment, which in 2014 was equal to about 5,800 m3 per person per year or 16,000 litres per person per day. Because about 2,000 to 5,000 litres of water is said to be used to produce a person's daily food and meet the daily drinking water and sanitation requirements, there is more than enough water available worldwide. But fresh water, like all natural resources, is very unevenly distributed, a reality that becomes obvious when water withdrawals from different economic sectors are measured.

Global water withdrawal increased from less than 600 km3/year in 1900 to almost 4,000 km3/year in 2010 (the use of fresh water has increased more than twice as fast as the population growth rate over the past century), with renewable internal fresh-water resources per capita plummeting in the last fifty years (Graph 6.1).

The distribution of water resources is marked by significant inequalities. To begin with, 70% of fresh water is used for irrigation, 22% for industry and only eight percent for domestic use. The United Nations report on water resources assessment (2012) estimated that if 86% of the population in developing regions would have access to drinking water by 2015, one billion people would not. In addition, health infrastructure is not keeping pace with global urban

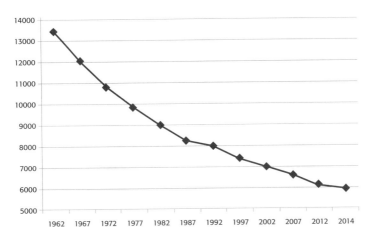

Graph 6.1   Renewable internal fresh-water resources per capita (cubic meters)

*Source*: FAO

development: More than 80% of waste water in the world is neither collected nor processed.

Large differences also exist with respect to water stress and water scarcity. Globally, more than 1.4 billion people currently live in watersheds where water use exceeds minimum recharge levels, leading to the drying up of rivers and the depletion of ground water. According to FAO, water stress starts when the water available in a country drops below 1,700 m3/year or 4,600 litres/day per person. When the 1,000 m3/year or about 2,700 litres/day per person threshold is crossed, water scarcity is experienced. Absolute water scarcity is considered for countries with less than 500 m3/year or roughly 1,400 litres/day per person. By this definition, 49 countries are water stressed, nine of which experience water scarcity and 21 absolute water scarcity. Africa has the highest proportion of countries experiencing water stress (41%), but Asia has the highest proportion of countries experiencing absolute water scarcity (25%).

Among social groups within countries, access to water is also very unequal. In sub-Saharan Africa, urban rich households are 329% more likely to have access to improved water sources compared with the urban poor (and 227% more likely to have access to improved sanitation facilities compared with urban poor households). In Guatemala, only 33% of indigenous populations have access to improved sanitation, compared to 70% of non-indigenous populations.[9] In the Democratic Republic of Congo, improved access to water in cities towers at 81%, compared to only 31% in rural areas. In Yemen, 63% of the population in the top 20% (household income group) has access to piped water, compared to 35% of the poorest. In India, 56% of the population in the top 20% (household income group) has access to piped water, compared to six percent of the bottom 20%.

Water inequality is also obvious in developed countries. In the US, mostly African-American residents of Flint, Michigan, were exposed in 2014 to lead contaminated water because of poor management, neglect, as, in the words of the Michigan Civil Rights Commission, the "result of systemic racism." By the same token, overwhelmingly non-white residents of Chicago and Detroit have been faced over the last decade with water unbearable rising prices (due to aging infrastructures and lack of public investment) and water shutdowns when they cannot pay their bills.

## Forests

The number of goods and services provided by forests, which still cover 30% of the planet, is large: wood and non-wood products (biomass-based energy), climate regulation (carbon sequestration, pollution control, soil protection and formation), erosion control, nutrients cycling, biodiversity protection, water regulation and supply, recreation, and disturbance regulation. Forest degradation, due primarily to extensive agriculture, is an obvious threat to biodiversity and an accelerator of climate change. It is also a threat for human well-being, as 40% of the extreme rural poor – some 250 million people – live in forest and savannah areas.

Covering 234 countries and territories, the Global Forest Resources Assessment 2015 carried out by the FAO shows "encouraging signs of improved forest management and a global slowdown in deforestation," although global tree cover loss reached a record 29.7 million hectares (73.4 million acres) in 2016. 129 million hectares of forest have been lost since 1990 on a net basis (239 million hectares of natural forest was lost), but the rate of net global deforestation has slowed down in the last 25 years, from 0.18% in the 1990s to 0.08% over the last five-year period (Table 6.2).

### Table 6.2 Evolution of global forest, 1990–2015

|  | Forest surface (thousand ha) | Net loss | Rate (%) |
| --- | --- | --- | --- |
| 1990 | 4,128 269 |  |  |
| 2000 | 4,055 602 | -7,267 (1990–2000) | -0.18 |
| 2005 | 4,032 743 | -4,572 (2000–2005) | -0.11 |
| 2010 | 4,015 673 | -3,414 (2005–2010) | -0.08 |
| 2015 | 3,999 134 | -3,308 (2010–2015) | -0.08 |

*Source:* FAO

## Land and soil

According to recent calculations, in 1700, only five percent of the biosphere land was occupied by intensive human activities (agriculture, cities), 45% were in a semi-natural state and 50% totally wild. In 2000, proportions dramatically changed: 55% of the biosphere was occupied by intensive human activities (crop and grazing land cover 35% of the planet's surface), 20% was in a semi-natural state and 25% wild.[10] Humans have colonized the planet, its land and soil.

According to the IPBES,[11] there are three major ways through which worsening land degradation caused by human activities are undermining the well-being of two fifths of humanity, driving species extinctions, and intensifying climate change: land abandonment, biodiversity degradation, and soil degradation.

The IPBES warns that rapid expansion and unsustainable management of croplands and grazing lands is the most extensive global direct driver of land degradation, causing significant loss of biodiversity and ecosystem services (food security, water purification, the provision of energy, and other contributions of nature essential to people), with negative impacts on the well-being of at least 3.2 billion people, of half of humanity (54% of wetland areas has been lost over the last century alone).

Here also, the pressure is all human: Rising per capita consumption, amplified by continued population growth in many parts of the world drive unsustainable levels of agricultural expansion, natural resource and mineral extraction, and urbanization, leading to greater levels of land degradation (more than 1.5 billion hectares of natural ecosystems has been converted to croplands).

## Agriculture

The "Haber process" (invented in 1909), synthesizing ammonia from nitrogen and hydrogen using iron as a catalyst in an environment of high temperature and pressure (resulting in artificial nitrogen fixation) was developed on an industrial scale by Carl Bosch. With it came the ability to manufacture fertilizer by using the abundant nitrogen reserves in the atmosphere, which then resulted in large increases in crop yields to support the growing population on our planet. It is estimated that the number of humans supported per hectare of arable land has increased from 1.9 to 4.3 persons between 1908 and 2008, because of Haber–Bosch nitrogen.[12]

But, as a result, nitrogen and phosphorus cycles have been radically altered and nitrogen and phosphorus pollute fresh waters and coastal areas. Around a quarter of all greenhouse gases emissions come from agricultural activity. And pesticides pollution destroys biodiversity.

This is maybe the best illustration of how counter-productive human economies blind to their life-support system destruction can become. Intensive agriculture relies on the heavy use of chemicals. It is now believed[13] that some of those chemicals, chief among them glyphosate (contained in popular herbicides) used around the world, are not only causing human cancer but also destroying bees (via the "colony collapse disorder"). But bees are the most important pollinators, helping humans grow 75% of their crops. By wanting to accelerate agricultural productivity, we are in fact threatening its survival.

There is an intricate relation between biodiversity, agriculture, and food.[14] While biodiversity for food and agriculture is indispensable to food security and many ecosystem services crucial to human well-being, many of its key components are in decline. A number of scenarios is being explored today to render compatible food supply and ecosystems sustainability. For instance, French institutes Inra and Cirad have created the Agrimonde-Terra scenarios, aiming at reconciling sufficient human nutrition in quantity and quality, developing agro-ecological production systems, and preserving forests in a context of climate change.[15]

While considerable progress has been made in the course of the twentieth century in feeding the global population (humans need on average 2,500 calories/day and the global average is 2,940 in 2015), large disparities remain. Food supply (kcal/capita/day) has increased in the last fifty years globally and in all regions of the world but not from the same level and at the same pace (Table 6.3).

| Table 6.3 Global and regional per capita food consumption (kcal per capita per day), 1964–2015 | | | | | |
|---|---|---|---|---|---|
| Region | 1964 | 1974 | 1984 | 1997 | 2015 |
| **World** | **2358** | **2435** | **2655** | **2803** | **2940** |
| Sub-Saharan Africa | 2058 | 2079 | 2057 | 2195 | 2360 |
| South Asia | 2017 | 1986 | 2205 | 2403 | 2700 |
| **Developing countries** | **2054** | **2152** | **2450** | **2681** | **2850** |
| Latin America and the Caribbean | 2393 | 2546 | 2689 | 2824 | 2980 |
| East Asia | 1957 | 2105 | 2559 | 2921 | 3060 |
| **Industrialized countries** | **2947** | **3065** | **3206** | **3380** | **3440** |

Source: FAO

Actually, evidence continues to signal a rise in world hunger, even though production capacities are large enough to cover humanity's needs. According to available data by the FAO, in 2017 the number of people suffering from hunger has been growing over the past three years, returning to levels from a decade ago. The absolute number of people in the world affected by under-nourishment, or chronic food deprivation, is now estimated to have increased from around 804 million in 2016 to nearly 821 million in 2017, around one out of every nine people in the world. The situation is worsening in South America and most regions of Africa; likewise, the decreasing trend in undernourishment that characterized Asia until recently seems to be slowing down significantly.

Food injustice is also a problem for developed countries. In a rich country like France, there are at least two issues of food justice: access to food (there is a ratio of one to two between the richest 10% and the poorest 10%, while food insecurity[16] reaches 12% of the adult population) and access to nutritional quality (there is no difference in energy density in the diet of different social categories, but of nutritional quality). In fact, energy and macro-nutrient inputs (carbohydrates, fats, proteins) vary little or not at all with the socio-economic position, whereas they have known significant historical variations for a century in France. Energy density is indeed financially accessible because of the low cost of energy-rich food ingredients and low management costs. On the other hand, the most nutritious foods and the least loaded with negative nutrients are reserved for the advantaged social classes. Although it may appear to be a paradox, food insecurity can also contribute to overweight and obesity. Nutritious, fresh foods often tend to be expensive. Thus, when household resources for food become scarce, people choose less expensive foods that are often high in calories and low in nutrients.

## Energy

The available energy globally is not shared equally. OECD countries, the richest in the world, accounting for about 12% of the world's population, now account for 40% of the energy consumed and for a little less in global $CO_2$ emissions. Global energy consumption is defined as the total energy used by an individual or organizations from around the world. Disparity between countries in the amount of per capita energy consumption are indeed vast (see Table 6.4).

### Table 6.4 Energy use (kg of oil equivalent per capita), 1980–2014

|                          | 1980  | 1990  | 2000  | 2014  |
|--------------------------|-------|-------|-------|-------|
| High income              | 4,337 | 4,473 | 4,935 | 4,638 |
| OECD members             | 4,142 | 4,241 | 4,586 | 4,145 |
| Upper middle income      | 789   | 1,369 | 1,288 | 2,204 |
| Middle income            | 569   | 976   | 907   | 1,396 |
| Low and middle income    | 568   | 952   | 877   | 1,325 |
| Lower middle income      | 328   | 550   | 525   | 646   |
| Sub-Saharan Africa       | 690   | 690   | 649   | 686   |
| World                    | 1,452 | 1,661 | 1,635 | 1,921 |

Source: FAO

The IEA defines energy access as "a household having reliable and affordable access to both clean cooking facilities and to electricity, which is enough to supply a basic bundle of energy services initially, and then an increasing level of electricity over time to reach the regional average." A basic bundle of energy services means, at a minimum, several lightbulbs, task lighting (such as a flashlight), phone charging, and a radio. Access to clean cooking facilities means access to (and primary use of) modern fuels and technologies, including natural gas, liquefied petroleum gas (LPG), electricity and biogas, or improved biomass cookstoves (ICS)2, as opposed to the basic biomass cookstoves and three-stone fires used in developing countries.

On this basis, the IEA estimates that about one billion people still live without electricity, while hundreds of millions more live with insufficient or unreliable access to it. At the same time, nearly three billion people cook or heat their homes with polluting fuels like wood or other biomass, resulting in indoor and outdoor air pollution that cause widespread health impacts. By 2030, 600 million out of the 674 million people without access to electricity will live in sub-Saharan Africa, a majority of them in rural areas.

But energy injustice is not only a problem for developing countries. It is estimated by the IEA that some 200 million people, over 15% of the total population in developed economies, suffer from energy poverty (see Box 6.2 for the case of the UK).

In France, the revolt of the so-called "yellow vests" that shook the country in the Fall of 2018 and early 2019 started because of a protest against a rise in fuel prices.[17] Close to 3.8 million French households (i.e. eight million people) are currently estimated to suffer from fuel poverty (close to 15% of the French population), with over 40% of households of the first income quartile considered fuel poor.

## Box 6.2 Fuel poverty in the UK

Fuel poverty in England is measured using the Low Income High Costs (LIHC) indicator. Under the LIHC indicator, a household is considered to be fuel poor if: it has required fuel costs that are above average (the national median level); were householders to spend that amount, they would be left with a residual income below the official poverty line.

Low Income High Costs is a dual indicator, which allows us to measure not only the extent of the problem (how many fuel-poor households there are), but also the depth of the problem (how badly affected each fuel-poor household is). The depth of fuel poverty is calculated by taking account of the fuel poverty gap. This is a measure of the additional fuel costs (in pounds) faced by fuel-poor households to meet the threshold that would make them non-fuel poor. It captures the fact that fuel poverty is distinct from general poverty: Not all poor households are fuel poor, and some households would not normally be considered poor but could be pushed into fuel poverty if they have high energy costs. Fuel poverty is therefore an overlapping problem of households having a low income and facing high energy costs.

In 2016, the average fuel poverty gap (in real terms) was £326. The aggregate fuel poverty gap (summed across all households in fuel poverty) was £832 million in 2016. The proportion of households in England in fuel poverty stood at 11.1% in 2016 (approximately 2.55 million households).

*Source:* UK Government (2017)

# 7

# Beyond EXPOWA (extraction, pollution, and waste)

Our current economic model could be labelled "EXPOWA": extract, pollute, and waste. More precisely, economic activity currently goes through four phases: extraction of primary materials renewable and non-renewable; transformation (production of goods and services); use (consumption); and waste (incineration, landfill, and recycling).

As it stands, this economic model is not only inefficient, but also unfair and unsustainable. But the nature of the problem should not be misunderstood. As highlighted by French philosopher Dominique Bourg and economist Christian Arnsperger,[1] most of the major current environmental disturbances do not result from pollution, but from the proportion of material flows generated by human activity. The source of the current ecological problem is essentially quantitative, not qualitative. What matters are quantities: Our environmental predicament (the general picture of which was presented in the previous chapter) now finds its source in the disproportionate flows of materials related to our activity as human beings. Neither carbon dioxide nor nitrogen are in themselves pollutants. They are, on the contrary, key constituents of major biogeochemical cycles. They become hazardous because of their volume. Pollutants can be naturally occurring substances or energies, but become contaminants when in excess of natural levels or absorption capacity by the biosphere. This is why, if we should improve production and consumption processes, we must mostly focus on reducing human-induced material flows. In essence, this is what the "perma-circular economy" advocated by Bourg and Arnsperger is about.

This chapter starts by presenting the magnitude of the flow problem, then looks at existing evidence on pollution and waste, and finally discusses strategies to reform current economic processes, especially the notion of decoupling.

A good place to begin to understand the flow problem is at the concept of socio-economic metabolism,[2] already alluded to in Chapter 3. Material resources (biomass, fossil fuels, metals, and non-metallic minerals) are the deep nutrients that feed the economy, which is only superficially nourished by labor and capital. Material flow accounting (MFA) allows us to estimate not just the "wealth" of nations but, more accurately, their "weight" (counting in tonnes rather than dollars, pounds, or euros). MFA traces the flow of materials through socio-economic systems, from their extraction in agriculture, forestry, and mining to their end-of-life discharge to the environment as waste and emissions.

Recent studies using this methodology show how far human societies have gone in "harvesting the biosphere" as Vaclav Smil put it. A recent UN Report highlights the fact that existing trends point globally to 88.6 billion tonnes of natural resources extracted in 2017, thrice the amount used in 1970.[3] This gigantic consumption results from human evolution: While hunters and gatherers extracted less than a ton of material per year, agrarian societies resulted in a three to six tonnes/capita/year natural resource use, modern industrial societies use on average between fifteen and 25 tonnes/capita/year.

Krausmann et al.[4] have compiled a long-term time series of global material extraction to show that, during the period of industrialization growth, global material use accelerated and increased from 3.7 Gt/year in 1850 to 7.1 Gt/year in 1900, to 14 Gt/year in 1950 to 70 Gt/year in 2010. According to authors, while growth in material use was partly driven by population growth (which increased 6.5-fold in this period), it is rising income and consumption in the industrial world in particular that accounts for the growth in the second half of the twentieth century.

The inequality among countries in this natural resource consumption is considerable: The table shows that industrial countries representing 16% of the global population consume 41% of all fossils but also that China now accounts for 44% of consumption of minerals, while its share in the world's population is only 20% (Table 7.1).

**Table 7.1 The share of country groups in global material consumption (DMC) by main material groups, population, and gross domestic product (GDP; in purchasing power parities and constant 2011 international dollars) in 2010**

|  |  | Global total | Industrial countries % | China % | Former Soviet Union % | Least developed countries % | Rest of the world % |
|---|---|---|---|---|---|---|---|
| Population | Billion head | 7 | 16 | 20 | 4 | 14 | 46 |
| DMC total | Gt/year | 70 | 26 | 34 | 5 | 4 | 32 |
| DMC total | tonnes/ capita/year | 10.0 | 15.9 | 17.3 | 11.5 | 2.6 | 6.8 |

Source: Adapted from F. Krausmann et al., 2017

Note: Direct material flow accounts is the amount of materials that is physically available to economies; these direct material flows comprise the extractions of materials inside the national economies and the physical imports/exports; direct supply of materials: Domestic Extraction Used (DEU) + Imports (IMP) = Direct Material Input (DMI). How materials are used is determined by the identity Direct Material Input (DMI) = Direct Material Consumption (DMC) + Exports (EXP).

This is a key evolution of our time: China, the first extractive power of the planet, has in a sense taken the lead from Western economies in the unequal consumption of the Earth's natural resources.

## Physical trade

This growth in consumption was accompanied by a buoyant trade, meaning that extraction was not entirely for domestic motives. Indeed, between 1970 and 2017, the quantity of traded materials more than tripled, growing from 2.7 billion tonnes to 11.6 billion tonnes. The growth of trade (3.2%) was in fact higher than the growth of extraction (2.6%).

But prominent importing regions changed. While in 1970, the group of high-income countries received 93% of all imports, the situation is more balanced today, with high-income countries receiving 52%, upper-middle-income countries 34% and lower-middle-income countries 13% of all imports. Overall, the three largest importing regions in 2017 are Asia and the Pacific (representing 48% of all imports), Europe at 28% and North America at eight percent.

The example of the European Union is especially interesting in this respect. While the European Union's (EU) trade balance in monetary values is more or less even, its physical trade balance is heavily asymmetric: The EU imports about three times more goods by weight from the rest of the world than it exports (physical imports amount to 3 to 4 tonnes per capita while physical exports are around one tonne per capita in the EU in 2017, Table 7.2).

| Table 7.2 Physical trade of goods by main material category and monetary trade of goods for the EU-28, 2000–2017 (tonnes per capita and euro per capita) | | 2000 | 2007 | 2017 |
|---|---|---|---|---|
| **Physical imports** | Biomass | 0.33 | 0.39 | 0.40 |
| | Metal ores | 0.51 | 0.61 | 0.49 |
| | Non-metallic minerals | 0.16 | 0.22 | 0.18 |
| | Fossil energy resources | 1.98 | 2.36 | 2.27 |
| | Other products and waste | 0.07 | 0.10 | 0.13 |
| **Physical exports** | Biomass | -0.21 | -0.22 | -0.33 |
| | Metal ores | -0.16 | -0.22 | -0.24 |
| | Non-metallic minerals | -0.12 | -0.13 | -0.17 |
| | Fossil energy resources | -0.29 | -0.38 | -0.52 |
| | Other products and waste | -0.07 | -0.08 | -0.10 |
| | | | | |
| | Monetary imports of goods | 5,300 | 7,605 | 9,192 |
| | Monetary exports of goods | -5,337 | -7,497 | -9,528 |

*Source:* Eurostat

This deficit in physical trade reveals a structural and growing dependency of the EU, especially when it comes to metal ores and fossil energy materials (see Table 7.3).

**Table 7.3 Import dependency by main material category for the EU-28, 2000–2017 (% of EU imports in total materials made available to EU-28 economy)**

|  | 2000 | 2007 | 2017 |
|---|---|---|---|
| Biomass | 8.6 | 10.5 | 10.7 |
| Metal ores | 62.4 | 68.5 | 54.4 |
| Non metallic minerals | 2.1 | 2.5 | 2.7 |
| Fossil energy materials | 48.1 | 56.6 | 63.8 |
| Total | 18.5 | 20.7 | 23.2 |

*Source:* Eurostat

This is typical of the developed–developing economic relation. The accounting in material footprints[5] reveals that despite the emergence of China, global material use is still dominated by North–South inequality. In 2017, despite more than half of global material use being directed to final demand in Asia and the Pacific, the material footprint of the region is estimated at 11.4 tonnes per capita. North America recorded 30 tonnes of material per capita for final demand, Europe 20.6 tonnes and all other regions measured under ten tonnes per capita. On a per capita basis, high-income countries continue to consume ten times more materials than low-income countries. Even more telling, the 1.2 billion poorest people account for one percent of the world's consumption, while the billion richest consume 72% of the world's resources (United Nations, 2013). This gigantic and unequal global extractive effort generates considerable amounts of pollutions and waste all along the process of our linear (rather than circular economic systems).

## Pollution and waste

Environmental pollution can be defined as "the contamination of the physical and biological components of the Earth/atmosphere system to such an extent that normal environmental processes are adversely affected." Any use of natural resources at a rate higher than nature's capacity to restore itself can result in pollution of air, water, and land.[6]

Sources of pollution are present in every economic sector: in *agriculture* and *food* (land-based farming, food and agro-industry, fisheries, and aquaculture); *energy* (combustion plants, fossil fuels, biomass, nuclear, domestic solid fuel heating); *industry* (chemicals, mineral extractives, forestry and paper products, cement); *manufacturing* (information technology, home electronics, construction and home-building products, batteries, textiles, apparel, footwear, and luxury goods); *pharmaceuticals* (for example antibiotics); *services* (retail, hospitality and tourism, hospitals and health-care services); *transport* (automobiles, fuel use and supply, engine emissions, road (tyres, surface), shipping, aviation, urban); and *waste* (improper management of municipal solid waste (which includes e-waste, plastics, food waste, organic waste, and open burning), industrial waste (which includes e-waste, construction and demolition waste), hazardous waste (which includes e-waste), sewerage effluents, landfills).[7]

Approximately 19,000,000 premature deaths are estimated to occur globally each year due to environmental and infrastructure-related risk factors that arise from the way societies use natural resources in production and consumption systems, including essential infrastructure and food provision. The specific impact the different forms of pollution have on human well-being are well documented and wide ranging;[8] we have already reviewed a number of them (especially air pollution), and we will explore this issue further in Chapter 10.

Waste is actually a source of pollution but also, as such, a symptom of our dysfunctional economic system. Waste generation is closely related to urbanization (Chapter 12), with cities generating globally 2.01 billion tons of solid waste every year including "e-waste."[9] In the OECD countries, municipal waste generation[10] has increased from 540,000 tonnes in 1990 to 675,000 in 2016 (a person generates, on average, 516 kg of municipal waste per year about 10 kg more than in 1990). While OECD cities are the most advanced in waste treatment, material recovery (recycling and composting) represents only a third of waste treatment with landfilling remaining the major disposal method in many countries (Table 7.4). Hence the need to make rapid progress on resource efficiency.

## Table 7.4 Waste treatment in the OECD, 2013

| | % of amounts treated | | | |
| --- | --- | --- | --- | --- |
| | Recycling and composting | Incineration with energy recovery | Incineration without energy recovery | Landfill |
| OECD | 34 | 20 | 2 | 44 |
| OECD Europe | 40 | 22 | 3 | 35 |

*Source:* OECD

## Resource efficiency

Because of the many adverse effects of pollution and waste, better and more efficient use of natural resources can be one of the most effective ways to reduce economic impacts on the environment and to advance human well-being. In general terms, resource efficiency means increasing human well-being while lowering the amount of resources required to do so and the environmental damage done in doing so.

As a matter of fact, in the course of the twentieth century, most economies of the world "dematerialized" the economic wealth produced by consuming fewer and fewer natural resources per unit output. In other words, productivity (or efficiency) grew. But, as we have seen, the volume of natural resources consumed by these economies continued to swell. There has, therefore, been only a relative decoupling between economic activity and the consumption of natural resources. The consumption has grown more slowly than the rate of economic development, but there has been no decline in the quantities consumed over time: on the contrary.

During the twentieth century alone, the volume of resources extracted has grown by almost a factor of seven, while the metabolic rate (material extraction per capita), taking into account population growth, has grown by 1.7. Material intensity, taking into account the wealth created, has declined by almost a factor of 2.5.[11] While natural resource consumption has grown less rapidly than population and significantly more slowly than economic wealth, the fact remains that humans consume ten times the amount of natural resources they did in 1900. The evolution of Western industrial European countries after the Second World War is typical of this illusion of dematerialization (Table 7.5).

| Table 7.5 Material flow accounting for Western industrial Europe, 1950–2010 | | | | | | | |
|---|---|---|---|---|---|---|---|
| | 1950 | 1960 | 1970 | 1980 | 1990 | 2000 | 2010 |
| Domestic Material Consumption (DMC) in kt/a | 5,886 686 | 8,266 201 | 12 116 416 | 13 751 320 | 14 827 101 | 15 800 373 | 14 744 638 |
| Per Capita Domestic Material Consumption (DMC) in t/cap/a | 9.7 | 12.1 | 15.9 | 16.6 | 167 | 16.6 | 14.8 |
| Material Intensity (DMC/GDP*) in kg/$/a | 1.8 | 1.6 | 1.5 | 1.2 | 1.0 | 0.8 | 0.6 |

| kt/a | metric kilotons (1,000 tons) per year |
|---|---|
| t/cap/a | metric tons per capita and year |
| kg/$/a | kilograms per dollar and year |

Source: Global Material Flows Database

Here also, inequality is large: While in the last six decades, global average material use increased from 5.0 to 10.3 tonnes per capita and year (t/cap/a), regional metabolic rates in 2010 range from 4.5 t/cap/a in sub-Saharan Africa to 14.8 t/cap/a in the Western industrial grouping.[12]

We can further look at three productivities (labor, energy, and natural resources) to see very clearly that, while economic systems have been characterized by a relative decoupling in the course of the twentieth century, this is no longer true after 2000. According to UN data, material productivity (the inverse of material intensity) grew by around 40% between 1900 and 2000 (by 25% between 1970 and 2000). It begins to decline in the early 2000s to decrease by about 12% between 2000 and 2015. At the same time, energy productivity starts to stagnate in the early 2000s while it had grown by 40% between 1970 and 2000. Only labor productivity continues to grow in the twenty-first century (it has grown by around 190% between 1970 and 2017 and by around 35% between 2000 and 2017). We will look further into this very interesting finding, in the light of the "digital revolution," in Chapter 11.

We can relate resources consumption and economic activity through material productivity/efficiency (or resource productivity/efficiency) comparing the amount of GDP generated per unit of material consumed, that is, GDP / DMC as we just did. But we can also move from static material accounting and the history of dematerialization to the dynamic of decoupling.

Reflections and work on the notion of decoupling between the economy and environment, goes back to the "environmental curve Kuznets." The basic idea of this curve is to link the economic development process (whose level is measured by per capita income) with the environmental degradations. A Bell-like relationship is then postulated: Environmental degradation is first expected to increase with rising per capita income before reaching a peak and then reduce. The idea behind this curve was introduced in 1992 in the report on the development of the United Nations and then formalized and illustrated empirically by an article by Grossman and Krueger published in 1995.[13] As for the initial "Kuznets curve," observing the U-inverted relation between growth and inequality in certain countries at a specific historical juncture, the second segment of the curve, where environmental degradations decline, depends on public policies being enforced.

There are at least three limits to this analysis. The first is that not all pollutions or degradations recede with the growth of national income. $CO_2$ emissions and waste for instance are heavily correlated to GDP and increase when national income does. The second is that improvements in technology and material efficiency, while reducing environmental impact in appearance, might trigger an accelerated consumption (this is the so-called "Jevons paradox," see Box 7.1).

## Box 7.1 Stanley Jevons and the "rebound effect"

In chapter VII of his book on the dependence of the British economy to a cheap but exhaustible coal, *The Coal Question* (1865), economist Stanley Jevons formulates the paradox that has kept his name since: Increasing efficiency technology in the use of a natural resource like coal may not reduce the demand for this resource, but instead increase it. Consumption is in a sense unleashed by the technological acceleration because of the lower costs that it causes. The demand is then carried away in a race that increases the impact of the consumption of natural resources and shortens the time between unsustainability and finally, in Jevons' mind, decline.

The "Jevons paradox" (also pictorially referred to as the "rebound effect") can be simply stated: The increase in energy efficiency (the decrease in the amount of energy used to produce a good because of the improvement in energy efficiency technologies) simultaneously generates energy savings in the short term and increases the consumption of the good in the medium term, which can cancel these savings and eventually lead to greater energy consumption.

With respect to climate change, a one percent energy efficiency improvement should result in a one percent reduction in energy use and energy-related emissions to provide the same energy services. A recent study[14] estimates that rebound effect magnitude (economy-wide) varies between the range of 15 and 350%: the rebound effect can lead to a backfire.

This relates to the difference between relative and absolute decoupling. There is decoupling when the rate of growth of a pressure on the environment (e.g. $CO_2$ emissions) becomes lower than that of its driving force (e.g. GDP growth). It is an absolute decoupling if the pressure on the environment (e.g. emissions $CO_2$ level) remains stable or decreases while the variation of the driving force is increasing (e.g. real GDP in volume). It is relative decoupling when the pressure on the environment increases but at a lower growth rate than the driving force (rate GDP growth rate > growth rate of emissions).

Related to this difference, the third limit of the "environmental Kuznets curve" is that the low level of degradations observed for rich countries may not be the end of the story: New levels of income might trigger new forms of degradations and encourage rich countries to transfer environmental degradations to low-income nations. This is a key point: A decoupling at national level, even absolute, may be the result of the displacement to other countries of consumption of natural resources and their environmental cost. A simple illustration of this idea can be given by the difference between the national and global evolution of greenhouse gas. It is a fact that some countries have been able to absolutely decouple GDP from $CO_2$ emissions (see Table 7.6).

Apart from the fact that GDP is not a good measure of human well-being (see Chapter 9), we can observe that most of these countries are European and that the emissions counted are production (or territorial) emissions, counted within national borders. Consumption-based emissions, instead, use a comprehensive approach to estimate emissions associated with national consumption of goods and services, regardless of where they were produced. If we use consumption emissions rather than production emissions for the European Union as a whole, the picture of decoupling changes substantially. The EU has reduced its GHG emissions by close to 20% in terms of production since 1990, but by only five percent when consumption emissions are considered. Actually, since the mid 1990s, the gap has indeed widened between emissions from domestic

| Table 7.6 Absolute decoupling between GDP and $CO_2$ in 21 countries | | | |
|---|---|---|---|
| | Change in $CO_2$ (2000–2014) % | Change in $CO_2$ (2000–2014) Mt | Change in Real GDP (2000–2014) % |
| Austria | -3 | -2 | 21 |
| Belgium | -12 | -20 | 21 |
| Bulgaria | -5 | -2 | 62 |
| Czech Republic | -14 | -18 | 40 |
| Denmark | -30 | -17 | 8 |
| Finland | -18 | -11 | 18 |
| France | -19 | -83 | 16 |
| Germany | -12 | -106 | 16 |
| Hungary | -24 | -14 | 29 |
| Ireland | -16 | -7 | 47 |
| Netherlands | -8 | -19 | 15 |
| Portugal | -23 | -16 | 1 |
| Romania | -22 | -21 | 65 |
| Slovakia | -22 | -9 | 75 |
| Spain | -14 | -48 | 20 |
| Sweden | -8 | -5 | 31 |
| Switzerland | -10 | -4 | 28 |
| Ukraine | -29 | -99 | 49 |
| United Kingdom | -20 | -120 | 27 |
| United States | -6 | -382 | 28 |
| Uzbekistan | -2 | -2 | 28 |

*Source:* World Resource Institute

production and emissions linked to the consumption of imported products in the EU (see Graph 7.1). This difference between production and consumption emissions is about twice as high in the European Union as in the United States and nearly four times higher than in Japan.

For a country like France, listed among the success stories of decoupling in Table 7.6, the picture is completely reversed when consumption emissions are used instead of production emissions: $CO_2$ emissions in France have not declined by ten percent between 1990 and 2015 as UN data show, but increased by 11% over this period (emissions of greenhouse gases per capita, which were

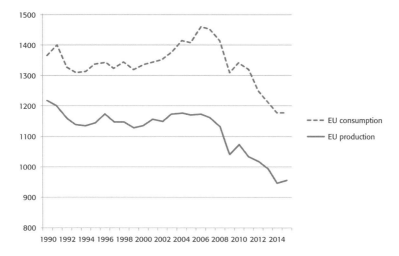

Graph 7.1   European Union emissions of GHG in production and consumption

*Source*: Global Carbon Project

only the equivalent of 7.7 tonnes of $CO_2$ in 2010, are 11.6, a third more, when carbon embedded in consumer products is also recorded).

To put it in simple terms, we should pay attention not only to the difference between absolute and relative decoupling, but also between net and gross decoupling (with respect to global flows). On this basis, we can therefore define four different forms of decoupling, ranging from the more trivial to the most demanding (Box 7.2).

## Box 7.2 Four types of decoupling

(1) Decoupling economic activity from environmental impact (or degradation): GDP increases while environmental degradation is reduced by the development of the green economy (circularity, etc.); but it can be only relative and gross and natural resources consumption can still increase;

(2) Decoupling economic activity from natural resources consumption: material productivity is increased; but it can be only relative and gross;

(3) Decoupling well-being from environmental impact: decoupling of well-being from the environmental impact in net and absolute terms; natural resources consumption can still increase;

(4) Decoupling well-being from natural resources consumption: Human well-being increases without an increase of natural resources consumption and the related environmental degradations in net and absolute terms.

## Circular or perma-circular economy?

Given previous developments, we can contrast two models of economic activity: The linear economy in which massive resource extraction leads to pollution and waste and the circular economy that minimizes the use of natural resources and toxic materials as well as the emissions of waste and pollutants over the life cycle of the service or product. But the circular economy itself is not without serious limitations. Hence the need for a third model: the perma-circular economy.

For the UN, the circular economy is: "the use of services and related products, which respond to basic needs and bring a better quality of life while minimizing the use of natural resources and toxic materials as well as the emissions of waste and pollutants over the life cycle of the service or product so as not to jeopardize the needs of future generations." But this definition is seen by some as too vague. Korhonen et al. (2018) note that the "circular economy is currently a popular concept promoted by the EU, by several national governments and by many businesses around the world. However, the scientific and research content of the concept is superficial and unorganized."[15]

Of even greater concern, focusing on the circularity of the economy might lead to obscuring real environmental problems. By focusing measures of circularity on micro levels (companies, sectors), one can overlook the multiple rebound effects and postponements of consumption of resources that propagate within the system as a whole. The main issue is not the circular nature of economic activity but how large the circle is (an economy might appear to be circular at the national level because it transfers waste and pollution to other countries).

This is why Dominique Bourg and Christian Arnsperger distinguish three levels of circularity. The first level of circular economy, which is consensual today, is that of the production sites, but without any systemic vision of global flows. The second one focuses on global flows of materials by advocating that the rate of growth of consumption of materials does not exceed one percent, at most 0.5% per year. On this condition, part of the economy can be made circular. The third level, the "perma-circular economy," considers the return to growth of 0.5% per year as a first step, but essentially aims at bringing down material flows that underpin our economic activities, degrade the biosphere and threaten our well-being. Of these threats, climate change has become the most visible.

# 8

# Energy, climate, and justice

As things stand, given current policies, global temperatures will reach 3.3 degrees above pre-industrial levels at the end of the twenty-first century.[1] The latest Assessment Report by the IPCC (2018)[2] estimates that, according to current trends, the 1.5 degrees threshold will be reached as early as 2040 (the planet has already warmed by 1.1 degrees compared to pre-industrial levels). What is more striking is that, if all countries fulfilled their pledges and reached their targets, the increase in temperatures would still be of three degrees (or twice the target agreed upon at the Paris Agreement in 2015). In other words, what is lacking is not just the political will but also the imagination. Policies thus need to change, decidedly and fast. For this to happen, key social drivers of climate change should be identified and mitigated and international negotiations need to be refocused and accelerated. All this is within our reach, provided we understand what the challenges are.

In August 2018, the *New York Times Magazine* ran a paper and online story[3] that received wide praise, about how climate science was "settled" but ignored during the period from 1979 to 1989. "Thirty years ago, we had a chance to save the planet" was the catchy headline promoting the publication. This is misleading on at least four important levels. First, science is not enough to trigger action. As French philosopher Jean-Pierre Dupuy profoundly remarked, we not only have to know, we have to believe what we know. Second, the planet will save itself; what is at stake is the hospitality of the planet for humans. Third, a number of important steps *were* taken after 1989, starting with the publication of the first IPCC Report (1990), the first Conference of Parties UN meeting (in 1995 in Berlin) and the drafting of the Kyoto Protocol in 1997. But, most importantly, this narrative ignores the kind of knowledge we need to avoid catastrophic climate change: It is not climate change science that we need to master, but human change science. And this is very much a work in progress.

Let us start with the link, comparable to a mathematical equation, between the use of fossil fuels and climate change. On each side of the equation are key parameters for analysis and policy, which this chapter aims to highlight.

## Energy and climate: The carbon problem

As was already mentioned but is worth repeating, the sun provides 8,000 times what humans need to operate their economies, yet human economies massively use fossil fuels (80% of the current global energy supply mix) for their needs, which gives rise to climate change that increasingly destroys human well-being.

The first parameter of the energy–climate equation is thus the global energy mix. Surprisingly it has not changed much over the last four decades (Table 8.1).

### Table 8.1 The global energy mix in 1973 and 2015

|  | 1973 | 2015 |
| --- | --- | --- |
| Oil | 46 | 31 |
| Coal | 24 | 28 |
| Natural gas | 16 | 21 |
| Nuclear | 0.9 | 4.9 |
| Hydro | 1.8 | 2.5 |
| Biofules and waste | 10.5 | 10 |
| Other (geothermal, wind, solar, tide, heat) | 0.1 | 1.5 |

Source: World Energy Outlook, International Energy Agency

The only notable evolution here is the relative and moderate increase in nuclear power, the substitution of natural gas for oil and the rise of other forms of energy, sometimes at a high speed in recent years, but to a very low level in the overall energy mix. And yet, in the last decade alone, renewable energies have become increasingly competitive, some doing even better with respect to this criterion for electricity generation than fossil fuels (Table 8.2).

### Table 8.2 Renewable energy competitiveness
### Global levelized cost of electricity from utility-scale renewable power generation technologies, 2010–2017 in 2016 USD/kWh

|  | 2010 | 2017 |
| --- | --- | --- |
| Fossil fuel cost range | 0.05 to 0.15 | 0.05 to 0.15 |
| Biomass | 0.007 | 0.007 |
| Geothermal | 0.05 | 0.07 |
| Hydro | 0.04 | 0.05 |
| Solar photovoltaic | 0.36 | 0.1 |
| Offshore wind | 0.17 | 0.14 |
| Onshore wind | 0.08 | 0.06 |

Source: IRENA

This is testimony to the fact that energy transitions are slow and cumulative processes: They occur by adding sources of energy gradually in time rather than by jumping from one source of energy to the next. But the pace of energy transition is anything but natural and largely depends on market incentives and public policy: Today in the global economy carbon taxation is too low, although it is spreading and gradually increasing worldwide, while fossil fuels subsidies remain high (Box 8.1).

## Box 8.1 Taxing and subsidizing carbon

Contrary to what is conveyed by contemporary economic mythology, there are no markets in the world governed by "free and undistorted competition." A market is, obviously, a set of rules of the economic game. No one, outside the public power, can create, impose, and administer these rules. This public creation and management of markets can take different forms (it can be done by commission or omission) and be more or less visible, but it is always there. The energy market is one where public intervention is the most prevalent. From an economic standpoint, there is little difference between taxing and subsidizing, except of course the direction of the effort (that is to say the sign of the sums involved): Both policies aim at altering behaviors using a price signal. But there is a considerable asymmetry today between carbon taxes and subsidies.

Subsidies to fossil fuels are estimated worldwide at $5.3 trillion in 2015, higher than the $4.9 trillion estimated for 2013, representing 6.5% of global GDP in both years.[4] Using a much more narrow definition accounting only for worldwide fossil fuel consumption subsidies, the International Energy Agency reports that they amount to 300 billion dollars, approximately twice the amount of subsidies going to renewable energy.

On the other hand, the World Bank estimates that in 2017, 53 carbon pricing initiatives were implemented or scheduled for implementation, with 46 national jurisdictions and 25 subnational jurisdictions covered by the initiatives selected. This represents close to 20% global GHG emissions for a total monetary value of 80 billion dollars (more than four times less than worldwide fossil fuel consumption subsidies alone).

The French think-tank I4CE has counted, in April 2018, 46 countries and 26 provinces implementing an explicit carbon pricing instrument (carbon tax or carbon trading system), these jurisdictions representing 60% of global GDP and 25 carbon pricing instruments announced for the coming years for an overall revenue of 26 billion euros.

The climate side of the equation derives from a physical fact: The biosphere can only absorb some of the $CO_2$ released by humans through the combustion of fossil fuels (and methane related to agriculture) via carbon sinks, for instance trees (when trees grow, they absorb $CO_2$ and release oxygen). The rest of the $CO_2$ goes into seas and oceans (where it creates acidification, see Chapter 6) and the lower levels of the atmosphere (where it creates climate change).

The main source of greenhouse gas is CO2 (representing close to 75% of all greenhouse gases) and it has two human sources: 90% of CO2 emissions come from industrial activities (heating, production, transport, waste) and the remaining ten percent from deforestation (when trees are burnt, they release part of the CO2 they have absorbed). Of these emissions, 26% are absorbed by seas and oceans (acidifying them), 31% by forests, while 44% get stuck in the lower parts of the atmosphere, changing the climate by warming the Earth, seas, and oceans' surface and fostering extreme climate events such as tornadoes, drought, or flooding.

Let us consider the emissions parameter of the energy–climate equation. Global emissions from fossil fuel and industry represent 36.2 GtCO2 in 2016, 62% above their 1990 level. Their average annual increase went from one percent between 1990 and 1999 to 3.3% between 2000 and 2009. After a very slight decrease during the "great recession" of 2009, GHG emissions began rising again at an annual rate of 2.5%.[5] Share of global emissions in 2016 among sources of energy are distributed the following way: coal (40%), oil (34%), gas (19%), cement (6%), flaring (1%).

In terms of concentration of greenhouse gases, global CO2 concentration increased from 277ppm in 1750 to 403ppm in 2016 (up 45%), with 2016 as the first full year with concentration above 400ppm.

Finally, in terms of temperature, the IPCC notes in its special assessment report released in the Fall of 2018 that "human activities are estimated to have caused approximately 1.0°C of global warming above pre-industrial levels, with a likely range of 0.8°C to 1.2°C. Global warming is likely to reach 1.5°C between 2030 and 2052 if it continues to increase at the current rate." The World Meteorological Organization notes in its 2018 annual statement that "Global mean temperatures in 2017 were 1.1 °C ± 0.1 °C above pre-industrial levels."[6]

## Climate policy: Mitigation

There are two essential and complementary (rather than substitutable) climate policies. The first is climate change mitigation defined by the IPCC as "an anthropogenic intervention to reduce the sources or enhance the sinks of greenhouse gases." The second is climate change adaptation defined as "adjustment in natural or human systems in response to actual or expected climatic stimuli or their effects, which moderates harm or exploits beneficial opportunities." John Holdren, a former advisor for science in the Obama administration, once grimly quipped that there were actually three types of climate policy: Mitigation that attempts to lower global warming and alleviate extreme climate events; adaptation, that faces the consequences of a changing climate not prevented by mitigation; and finally, suffering, the sum of the combined failures of mitigation and adaptation.

The various instruments of climate change mitigation have been reviewed in Chapter 5. But what are the major drivers of greenhouse emissions? To answer this question, one can use the variables of the Kaya equation (1990) that breaks down the components of emissions:

Energy related CO2 emissions = GDP * Carbon intensity of growth

Energy related CO2 emissions = GDP * Energy intensity of growth * Carbon intensity of energy

Energy related CO2 emissions = GDP per capita * population * total primary energy supply per unit of GDP * CO2 emissions per unit of total primary energy supply

Growth rate of emissions $\approx$ Sum of growth rate of 4 components.

Once these determinants and their respective importance have been identified, mitigating climate change does not look easy but is certainly possible (Box 8.2).

## Box 8.2 How to mitigate climate change: A policy toolbox

Data show that between 1970 and 2010, CO2 emissions per year grew by three percent as the result of a strong population growth and growth of GDP per capita (for a combined growth of close to four percentage points), mitigated by the de-growth of energy intensity and carbon intensity for a combined subtraction of close to one percentage point. According to EIA projections for 2010 to 2040, carbon intensity could continue to decrease, but by much less than energy intensity, while income per capita will grow much more than population (see table).

|                          | 1970–2010 | 2010–2040 |
|--------------------------|-----------|-----------|
| Population               | 2.1       | 0.8       |
| Income per capita        | 1.8       | 2.8       |
| Growth of accelerators   | 3.9       | 3.6       |
|                          |           |           |
| Energy intensity         | -0.5      | -2.1      |
| Carbon intensity         | -0.37     | -0.2      |
| De-growth of mitigators  | -0.87     | -2.3      |
|                          |           |           |
| Growth of emissions      | 3.03      | 1.3       |

Source: World Bank and EIA

How to solve climate change? By acting on these four drivers:

- The first policy is obviously to control *population* (although its contribution to the problem will be significantly lower in the next three decades than it has been in the previous four decades). This can be done most efficiently by investing in the education of women in order to reduce fertility rates (an investment that entails educating men to the benefits of women's emancipation);

- The second policy is twofold: First, policy-makers can design tax and social policy aiming at sharing income and wealth more equally in order to decrease average *income per capita* while maintaining living standards. Inequality inflates the need for economic growth. If income and wealth in a given country are increasingly captured by a small fraction of the population, the rest of the population will need to compensate with additional economic development. Since, as we have seen, virtually no country in the world has managed to decouple (in absolute or net terms) economic growth from its negative environmental impacts, this additional economic growth will translate into more environmental degradations, starting with climate change (the correlation between GDP level and $CO_2$ emissions is close to one). In the United States for instance, between 1993 and 2011, one percent of the population managed to capture 75% of economic growth. A more even distribution of income (i.e. a growth of income of two percent for the top ten percent and bottom 90% of the income distribution alike) would have reduced the total growth necessary to meet the needs of the vast majority of Americans and led to a small decline in $CO_2$ emissions[7] (on this point, see Chapter 10). The second sub-policy that is needed is to change the very definition of income and wealth (see Chapter 9) to reduce their environmental impact;

- The third policy is to increase *energy efficiency* and *energy savings*. Innovation, driven by adequate incentives informed by justice principles, can result in efficient and fair outcomes (see Chapter 5);

- Finally, economies around the world have to increase their *carbon efficiency* (or decrease their carbon intensity) by deploying and using renewable energy in lieu of fossil fuels. Again, efficient and fair policy is possible on this front.

To say, as is often done, that individual actions are meaningless, given the magnitude of the climate problem is not accurate: All actions are individual in the end it is their aggregation that produces collective change. What is true is that the obstacles to solving climate change are neither technological nor economic, they are the usual intellectual and political hurdles to any change or progress: ideas, interests, and institutions. But the fact remains: We have every lever we need to solve climate change.

Because, as we have seen, climate is a pure public good (non-excludable and non-rival), the key to mitigating climate change is international cooperation.

## Negotiating climate

For twenty years (from 1997 to 2016), the framework for climate negotiations has been the Kyoto Protocol. The thinking today is that Kyoto, which guided negotiations following the United Nations Framework Convention on Climate Change (decided at the 1992 Rio Summit), has been a resounding failure. However, that is only a partial truth: In fact, Protocol-bound Annex 1 countries[8] did live up to their commitments – albeit only by resorting to a sleight of hand. In the Kyoto Protocol, the most economically developed countries made a first – and supposedly binding – greenhouse gas (GHG) emission reduction commitment while the less developed countries were exempted from such commitments due to their lower development levels and lower GHG emissions. In 1990 – the baseline year for calculating emissions – the first-group of nations (comprising OECD countries and former Soviet Union members) were deemed responsible for 60% of the total GHG emissions.

Under the Kyoto Protocol, these countries (called "Annex 1 countries") committed to reduce their emissions collectively by approximately five percent by 2012, compared to 1990 levels. What is not always understood today is that this objective was actually met. Even better, the latest available data show that the reduction almost reached ten percent (even 15% according to some estimates): Annex 1 countries thus did twice as well as was expected from them, but almost entirely because of the collapse of the USSR that completely biased Annex 1 countries' performance.[9]

What is more, while this dubious reduction was taking place, a much more significant increase of emissions, driven by the economic expansion of China, was taking place in the rest of the world (see Table 8.3).

In other words, a great reversal occurred between developed countries (Annex 1 countries) and developing countries, from the time the Kyoto Protocol was drafted until the moment it was supposed to be achieved: In the mid 1990s, Annex 1 countries represented two-thirds of emissions, 25 years later, they represent a third of the total emissions (Table 8.3). The geopolitical vision (and data) that informed the Kyoto Protocol had become totally obsolete. After the failure of the Copenhagen summit in 2009, where developed and emerging countries clashed over their respective burdens in mitigating climate change, a positive negotiation dynamic, driven by the US–China bilateral talks, emerged and culminated at the COP 21 in Paris in December of 2015. The first ever universal climate treaty, the Paris Agreement, was adopted on December 12, 2015.

If the contents of the 32-page text had to be summarized in a single phrase, one could say that never have the ambitions been so high but the commitments so low. This is the basic trade-off in the text, and this was undoubtedly the condition for its adoption by all the world's countries. The expectation had been that the aim of COP 21 was to extend to the emerging markets,

| Table 8.3 Global emissions of $CO_2$ in 2016 | | | |
|---|---|---|---|
| | **Emissions 2016** | | |
| Region/country | Per capita | Total | |
| | $tCO_2$ per person | $GtCO_2$ | % |
| Global (with bunkers) | 4.8 | 36.18 | 100 |
| | **Annex 1 countries** | | |
| **Total Annex 1** | 9.8 | 12.56 | **34.7** |
| USA | 16.5 | 5.31 | 14.7 |
| OECD Europe | 7.0 | 3.42 | 9.5 |
| Japan | 9.5 | 1.21 | 3.3 |
| South Korea | 11.7 | 0.60 | 1.6 |
| Canada | 15.5 | 0.56 | 1.6 |
| | **Non-Annex 1 countries** | | |
| **Total non-Annex 1** | 3.6 | 22.25 | **61.5** |
| China | 7.2 | 10.15 | 28.1 |
| India | 1.8 | 2.43 | 6.7 |
| Russia | 11.4 | 1.63 | 4.5 |
| Iran | 8.2 | 0.66 | 1.8 |
| Saudi Arabia | 19.7 | 0.63 | 1.8 |
| | **International bunkers** | | |
| Aviation and shipping | | 1.37 | 3.8 |

* Emissions in $GtCO_2$, from fossil energy consumption and cement production.

*Source:* Global Carbon Project

starting with China and India, the binding commitments agreed in Kyoto eighteen years ago by the developed countries. What took place was exactly the opposite: Every country is now effectively out of Annex 1 of the Kyoto Protocol, released from any legal constraints on the nature of their commitments which now amount to voluntary contributions (Intended Nationally Determined Contributions or INDC) that countries determine on their own and without reference to a common goal.

This can indeed be seen as a victory for US negotiators, who have insisted that a legally binding text – which would have required at the time the approval of the Republican controlled Senate – had no chance of being adopted. The US position was contested by the EU and its member states, which, in their Intended Nationally Determined Contribution released on March 6, 2015, called for "adopting a global legally binding agreement applicable to all Parties."[10] China also called for a "legally binding agreement" in a clear challenge to the US position.[11] But the US position prevailed in Paris, meaning that the Paris Agreement is weaker, in terms of legal force, than the Kyoto Protocol – itself deprived of any sanction for non-abiding parties.

Of more concern, there is a glaring gap between the main ambition of the Paris Agreement: "Holding the increase in the global average temperature to well below 2°C above pre-industrial levels and pursuing efforts to limit the temperature increase to 1.5°C above pre-industrial levels" (Article 2) and the reality of existing commitments (current policies lead to a 3.4 degrees world and current pledges to an only slightly better 3.2 degrees world).

Yet, at the 2011 Durban Conference (COP 17), the parties acknowledged the gap between their commitments and achieving the two-degree Celsius objective. In the preamble of their joint statement, they expressed "grave concern" and promised to "raise the level of ambition" to bridge this gap. At the Lima Conference (COP 20) in December 2014, the parties reiterated[12] the same "grave concern" about "the significant gap between the aggregate effect of Parties' mitigation pledges" and the goal of holding the increase in global average temperature below the two-degree Celsius limit. But the ambition–commitment gap has so far survived all virtuous proclamations.

This is in part due to the fact that climate negotiations have so far revolved crucially around volumes of carbon emitted: Under the Kyoto Protocol, a country's climate performance is assessed in terms of emission reduction targets compared to their 1990 levels and climate commitments are being framed in terms of emission reductions up to 2030 or 2050. Under the Paris Agreement, almost all INDCs are labelled in volume of emissions reduction (the need to put a price on carbon, and thus give it social value, disappeared from the final version of the Paris Agreement under the combined pressure of Saudi Arabia and Venezuela).

There are two reasons why this volume-based approach can be insufficient: It does not specify the instruments that are supposed to be used to match the volume targets; and it does not take into account carbon flows, that are emissions resulting not only from national production, but also from national consumption (as we have seen with the case of the EU in the previous chapter, this gap can be quite large). The current weaknesses of the existing climate negotiation framework could be remedied in large part by introducing into climate negotiations the goal to develop a robust global carbon pricing system. The new system would rely on a few simple principles (see Laurent 2017):

> The common climate objective is now officially to limit global warming to between 1.5 degrees and two degrees Celsius above pre-industrial levels; a global carbon price must therefore aim at meeting that objective.

Because the internationally agreed principle of *Common but Differentiated Responsibilities* would make it very difficult to set a single price immediately, it would be more realistic to consider a price convergence-based process stretching over a number of years, as proposed by such international bodies as the International Energy Agency; a carbon budget set to the two-degree limit leads to the establishment of a differentiated trajectory of gradually converging global pricing of carbon, each country freely determining the mix of instruments used to raise its price.

Given that developed countries have pledged to provide one hundred billion dollars yearly to help the most vulnerable countries deal with climate change without specifying a stable resource to back this pledge, a global carbon price would be a good instrument to meet – or even surpass – this commitment.

In short, negotiators need to follow up on the Paris Agreement with one main principle: climate justice.

## Climate justice: Fair and efficient

The Paris Agreement mentions the term "justice" only a single time, to affirm that signatories recognize "the importance for some of the concept of 'climate justice.'" This is clearly a misinterpretation. The whole point of climate justice is precisely that it is not confined to a few nations or important for a few people: It should be the concern of all involved in climate negotiations. Two related issues indicate why justice should be put at the heart of the climate negotiations.

The first has to do with climate mitigation and the choice of the criteria for allocating the remaining "carbon budget" between countries (the approximately 1,200 billion metric tons of carbon that remain to be emitted over the next three decades so as to limit the rise of ground temperatures to around two degrees by the end of the twenty-first century).

The unequal nature of the distribution of global emissions is striking. The top four emitters in 2016 covered 59% of global emissions: China (28%), United States (15%), EU28 (10%), India (7%). The first top twenty emitters represented close to 80% of emissions. Climate change is thus the responsibility of a small minority of countries (10% of nations comprising 63% of global population) imposing a huge cost on the rest of the world[13] (Table 8.4).

Given this reality, various indicators can be used both to estimate the carbon budget and to distribute it equitably among top emitters (something that the Paris Agreement is silent about). It can be shown that the application of a hybrid but relatively simple criteria on climate justice would lead to substantially cutting global emissions in addition to the carbon budget (by 36%) over the next three decades which would ensure meeting the goal of

## Table 8.4 Emissions of carbon dioxide in 2015, country ranking and shares

| Country rank | Country | 2015 CO$^2$ emissions from fuel combustion | | | |
|---|---|---|---|---|---|
| | | (2015, million metric tons) | Share of total emissions (in %) | Share of total population (in %) | Share of total countries (in %) |
| 1 | China | 9040.74 | 28 | 18.5 | 0.5 |
| 2 | United States | 4997.50 | 15 | 4.3 | 0.5 |
| 3 | India | 2066.01 | 6 | 17.9 | 0.5 |
| 4 | Russia | 1468.99 | 5 | 1.9 | 0.5 |
| 5 | Japan | 1141.58 | 4 | 1.7 | 0.5 |
| 6 | Germany | 729.77 | 2 | 1.1 | 0.5 |
| 7 | South Korea | 585.99 | 2 | 0.9 | 0.5 |
| 8 | Iran | 552.40 | 2 | 1.1 | 0.5 |
| 9 | Canada | 549.23 | 2 | 0.5 | 0.5 |
| 10 | Saudi Arabia | 531.46 | 2 | 0.5 | 0.5 |
| 11 | Brazil | 450.79 | 1 | 2.8 | 0.5 |
| 12 | Mexico | 442.31 | 1 | 1.7 | 0.5 |
| 13 | Indonesia | 441.91 | 1 | 3.5 | 0.5 |
| 14 | South Africa | 427.57 | 1 | 1 | 0.5 |
| 15 | United Kingdom | 389.75 | 1 | 1 | 0.5 |
| 16 | Australia | 380.93 | 1 | 0.5 | 0.5 |
| 17 | Italy | 330.75 | 1 | 1 | 0.5 |
| 18 | Turkey | 317.22 | 1 | 1.1 | 0.5 |
| 19 | France | 290.49 | 1 | 1 | 0.5 |
| 20 | Poland | 282.40 | 1 | 0.5 | 0.5 |
| **Top 20** | | | 78 | 63 | 10 |
| **Rest of the world** | | | 22 | 37 | 90 |

*Source:* CO$^2$ Emissions from Fuel Combustion, IEA, and author's calculations

two degrees, and even targeting 1.5 degrees, thereby enhancing the fairness of this common rule with respect to the most vulnerable countries and social groups (see Table 8.5).

| Table 8.5 A simple model of fair and efficient climate justice | | | | | | |
|---|---|---|---|---|---|---|
| Top twenty $CO_2$ emitters: 76% of global emissions | % of the global average of consumption emissions per capita, averaged over 1990–2012 | % of the global average of HDI, averaged over 1990–2012 | Average distance to 100 of (1) and (2) | Projected population increase until 2050 | Equal distribution of 75% of 1,200bn tonnes of $CO_2$ | Carbon budget per country : = (5) + or – (3) + or – (4) |
| | | | (in %) | (in %) | (in bn tonnes) | (in bn tonnes) |
| | (1) | (2) | (3) | (4) | (5) | |
| India | 27 | 75 | 49 | 24 | 45 | 78 |
| Indonesia | 30 | 95 | 38 | 22 | 45 | 72 |
| Brazil | 43 | 106 | 26 | 12 | 45 | 62 |
| Thailand | 70 | 102 | 14 | -5 | 45 | 49 |
| China | 85 | 97 | 9 | -2 | 45 | 48 |
| Mexico | 83 | 108 | 5 | 27 | 45 | 59 |
| Turkey | 96 | 104 | 0 | 20 | 45 | 54 |
| Iran | 123 | 103 | -13 | 17 | 45 | 47 |
| South Africa | 137 | 94 | -15 | 28 | 45 | 51 |
| France | 187 | 122 | -55 | 9 | 45 | 24 |
| Italy | 210 | 121 | -65 | -8 | 45 | 12 |
| UK | 232 | 123 | -78 | 14 | 45 | 16 |
| South Korea | 233 | 121 | -77 | 0 | 45 | 10 |
| Russia | 253 | 112 | -82 | -8 | 45 | 5 |
| Japan | 249 | 123 | -86 | -16 | 45 | -1 |
| Germany | 280 | 124 | -102 | -3 | 45 | -2 |
| Saudi Arabia | 296 | 114 | -105 | 36 | 45 | 14 |
| Australia | 319 | 127 | -123 | 33 | 45 | 5 |
| Canada | 361 | 125 | -143 | 22 | 45 | -9 |
| US | 391 | 125 | -158 | 20 | 45 | -17 |
| Total | | | | | 900 | 576 |

Reading: The 1990–2012 average of per capita consumption emissions can be compared with the average level of the human development index for this period, relying on the idea of the carbon budget as a development budget. Two global average deviations are calculated for each of the twenty largest emitters: the emissions gap and the human development gap, the average of which determines the national carbon budget (either positive or negative) to be used until 2050 (countries with a negative carbon budget may have to pay by investing in carbon sinks or by transferring technology and/or financing to accelerate emission reductions in carbon positive carbon budget countries). Countries receive the same carbon endowment up to 2050 regardless of population size, this equal endowment corresponding to an equal sovereign right to develop. But this initial equal endowment is adjusted by the projected increase of population until 2050 for each country (notice that population size has already been taken into account with per capita emissions in column 1). India for instance has emitted 27% of the world average from 1990 to 2012 and reached 75% of the world average level of human development over the same period. Its population will increase by 24% until 2050, it is therefore allocated 78 billion tonnes of $CO_2$ to be emitted by 2050. In contrast, the United States owes 17 billion tonnes of $CO_2$ to the rest of the world. Applying these criteria (and justice principles) makes it possible to determine the carbon budget of each state, and leads to a reduction of 36% global emissions, from 900 billion metric tons to 576 billion metric tons.

*Source:* Human Development Report, Global Carbon Project, and author's calculations, UN Population Division

Within nations, there is also a link between wealth and emissions. In the UK for instance, it can be shown that the distribution of mean household $CO_2$ emissions from all sources, in metric tons, varies according to net disposable household income decile, with a clear upward trend in emissions across the income deciles from all sources (with the exception of public transport). Households within the highest disposable income decile have mean total $CO_2$ emissions more than three times that of households within the lowest income decile (emissions from private road travel and international aviation account for a high proportion of this differential: International aviation emissions of the highest income decile are more than ten times that of the lowest income decile, while emissions from private vehicle travel are around seven to eight times as high).

An Oxfam report, combining the two sets of data (international and intra-national), has shown that the poorest half of the global population – around 3.5 billion people – are responsible for only around ten percent of total global emissions attributed to individual consumption. Around 50% of these emissions can be attributed to the richest ten percent of people around the world, who have average carbon footprints eleven times as high as the poorest half of the population, and sixty times as high as the poorest ten percent. The average footprint of the richest one percent of people globally could be 175 times that of the poorest ten percent. This climate injustice must take center stage in international negotiations if decisive progress is to be made in halting catastrophic climate change.

The second issue of climate justice concerns adaptation to climate change, that is to say, the differentiated exposure and sensitivity to extreme weather events and rising global temperatures of individuals and groups. Here too it is important to select relevant indicators of climate vulnerability in order to allocate fairly the available funding (which should increase to $100 billion per year by 2020). But it will be very difficult to mobilize the necessary sums without shifting the climate negotiations from the current quantitative logic to a price logic. In Copenhagen (COP 15) and Cancún (COP 16), the developed countries committed to a contribution of US$100 billion per year beginning in 2020, to help developing nations fight – and adapt to – climate change. A fund – the "Green Climate Fund" – has been created for this purpose, to provide developing countries with the substantial financial and technological assistance they require. Developing countries take this commitment very seriously. They have made it known that no agreement will be possible in Paris without the conclusion of a clear plan for the delivery, through the Green Climate Fund, of the committed US$100 billion per year by 2020. Unfortunately, despite years of ongoing discussion over this agreed-on $100 billion target, nobody knows how much each developed country is supposed to contribute, and the Paris Agreement has done little to clarify this question.

And yet, the risks populations will have to face are unequally distributed and are generally more significant for underprivileged communities and people at all levels of development: "people who are socially, economically, culturally, politically, institutionally, or otherwise marginalized are especially vulnerable to climate change and also to some adaptation and mitigation responses" (IPCC, 2014). And there is no doubt that such inequalities will increase, along with the amplitude of future global warming. One can cite food security and risks linked to heat stress, extreme precipitation, floods, landslides, droughts, water scarcity, sea-level rise, and violent conflicts. These risks could affect people, ecosystems, goods, and economies both in urban and rural areas and they are amplified for those without vital services and infrastructures or those who live in poor-quality housing or in exposed areas (IPCC, 2014). Indeed, once impacts of climate change are aggregated, the most important consequence could be this increase of inequalities between poor and marginalized populations and those populations who can relatively easily adapt.

Adger et al. (2009) usefully recall that there are two basic coping strategies in the face of climate change. The first is private in nature and does not involve social co-ordination between individuals: Individuals and businesses can decide on adaptation measures depending on the resources available to each other (rich families will be more protected than poor families, the employees of one company more than those of another). On the other hand, individuals and organizations can engage in a collective process of adaptation, possibly resulting in the redistribution of adaptation resources according to criteria of effectiveness or justice. Following the devastation of hurricane Katrina in New Orleans, Mutter (2010, 2015) pointed out the propensity of natural disasters to hurt the poorest and most vulnerable.

Using emissions and vulnerability metrics, Althor et al. (2016) have profiled "climate free riders" as countries with emissions in the highest quintile and vulnerability in the lowest quintile, and "climate forced riders" as countries with emissions in the lowest quintile and vulnerability in the highest quintile. This typology provides a rationale as to why some countries may not act as much as they should regarding climate mitigation, imposing the cost of inaction on others.

Putting climate justice front and center in climate negotiations is not an easy task but it should be done for the sake of both fairness and efficiency: Cooperation is simply impossible without reciprocity.

# 9

# Well-being and our environment: From trade-offs to synergies

Contrary to what a number of conventional economists and some uninformed policy-makers still think, preserving the biosphere is not incompatible with human well-being: it is its pre-requisite. The "double-dividend" or "co-benefit" logic allows us to understand this reality: Mitigation of ecological crises can provide massive health gains (or prevent considerable losses), energy transition can lead to substantial job creation and new indicators of well-being, resilience, and sustainability can change policy for the better, advancing human well-being within the limits of the biosphere. Economic systems, in short, need to move from a logic of trade-offs to a logic of synergies between our environment and our well-being.

## Well-being and sustainability: From a vicious to a virtuous cycle

Nothing expresses better the current relationship between well-being and sustainability than the idea of a vicious circle whereby humans destroy the very foundation of their own well-being (see Figure 9.1). If a sustainable system is a system whose features tend to self-perpetuation, an unsustainable one has features leading to self-destruction.

Yet there is nothing inevitable about this self-defeating logic of human action: Global environmental stewardship leading to climate change mitigation and adaptation as well as biodiversity and ecosystems preservation can foster the vitality of both the biosphere and human well-being (Figure 9.2) provided we profoundly change our approach to the economy, focusing on social cooperation and human well-being.

This was obvious for the drafters of the Declaration of the United Nations Conference on the Human Environment (Stockholm, June 15–16, 1972), which proclaims that:

(1) Man is both creature and molder of his environment, which gives him physical sustenance and affords him the opportunity for intellectual,

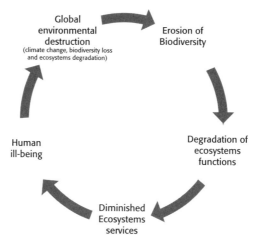

Figure 9.1   Human well-being and the biosphere: The self-destructive vicious circle

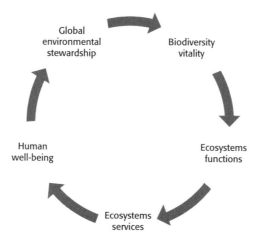

Figure 9.2   Human well-being and the biosphere: The virtuous circle of sustainability

moral, social, and spiritual growth. In the long and tortuous evolution of the human race on this planet a stage has been reached when, through the rapid acceleration of science and technology, man has acquired the power to transform his environment in countless ways and on an unprecedented scale. Both aspects of man's environment, the natural and the man-made, are essential to his well-being and to the enjoyment of basic human rights, the right to life itself.

(2) The protection and improvement of the human environment is a major issue which affects the well-being of peoples and economic development throughout the world; it is the urgent desire of the peoples of the whole world and the duty of all Governments.

# The health-environment double dividend

*The Lancet* has embarked on a mission to accelerate the convergence of environmental and health studies by launching or re-launching the work of three of its Commissions: the Commission on Health and Climate Change, the Commission on Pollution and Health and the Global Health Commission. Each of these commissions, which includes dozens of researchers from around the world, has recently produced a reference report. Their message can be summarized in the following way: Contemporary ecological crises have the power over the next fifty years to nullify the considerable progress of human health in the last fifty years.

The World Health Organization (WHO) recognized as early as 1994 the concept of "environmental health": At the Second European Conference on Environment and Health held in June 1994 in Helsinki, a "Charter on Environment and Health" was adopted. Its first article reads: "Good health and well-being require a clean and harmonious environment in which physical, psychological, social, and aesthetic factors are all given their due importance. The environment should be regarded as a resource for improving living conditions and increasing wellbeing." Following up, in 1999, the WHO deemed the improvement of environmental conditions "the key to better health."

WHO has accompanied this conceptual recognition by methodological innovation, designing and popularizing an empirical method aimed at isolating the actual environmental burden of disease burden (WHO estimates morbidity today at 24% of the global burden and deaths due to environmental factors at 23%). According to the latest estimates released in March 2016, 12.6 million people died in 2012 from living or working in an unhealthy environment, nearly one in four of total global deaths (children and the elderly being the most exposed to environmental risks).

The diseases with the largest environmental fraction include cardiovascular diseases, diarrheal diseases, and lower respiratory infections. Ambient and household air pollution, and water, sanitation, and hygiene are the main environmental drivers of those diseases (Table 9.1).

## Table 9.1 Environmental contribution to some diseases

|  | % |
| --- | --- |
| Stroke | 42 |
| Ischaemic heart disease | 35 |
| Diarrheal diseases | 57 |
| Lower respiratory infections | 35 |
| Cancers | 20 |
| Malaria | 42 |
| Asthma | 44 |

*Source*: WHO

There is, again, a strong inequality among certain categories of the population and geographical areas with respect to environmental deaths: The burden attributable to the environment is almost three times as high in South East Asia as it is in OECD American and European countries (see Table 9.2).

| Table 9.2 Environmental deaths in different regions of the world (in millions) | | | | | | |
|---|---|---|---|---|---|---|
| | World | World Children 0–4 years | South East Asia | Sub-Saharan Africa | Europe OECD | America OECD |
| Population | 7,044 | 651 | 1,833 | 903 | 479 | 369 |
| Total deaths | 55 | 6.5 | 13.76 | 9.4 | 4.4 | 3 |
| Total environmental deaths | 12.6 | 1.7 | 3.8 | 2.1 | 0.538 | 0.320 |
| Burden attributable to the environment | 22.7% | 26% | 28% | 23% | 12% | 11% |

*Source:* WHO

The case of climate change clearly illustrates the importance of environmental conditions for human health. The Multidisciplinary Commission set up by *The Lancet*, whose updated work was published in June 2015, details direct effects (heat waves, floods, drought, hurricanes, and storms, all causing morbidity and mortality) and indirect effects on health (pollution airborne diseases, dengue-type vector-borne diseases, food insecurity and malnutrition, population displacement, and mental illness, all resulting from extreme weather events and global warming). Recent research provides striking illustrations of this impact. Globally, between 2030 and 2050, climate change is expected to cause an estimated 250,000 additional deaths per year due to malnutrition, malaria, diarrhea, and heat stress. The overall risk of heat-related illness or death for instance has climbed steadily since 1980, with around 30% of the world's population now living in climatic conditions that deliver potentially deadly temperatures at least twenty days a year. Between 2000 and 2016, the number of vulnerable people exposed to heat-wave events has increased by approximately 125 million.[1]

Heat-wave frequency and intensity in developed countries is one facet of this global issue. In August 2003, Europe recorded one of its most severe heat waves. It is now estimated that 70,000 people died from it. The case of France is particularly interesting because its health system, considered one of the best in the world, should logically have mitigated the human impact of this disaster. But the duration, intensity, and geographic scope of this heat wave caused an excess mortality of 14,800 people in France (2,000 people died in a single day – August 12).[2] Health studies on excess mortality in France in the first half of August (under the effect of temperatures exceeding 35°C for more than ten consecutive days), indicate that 80% of the victims were aged over 75 years (90% of the victims were over 65).

The analysis of the disaster in terms of socio-economic inequalities is even more revealing: the Institute for Public Health Surveillance (INVS) statistically established the variables explaining the deaths. They were, in order of importance, the socio-professional category and the degree of autonomy of the elderly. Hence, from the proven importance of environmental factors for the health of citizens naturally arises the ethical and political question concerning the socially differentiated exposure and vulnerability of individuals and groups.

Health inequities are defined by the WHO as "avoidable inequalities in health between groups of people within countries and between countries." They arise from inequalities within and between societies. In other words, social and economic conditions and their effects on people's lives determine their risk of illness and the actions taken to prevent them from becoming ill, or to treat illness when it occurs. Among these "social determinants of health" (the circumstances in which people are born, grow up, live, work, and age, and the systems put in place to deal with illness that are shaped by economics, social, and political factors), environmental conditions play an important and growing role.

Because environmental risk factors, such as air, water, and soil pollution, chemical exposures, climate change, and ultraviolet radiation, contribute to more than one hundred diseases and injuries, the notion of a health-environment double dividend or "co-benefits" appears intuitive: Improving the environment (or contributing to halting its degradation) is a lever to improve health.[3] By focusing on reducing environmental and social risk factors, nearly a quarter of the global burden of disease could be prevented. To quote authors from the aforementioned *Lancet* Commission: "tackling climate change could be the greatest global health opportunity of the twenty-first century." What is more, the health–pollution–climate nexus, which revolved around the notion of "co-benefit," is the lever of action of the national and local public authorities against climate change (it is the improvement of the health at the local level via the fight against atmospheric pollution that holds the key to global mitigation of climate change).

For instance, the Air Quality Life Index measures the potential gain in life expectancy that communities could see if they reduced air pollution to comply with the World Health Organization guideline or national standards. Studies based on this index find that sustained exposure to an additional 10 µg/m3 of PM2.5 reduces life expectancy by 0.98 years. This means that a country like China, whose air is heavily polluted, can act against climate change on the basis of the improvement of the local living conditions of its urban residents.

Accounting for ecological issues into health-care systems therefore means revealing the visible and hidden social costs of environmental crises, such as climate change, in order to mutualize and ultimately reduce it. This was one of the major arguments put forward by the Obama Administration to justify its 2014 Clean Power Plan. (An in-depth analysis by the EPA found that the combined climate and health benefits of the Clean Power Plan will far outweigh the costs of implementing it. and that it will deliver billions of dollars in net benefits each year, estimated at $26 billion to $45 billion in 2030.)[4]

Many reports highlight the beneficial effect of environmental regulations on health and, more generally, physical and mental well-being. 2017 marked the thirtieth anniversary of the Montreal Protocol, which protects the ozone layer and allows for its gradual regeneration.[5] This is the biggest success story in global environmental governance, with almost all ozone-depleting substances now phased out. But it is also, and above all, a health victory: The Montreal Protocol has allowed, allows, and will notably prevent hundreds of millions of cases of skin cancer around the world.

## Energy transition and job creation

Since production and consumption systems must be shifted toward a low-carbon economy to avoid a climate catastrophe (see Chapter 8), there is a great opportunity to turn this constraint into a lever for employment. IRENA for instance estimates that "The total share of renewable energy must rise from around 18% of total final energy consumption (in 2015) to around two-thirds by 2050. Over the same period, the share of renewables in the power sector would increase from around one-quarter to 85%, mostly through growth in solar and wind-power generation. The energy intensity of the global economy will have to fall by about two-thirds, lowering energy demand in 2050 to slightly less than 2015 levels."

But it is first necessary to pull out the energy transition from the trap of cost-benefit analysis advocated by conventional economics. Many economic models commonly used by public and private decision-makers lead to the discrediting of the energy transition on the grounds that the ecological constraint would be an obstacle to economic dynamism. The example of Sweden shows, on the contrary, how to turn the ecological challenge into a force for innovation: The higher the level of environmental constraint, the more the innovation is stimulated. Because it is necessary to find new ideas to save energy or promote energy efficiency, and new forms of organization to bring new technologies to life, environmental constraint can be economically fruitful.

More fundamentally, it is the entire economics of energy transition that must be reconsidered in the light of a truly updated analysis by current scientific knowledge. Conventional cost-benefit analysis indicates that the energy transition may be necessary in the medium term, but could be very costly or even ruinous at least in the short term. This appreciation calls for several refutations.

First of all, if they are so "un-competitive," why is there so much investment in renewables when the price of carbon is still so low? Various reports have tracked a record of investments in renewables, bringing their total to more than 330 billion dollars in the world in 2015, a factor of six more than the level of 2004. The last decade thus witnessed an explosion of investments in renewable energies. This is all the more remarkable as the sharp and prolonged decline in the price of oil has played against the diversification of the energy portfolios of nations. Renewable energy capacity additions are exceeding fossil fuel generation investments by a widening margin and the record 162GW of new renewable power added in 2016 represented 60% of all new power capacity additions in that twelve-month period.

But, as was mentioned in Chapter 8, the energy transition is slow: After forty years, renewable energy share is still meagre. Is it not precisely because of their excessive cost? But what are the "costs" taken into account in this analysis? What are the benefits? What to count? How to value?

When the benefits and costs of each energy are correctly accounted for (notably by updating their cost over time to take into account, for example, in the case of nuclear power, the cost of dismantling power stations or the long-term impact of burial and storage of waste), the latest available results show that land-based wind is less expensive than coal and gas and that photo-voltaics are cheaper than nuclear energy (offshore wind is currently more expensive than other energy sources).[6]

The cost of electricity production, for example in France, if it is to be sincere, must include the cost investment in a means of production, the cost of operation (fuels, maintenance), the cost of dismantling nuclear installations, the cost of damage to the environment and health generated by the production of electricity and finally the cost (or profit) generated by the insertion of the production unit into the electrical system. Once these elements are taken into account, the low carbon transition is a very good deal. Even more importantly, it has the power to generate hundreds of thousands of jobs (Box 9.1).

## Box 9.1 Energy transition in France: The négaWatt scenarios

For fifteen years, the négaWatt Association has published renowned energy transition scenarios for France. They are meant to envision a different energy future in which environmental risks (climate change, biodiversity loss …), technological risks (e.g. nuclear accidents), and dependency on foreign resources is history. They are based on three main pillars:

Sufficiency: Reducing the overall need for energy-using services, through better sizing, using, and sharing equipment, and better organizing of land and society.

Efficiency: Avoiding as much energy losses as possible all along the chain in the way energy services are provided, through improved equipment, buildings, and vehicles.

Renewables: Prioritizing green energies for supplying the remaining energy demand.

The 2017–2050 négaWatt scenario modelling output shows a halving of the final energy consumption by 2050, driven by sufficiency (60%) and efficiency (40%). The contribution of renewable sources to the energy supply is multiplied by 3.4, and allows 99.7% of the primary energy demand to be covered by 2050. Half of the supply comes from primary electricity sources, and 40% from biomass. This notably means that the country becomes fully independent for its energy supply, and the production is more homogeneously spread over the country land. This allows the country's nuclear reactors to be progressively shut down, with no life extension over forty years. The last one terminates in 2035.

Combined with the Afterres2050 scenario developed by Solagro on agriculture, food and land use, the négaWatt scenario reaches a level where remaining greenhouse gas emissions (mostly from agriculture) are fully offset by national carbon sinks. Then the amount of carbon in soils flattens, and carbon sink potentials finally diminish over 2050 to 2100, leaving open the issue of further action.

A detailed economic analysis based on the scenario outputs concludes that its implementation would require around €1.160 billion investments in the energy sector until 2050, compared to 650 in the business-as-usual trend. But it would halve the national energy bill over the 2017–2050 period, with a net profit of €1.130 billion. When including all sectors covered by the energy transition (buildings, transport, and so on), total expenses in the négaWatt scenario are, until 2030, quite similar to those in the business-as-usual scenario (first investments are offset by sufficiency and efficiency savings).

Then négaWatt starts to become more economical as early investments deliver their full effect. The cumulative savings until 2050 reach €370 billion (with a flat energy price assumption). The outcome is favourable for the economy. The overall benefit would only cease to exist if imported fossil fuels were to become twice cheaper than today in the future. The impact on jobs is clearly positive: A net outcome of 100,000 full-time equivalents in 2020, rising to about 400,000 by 2030 and 500,000 by 2050, mainly due to the stimulation of more job-intensive sectors.

*Source:* 2017–2050 négaWatt scenario, https://negawatt.org/IMG/pdf/negawatt-scenario-2017-2050_english-summary.pdf

It is also necessary to broaden the perspective further to accommodate other dimensions of well-being: There is a fundamental link between climate change and health, and therefore between energy transition and health. Thanks to the transition to renewable sources, local pollution (like fine particles), as well as global pollution (like greenhouse gas emissions), inherent to the combustion of fossil fuels can be reduced. When these benefits are taken into account (as they should be), the transition to renewable energies leads to saving fifteen times the cost of their deployment (according to IRENA).

Moreover, a global study linking health, employment, safety, and sustainability has been undertaken. Mark Jacobson (Stanford University), one of the world's leading experts on both air pollution and renewable energy economics, has developed a roadmap for the transition to one hundred percent of renewable energies by 2050 for 139 countries in the world and fifty US states. This study shows that this transition would lead to the elimination of four to seven million premature deaths related to air pollution and the main sources of climate change, while creating twenty million jobs and stabilizing energy prices.[7]

## Measuring well-being, resilience, and sustainability to change policy for the better

In the Paris Agreement (see Chapter 8), the first universal treaty on climate change agreed upon after the COP 21 in December 2015 and ratified to date by 175 countries, there are only two numbers and none has to do with national income or economic growth.[8] Both can be found in Article 2 of the text that spells out the fundamental consensus among parties: "Holding the increase in the global average temperature to well below 2°C above pre-industrial levels and pursuing efforts to limit the temperature increase to 1.5°C above pre-industrial levels." These numbers are not just scientific data but policy indicators, the new compasses to the twenty-first century: They represent a physical limit of the biosphere and they are *de facto* conditioning economic policy for countries that have collectively and individually agreed to the text, including their growth strategy. The underlying new reality put forward in Article 2 of the Paris Agreement is that in a world warmer by three degrees, a Gross Domestic Product (GDP) larger by three percent is of little importance, if any.

Yet, two key features are missing from the Paris Agreement. The first one is a robust institutional framework linking targets/objectives to adequate policy instruments so that new visions of the world can translate into effective change. The second missing feature is a compelling narrative explaining why countries should now pursue a 1.5 to two degrees world so as to engage citizens and ensure the viability of what was agreed upon by states.

As such, the Paris Agreement is a testimony of what has been achieved and what remains to be done in the course of what can be called the *well-being transition*: A refocusing of global, national, and local policy on human well-being under a severe and increasing ecological constraint.

Why is a well-being transition needed? Because the twenty-first century challenges cannot be understood, let alone addressed with twentieth-century policy indicators such as growth of Gross Domestic Product (GDP) conceived in the mid 1930s. To put it differently, while policy-makers govern with numbers and data, they are as well governed by them. These data thus should be relevant and accurate. Such is no longer the case for GDP. Consider the crisis of inequality and the crisis of the biosphere on which this book is focused. Neither can be analyzed nor mitigated with growth (of GDP) simply because GDP was not designed to assess either. As a result, focusing on growth leads to analytical and policy mistakes: Policy-makers neglect equality and distributional issues, confusing growth with social progress, and degrading ecosystems for short-term economic gains, harming human well-being, while hoping to improve it. Policy ends up divorcing from citizens' aspirations and scientific knowledge. But there is nothing inevitable about this: We can change what we measure to reform what we manage and put human well-being back at the center of policy at all levels of governance. We can measure what really counts to protect what truly matters.

What is human well-being?[9] It stems from an eternal question: What are the real drivers of human development and success beside material conditions? Exploring human well-being means articulating a multidimensional vision of human welfare casually referred to as "quality of life." Human well-being can be assessed at different geographic scales: Objectively (via measures of health status or educational attainments), or subjectively (through the assessment of happiness or trust), but it is in all cases a static metric that tells us nothing about its evolution over time.

For a dynamic approach that sheds light not only on the current state of well-being but also on its future, one has to turn to the concepts of resilience and sustainability. The questions asked by citizens and policy-makers then become substantially more complex: "Can we project our well-being over time?" Resilience is a first step in this direction, as it tries to determine if well-being can resist and survive shocks. More precisely, it assesses the ability of a community, a territory, a nation, or the whole planet to cope with economic, social, or environmental shocks and their capacity to return afterward to their pre-shock level of well-being without seeing it degraded or destroyed. One typical, pressing, resilience issue is how human communities around the world can adapt to climate change.

The measurement of sustainability is even more ambitious, in that it seeks to evaluate well-being in the long run, both after the occurrence of shocks and during normal times. Attempting to assess sustainability is about trying to understand how these stocks can be maintained or even increased over time, such as how services freely provided by ecosystems can continue benefiting future generations. (Consider, for example, pollination, on which 75% of the world's crops at least partially depend.) From this perspective, resilience can be understood as the short-run horizon of sustainability: Resilience is concerned with shocks and sustainability with stocks.

The meaning of the well-being transition is thus the following: Instead of growth, policy-makers should be concerned with the advancement of well-being (human flourishing), resilience (resisting shocks), and sustainability (caring about future well-being by preserving the biosphere). In our time, regardless of its current or future level and the enthusiasm that greets it, economic growth is indeed outdated as a collective horizon and it is a broken compass for policy.

Conceived in the mid 1930s by Harvard development economist Simon Kuznets to take stock of the Great Depression, and improved by a team of British economists around John Maynard Keynes in the midst of the war effort, GDP was crowned king of all economic data at the Bretton Woods conference in July 1944, when Western nations embraced it as their common currency of power and success. From then on, to be "developed" meant to have developed its GDP. It took three decades for the "beyond GDP" to emerge. In a series of papers published between 1972 and 1973, economists William Nordhaus and James Tobin suggested that "growth" (understood narrowly as the increase of GDP) had become "obsolete" and attempted for the first time to offer not just an ethical or theoretical alternative to growth, but an empirical one (Nordhaus and Tobin, 1973).

This research and policy-making agenda has greatly expanded since then (see Gadrey and Jany-Catrice, 2006), and gained momentum in the last decade, starting with the organization of the "Beyond GDP" conference under the auspices of the European Union in December 2007, aimed at taking stock of existing alternative indicators to GDP.[10] Today, dozens of well-being indicators (i.e. well-being, resilience, and sustainability indicators) are being produced and updated each year.[11] But what exactly do they measure? How to map this burgeoning field? A possible analytical and visualization framework is offered at Figure 9.3 (the table attached to Figure 9.3 gives for each dimension of well-being an example of existing indicator).[12]

This representation is organized to mirror a gradual understanding of the complexity of human well-being, from core economic well-being to the frontiers of sustainability analysis. This figure reflects the belief that we need to move "beyond GDP," not so much by building a single alternative composite indicator (replacing GDP with a counter-GDP), but by relying on policy area-specific indicators that form the building blocks of well-being and sustainability. In other words, we should not so much be looking for what Costanza et al. (2014) have called "the successor of GDP" than for its alternatives. This pluralistic approach appears to be the best way to desacralize GDP, not just in terms of substance but also form.

In this overall picture, GDP appears small. Indeed, it captures only a tiny fraction of what goes on and matters in our complex societies: It tracks some but not all of economic well-being (saying nothing about fundamental issues such as income inequality); it does not account for most dimensions of well-being[13] (think about the importance of health, education, or happiness for quality of life); and it says exactly nothing about "sustainability," which basically means well-being not just today but also tomorrow (imagine the quality of human life on a planet where the temperature would be four degrees higher or where there would be scant drinkable water or breathable air).

Figure 9.3 has two essential meanings. First, well-being dimensions are cumulative: We can choose to look at (and take care of) only economic

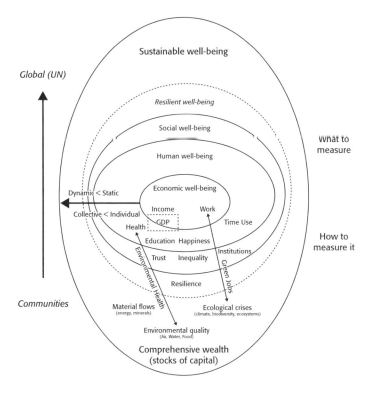

Figure 9.3   Three horizons for humanity: Well-being, resilience, and sustainability

well-being or capture human well-being and social well-being as well (in this latter case, it means embracing not just an individual approach to well-being but a collective one also, for instance by measuring the quality of our institutions such as the judiciary system or the Parliament). Then we can choose to enlarge further our concern and add a time component to our analysis by trying to measure if our interactions with the biosphere can be sustained tomorrow and the day after without damaging our well-being. By doing so, we move from a static approach of well-being to a dynamic one. But why should one care about the quality of education, the reduction of inequality or the depletion of trust if indicators related to ecological crises reveal that a near collapse of the biosphere is on the horizon?

This is where the second meaning of this framework comes in. It represents an attempt at linking together well-being, resilience, and sustainability to understand their synergies (the connection between well-being and sustainability is made explicitly with "environmental health" and "green jobs").

Well-being without sustainability (and resilience understood as short-term sustainability) is just an illusion. The climate crisis has the potential to destroy the unprecedented contemporary progress in human health in a mere few decades. If China's ecosystems collapse under the weight of hyper-growth with no unpolluted water left to drink and no clean air to breathe,

| Well-being Dimensions | Existing Indicator | Statistical Source |
| --- | --- | --- |
| Income | Household income | For the US: BLS<br>For the EU: Eurostat<br>For the OECD: OECD<br>For the ROW: national sources |
| Work | Employment rate | For the US: BLS<br>For the EU: Eurostat<br>For the OECD: OECD<br>For the ROW: national sources |
| Health | Life expectancy | WHO |
| Education | Skills and knowledge of 15-year-old students | Program for International Student Assessment (PISA), OECD |
| Happiness | Life satisfaction | World Happiness Report 2018 |
| Time use | Time use survey (amount of time people spend doing various activities) | For the US: BLS<br>For France: INSEE<br>For the ROW: national sources |
| Trust | Trust in people and institutions | World Values Survey |
| Inequality (income and wealth) | Percentiles share of national income and wealth | World Inequality Database |
| Institutions | Quality of governance | Governance Matters Database, World Bank |
| Resilience | Resilience index | Hallegatte, Stephane; Vogt-Schilb, Adrien; Bangalore, Mook; Rozenberg, Julie. 2017. Unbreakable: Building the Resilience of the Poor in the Face of Natural Disasters. Climate Change and Development, Washington, DC: World Bank |
| Material flows | Material footprint | Thomas O. Wiedmann, Heinz Schandl, Manfred Lenzen, Daniel Moran, Sangwon Suh, James West, Keiichiro Kanemoto, "The material footprint of nations," Proceedings of the National Academy of Sciences May 2015, 112 (20) 6271-6276 |
| Ecological crises (climate, biodiversity, ecosystems) | Climate change, biodiversity, and ecosystems data | IPCC and IPBES reports and assessments |
| Environmental quality | Environmental health and ecosystem vitality | 2018 Environmental Performance Index (EPI) |

the hundreds of millions of people who have escaped poverty since the 1980s in the country will be thrown back into it. In Figure 9.3, if the outer circles collapse then the inner ones will follow suit, while the opposite is not true.

But sustainability without well-being is just an ideal. Human behaviors and attitudes will not become more sustainable to "save the planet" but to preserve human well-being. What is more, as argued convincingly by the late

Elinor Ostrom (Ostrom, 2010), social cooperation is the key to sustainable practices and social cooperation depends critically on education, equality, trust, and good institutions (which are to be found in Figure 9.3 inner circles). Comprehensive wealth, the ultimate metric representing sustainable well-being, means both that well-being is approached in a multidimensional way and tracked through time in a dynamic manner.

Mapping well-being indicators is a first necessary step that leads to two questions: Do these metrics help us see the world differently? (What is their analytical value added?). Can they help us change it? (What is their perform-ative power?)

To attempt to answer the first question, let us consider health. Simple metrics such as life expectancy or mortality rates tell a whole different story about what has happened in a given country in the last thirty years than economic growth. Consider the United States. The recent discovery by economists Angus Deaton and Anne Case of very high mortality rates among middle-aged Whites in the US (Case and Deaton, 2015), all the while GDP was growing, is proof that health status must be studied and measured regardless of a nation's perceived wealth status.

Indeed, the standing of the US with respect to economic prosperity can be questioned more deeply using well-being indicators, for instance inequality and trust in institutions. Recent data show that income inequality is higher today than it was during the Gilded Age, relentlessly fracturing the American society and blocking social mobility, and that the level of trust in Congress has been divided by three and a half since the mid 1970s, with political polari-zation at an all-time high, while all the while Growth Domestic Product per capita roughly doubled.[14]

Well-being paints a much more extensive, accurate, and up-to-date picture of economic development in the US using a plurality of indicators to answer key questions: Is income fairly shared? Are workers healthy? Are institutions underpinning markets robust? Are ecosystems sustaining human well-being vigorous?

On all these counts for the last three decades, strong growth in the US has obscured the reality of weak well-being. Income inequality is at an all-time high and second to none among the world's comparable countries. Life expectancy is declining, while scores of Americans have been dying of "social despair." Trust in Congress and confidence in democracy is dismal, with political polari-zation stronger than ever. Ecosystems are weakened and increasingly suffering from the loss of biodiversity and the impact of climate change. This is nothing to dream about.

The fixation of the US public debate on growth data is not only misleading but perilous. Because it captures and reflects so little of what happens and matters in our complex societies, growth is now fake news: It is not progress, it is the illusion of progress. And the US has become the poster child of this deception.

Another example is China, which has experienced between 1978 and now the highest economic growth of all times, and is a strong testimony against the mirages of economic growth (Box 9.2).

## Box 9.2 Three lessons from the Chinese growth experiment

Almost forty years ago, on December 29, 1978, the 11th Central Committee of the Communist Party of China released the official communiqué from its third plenary session. In newspeak understandable to CPC insiders, the country's leaders, loyal to Deng XiaoPing, channelling the wishes of Deng Xiaoping, announced through the voice of comrade Hua Kuo-feng a series of unprecedented "modernizations" that would transform one of the world's least developed countries into a leading economic power. The greatest experiment of economic growth in the history of humankind has just begun.

In four decades, China, one of the least developed countries on the planet, would become the world's leading economic power (knocking the US out this position in 2014; see graph).

**GDP in purchasing power parity, China and the United States, in billions of international dollars**

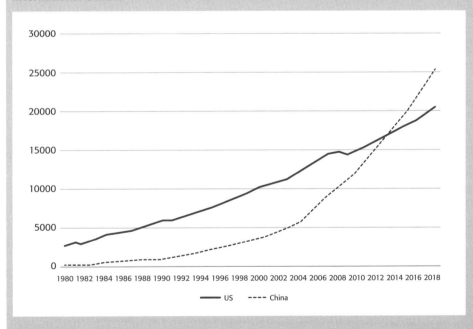

*Source:* IMF

Its gross domestic product per capita would be multiplied by 58 (in 2018 it is only 3.4 times lower than that of the United States, whereas it was forty times lower in 1980; see graph).

**GDP per capita in purchasing power parity, China and the United States, in international dollars**

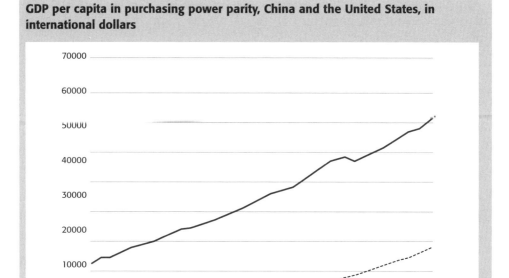

*Source:* IMF

To sum up: 15% of humanity propelled at ten percent annual growth on average for forty years. All the theoretical models and empirical controversies in the world will never have the force of demonstration of the Chinese experience. What does it teach us? To put it simply, China is the most striking and illuminating illustration of the fundamental limits of economic growth.

More precisely, the vertiginous trajectory of Chinese development makes it possible to dispel three economic mythologies attached to growth.

(1) Economic growth reduces inequality and increases happiness.
In 1955, Harvard economist Simon Kuznets put forth the hypothesis of an initial increase and then a gradual reduction of income inequality as countries progress in economic development: The higher the standard of living, the more, at first, inequality increases before being reduced in a second time, describing a reassuring and familiar "Bell curve."

The Chinese experience, like so many others, disproves Kuznets' reasoned optimism. China is today one of the most unequal countries in the world, with a Gini index estimated at around 0.5 (it was around 0.3 in 1980), and stagnating around this value for the last ten years (by a troubling historical coincidence, the United States and China have about the same Gini index today). Even more problematic, the relationship between growth and inequality over time has followed a peculiar pattern: China's Gini coefficient has increased with growth, and decreased when growth has slowed.

The evolution of the distribution of national income between social categories allows us to specify these stylized facts. According to the World Inequality Database, while the share of national income of the richest ten percent increased between 1978 and 2015 from 27 to 41% (the share of the top one percent doubling over the period), the share of the national income of the poorest 50% of the Chinese fell from 26 to 14%. These data are consistent with other sources that show, for example, that while GDP per capita was multiplied by fourteen between 1990 and 2010, the top three quintiles of distribution saw their share of national income fall, and the fourth quintile saw its own stagnate in favor of a sharp increase in the income of the richest 20% of Chinese.

But these are of course relative inequalities and no one can ignore the undeniable role that China has played in the considerable reduction of monetary poverty in the world for a quarter of a century. The temporal dynamics of this reduction, however, do not fit well with economic growth: The number of poor has been reduced from 750 to 400 million from 1992 to 2002, with a declining growth rate (from 14% to 9%), then, while oscillated from nine to ten percent from 2002 to 2010, the number of poor decreased by 250 million. Finally, from 2010 to 2015, poverty was reduced by an additional 150 million people, with a growth rate dropping from ten to seven percent.

But, at least it is certain that the Chinese, escaping their equality in misery and more unequally rich than in 1978 (the income of the poorest 10% has increased by 65% between 1980 and 2015) are happier today? The opposite seems to be true. The recent work of William Easterlin (see chapter in Helliwell at al., 2017) is very convincing on this point: While GDP has been over-multiplied for twenty-five years, the subjective well-being of the Chinese has declined, this being especially true among the poorest and oldest social classes. Even more surprisingly: Subjective well-being has picked up over the past decade (but has not returned to its 1990 level), while economic growth is clearly lagging behind in the period from 1990 to 2005. Happiness declines when growth is strong and regains strength when it weakens.

(2) Economic growth fueled by economic liberalism breeds political liberalism.
1989 is a major year in the formation of our geopolitical reality. In November, the Berlin Wall collapsed, leading to the inexorable collapse of the USSR. But a few months earlier, in June, the other great communist power of the planet crushed the student revolt of Tian'anmen Square in Beijing (10,000 deaths). The political inertia of the country over the last forty years, astonishing given the economic upheavals at work, is perfectly illustrated by the data of the Polity IV project: a flat authoritarian encephalogram.

Yet this image is misleading: The Chinese state has managed to become much more efficient, while remaining arbitrary and unfair. "Socialism with Chinese characteristics" is precisely characterized by a strong state in both senses of the term, technically effective but put at the service, on the one hand, of economic expansion and, on the other hand, of political regression measured by the muzzling of civil liberties and stifling of political rights. This is clearly shown by the data of the World Bank's Worldwide Governance Indicators project (table). While it was thought that China would be the last state to crown the inevitable advent of liberal capitalism after the Cold War, it was in fact the first country to open the authoritarian neoliberal we are currently witnessing, from Turkey to Brazil, from Hungary to India.

| Three indicators of Chinese governance, 1996–2017 | | | |
|---|---|---|---|
| | | Score | Relative ranking (in percentiles of the countries of the world) |
| Voice and accountability | 1996 | -1.36 | 12 |
| | 2007 | -1.72 | 4.81 |
| | 2017 | -1.50 | 7.88 |
| Government effectiveness | 1996 | -0.35 | 43.17 |
| | 2007 | 0.18 | 59.22 |
| | 2017 | 0.42 | 68.27 |
| Regulatory quality | 1996 | -0.27 | 45.11 |
| | 2007 | -0.17 | 50.97 |
| | 2017 | -0.15 | 48.56 |

Source: Worldwide Governance Indicators (WGI), World Bank

(3) Economic growth is the solution to ecological crises.
The Chinese development, denounced by Prime Minister Wen Jiabao more than a decade ago as "unstable, unbalanced and unsustainable," is based on a kind of physical law: The human mass multiplied by the speed of growth is equal to the ecological impact. But economic growth was supposed to prevent, or at least mitigate, the Chinese environmental disaster. It turned out not to be the case.

First, consider material flows and economic metabolism. Data referred to in Chapter 7 show that China has become the first extractive power of the planet in a global economy that, far from the fantasies of digital dematerialization, has never been more resource-intensive. While China represented 14% of global GDP in 2010, it consumed 17% of biomass, 29% of fossil fuels and 44% of metal ores. Its domestic consumption swallows a third of global natural resources (compared to a quarter for all developed countries).

Then there is climate. China now accounts for 28% of global carbon dioxide emissions (twice as much as the United States, three times more than the European Union, four times more than India). It increased its emissions from 1.5 billion tonnes of $CO_2$ in 1978 to ten billion tonnes in 2016 (and from 1.8 tonnes per capita to 7.2, well above the world average, at 4.2 tonnes per inhabitant).

As is well documented, the pollution of water, ground water, and air is critical (see Yuyu et al., 2013). Incidentally, the Chinese experiment is as much of a problem for the proponents of the "Kuznets Environmental Curve" as for the promoters of the "Capitalocene" concept (see Chapter 11): The most ecologically unsustainable country in economic history is communist, not capitalist. China has this in common with the former USSR: to have demonstrated that authoritarian communism manages to destroy the biosphere as effectively as liberal capitalism.

As colossal as the destruction of Chinese ecosystems by a blind hyper-growth regime has been, it is surprising that the situation, improving since growth has receded (especially with respect to air pollution), has not been more dramatic. This is because the Chinese population deceleration is among the fastest in the developing world. The annual growth rate of the Chinese population in 2015 is half of the global rate and about one-sixth of the average population growth rate of the African continent. Over the last forty years, the Chinese population growth rate has been divided by about three (graph).

**Population growth rate in %, annual average over 5-year intervals**

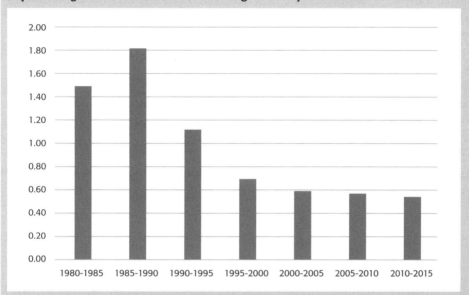

China has therefore somewhat limited the environmental damage of its economic growth only by means of a Malthusian policy that it is now trying to relax, while at the same time it is engaging in a conquest of the world's natural resources (via a number of trade routes and infrastructures network that it is currently assembling and by its bi-lateral relations with many African countries). Chinese ecological imperialism against the backdrop of an aging population is arguably the most important geopolitical phenomenon of the next forty years.

On October 18, 2017, at the opening of the Chinese Communist Party Congress in Beijing, Xi Jinping declared: "What we now face is the contradiction between unbalanced and inadequate development and the people's ever-growing needs for a better life." In a perfectly intelligible language, the Chinese President confirmed to the nation and the world the transition to "ecological civilization" begun by the 13th Five-Year Plan of 2016. The greatest experiment of economic growth in the history of humankind had just ended.

Paying attention to well-being rather than just growth can also help us to understand the importance of social well-being and, more specifically, the human aspiration for civil rights and political liberties. This aspiration explains why the Arab Spring erupted in Tunisia in 2011, a country where

GDP growth was strong and steady but where civil liberties and political rights clearly deteriorated before the revolution. Finally, considering environmental quality helps us assess accurately the true quality of life: In beautiful and opulent cities like Paris, air pollution (especially particulate matters) has reached life-threatening levels, clouding the future of tens of thousands of resident children.

Measuring well-being simply changes the way we see the world. But alternative indicators should also be performative: They should inform and reform policy. Measuring, indeed, is governing, and well-being indicators have already started to deliver progress.

It is now a scientific fact that smoking causes health to deteriorate, and thus affects human well-being. WHO estimates that tobacco use is causing the death of seven million people each year (tobacco kills roughly half of its users). But the WHO also estimates that countries that have implemented tobacco control policies, including taxation, graphic pack warnings, and no smoking areas, have greatly reduced consumption. Only two decades ago, 36% of young Americans were smoking, they are only ten percent now (in the OECD, daily smokers represented around 40% of the population aged 15+; in the early 1980s, this figure has plummeted to around 15% today). If this transition has actually happened, it is thanks to the design and dissemination of metrics that highlighted not only the prevalence of smoking but the causal link between smoking and illnesses, and the collective cost of these illnesses. Then, policy instruments were carefully conceived and resolutely implemented. And, all along, powerful lobbies with considerable economic interests at risk have been fought and eventually overcome. Smoking is still a serious health problem in countries where no political will exist to address it, but in countries that opted for action based on data-driven science, human well-being has been improved. Looking at the past 25 years, GBD (2017) note that: "The scale-up of tobacco control … is a major public health success story." Why would carbon control be so different from tobacco control?

Of course, mitigating climate change is a global sustainable well-being problem. But the challenges of time and space were also standing in the way of control of the substances causing ozone layer depletion, and they have been overcome. The Montreal Protocol on Substances that Deplete the Ozone Layer, signed by only 24 countries and the European Economic Community in September 1987, became the first universal treaty (with 196 parties) in September 2009. It is based on indisputable science (i.e. ground and satellite data demonstrating the ozone layer depletion), grounded in efficient governance (assigning quantitative and transparent targets for developed and developing countries alike), and realistic economics (taking into account national production and imports and exports but also allowing for financial transfers between parties and revision of targets according to science and achievements). The result has been the elimination of 97% of ozone depleting substances (ODS), the gradual reconstruction of the ozone layer, and the prevention of hundreds of millions of cancer cases around the globe. Why would carbon control be so different from ODS control?[15]

These two examples show how well-being metrics can become new visions, informing and changing policy, while overcoming powerful economic interests that contribute positively to GDP and growth (tobacco control and ODS control both end up decreasing GDP, at least in the short run). For a comprehensive well-being transition to take place, what is needed is thus the design of metrics of input (drivers) and outcomes (results), relying on an analytical framework establishing causal links between the two, and using policy instruments able to change behaviors and attitudes so that drivers are altered and outcomes improved. Despite its complexity, there is no reason why climate change, a scientifically proven ecological crisis with identified causal indicators and considerable health consequences, cannot be addressed with powerful regulation instruments (including pricing carbon) in order to be mitigated. Such transition is technically feasible and there is no reason other than policy-makers (mis)giving the priority to other policy indicators, such as growth of GDP. As a matter of fact, a considerable literature now exists[16] on how to translate carbon metrics into carbon policy through pricing, taking into account effectiveness as well as equity (Boyce, 2018).

Actually, the well-being transition is already under way: Examples abound of regions, nations, and cities changing their policy by adopting new well-being metrics, from the European Union to the UK, and Australian governments to the province of British Columbia or the city of Santa Monica.

The basic course of action is to make visible what matters for humans and then make it count. Un-measurability means invisibility: "What is not measured is not managed," as the saying goes. Conversely, measuring is governing: indicators determine policies and actions. Measuring, done properly, can produce positive social meaning. It does not mean that everything should be monetized or marketed but understanding how what matters to humans can be accounted for is the first step to valuing and taking care of what really counts. There is no accountability without accounting.

A key distinction should be made here between quantification, monetization, and commodification (or marketization). It is important to quantify invisible value so that it is not ignored or blindly destroyed (this is the example of health in the US and happiness in China). But this quantification should not necessarily imply monetization. And this monetization, when necessary, does not lead inevitably to commodification.

Consider food labelling. If the only dimension of food resources that receives recognition is their monetary cost, the health dimension will never be reflected in production and/or consumption behavior. Appropriate labelling on the other hand (such as the one being implemented currently in France and other European countries in the form of a Nutri-score ranging from A to E), will inform the consumer about important aspects of the food that manufacturers may have an interest in concealing, such as the presence of chemical additives, the total caloric value, or its salt or fat content.

Or consider ecosystems valuation. To destroy a wetland rich in biodiversity on the basis of the economic value of the housing that can be built on it is to rely on one value (the immediate economic one) against all the others that have just as much bearing on human well-being. Revealing the plural values of biodiversity or ecosystems, monetized or not, amounts in this case to protecting them from blind destruction.

In fact, the performative power of well-being indicators does not depend only on the technical quality but, much more importantly, on their embedment in public debate and the democratic process. This can be done by integrating indicators in policy through representative democracy, regulatory democracy, and participatory democracy. Applied carefully by private and public decision-makers, well-being indicators can foster genuine progress.

For instance, we should be rethinking the way we vote the budget. Most parliaments' members around the world know very little about the true state of their country apart from aggregate macroeconomic indicators when they make key decisions on public finance. In an old democracy like France, the statistical information given to MPs amounts to GDP and its components. In the European Union, common economic governance rules of member states take the form of budgetary discipline metrics in percentage of GDP, a double mistake. It would not be difficult to select well-being indicators in key dimensions relevant for public finance, starting with inequality and the state of the environment, and embed those indicators in the budgetary procedure so that they are made public and discussed prior to voting. A permanent parliamentary body could even be created that could become a place of continuing deliberation on public choice impacting well-being, bringing together experts and citizens to mobilize the right indicators on the right issues in order to provide policy-makers with the relevant information to make their choices. This could take place at the national level as well as the regional level (e.g. the European Union).

The second reform concerns regulatory democracy and, more precisely, the reform of economic instruments used routinely by the executive branch of governments to design public policies once laws have been adopted. Public policies today too often rely on simplistic models framed by cost-benefit analysis (see Chapter 5).

Finally, participatory democracy must strengthen these reforms of the legislative and executive branch. Democracy is not just one dimension of well-being, but also the method that must govern its definition and governance: it is at once an outcome and an input. An example of participatory method are "citizens' conferences," a setting that includes a panel of citizens, experts, and decision makers discussing the respective importance of different dimensions of well-being and agreeing on a common dashboard to be implemented (such method was implemented in the French region of Nord-Pas-de-Calais in 2010).

It is of crucial important to build tangible transitions at the local level, since well-being is best measured where it is actually experienced. The well-being transition is, in the words of Elinor Ostrom (2012), a "polycentric transition": Each level of government can seize this opportunity to reform policy without waiting for the impetus to come from above (see Chapter 12).

To make way for the well-being transition, economics firmly detached itself from its passion for growth. Environmental economics itself, practiced and honored at the highest professional level, is tainted by this attachment, as the attribution of the 2018 Sveriges Riksbank Prize in economics makes clear (see Box 9.3).

## Box 9.3 The Sveriges Riksbank Prize in Economic Sciences 2018

As much as economists want to believe it, there is actually no Nobel Prize in Economics. When Alfred Nobel (1833–1896) decided to create the "Nobel Prizes," he wanted first and foremost to redeem his soul from the invention of dynamite (in 1866) that would end so many human lives. In his testament, he directed that his fortune be used to award "prizes to those who, during the preceding year, have conferred the greatest benefit to humankind" in the field of physics, chemistry, physiology or medicine, literature, and peace.[17] Economists were not on that list. It has been recently shown[18] that the creation in 1969 of "The Sveriges Riksbank Prize in Economic Sciences in Memory of Alfred Nobel," established more than six decades after the first Nobel Prize could be awarded in 1901, was the result of ideological tensions between Sweden's central bank (Sveriges Riksbank) and social democratic governments and an attempt to endow economic analysis with a scientific appearance.

Environmental economics has been largely ignored by the Sveriges Riksbank Prize. Some recipients, like Joseph Stiglitz and Robert Solow, made important contributions in environmental economics but were not honored for those contributions. One of the major inspiratory figures of environmental economic policy-making, Ronald Coase, was distinguished "for his discovery and clarification of the significance of transaction costs and property rights for the institutional structure and functioning of the economy." The only straightforward prize in environmental economics before 2018 was Elinor Ostrom, the only woman to ever receive the award, "for her analysis of economic governance, especially the commons."

The prize of 2018, awarded to leading climate economist William D. Nordhaus, was therefore welcome. Yet this recognition raises two serious caveats. The first has to do with Nordhaus' won contribution. The Yale economist was honored "for integrating climate change into long-run macroeconomic analysis." But a number of fellow economists has criticized the nature of this "integration." James Boyce[19] for instance shows that the DICE model designed and refined over the years by Nordhaus "recommends a carbon price that rises from \$37/t $CO_2$ in 2020 to about \$100/t in 2050. To meet the 2.5° target, the price would start more than six times higher, at about \$230/t in 2020, and rise to more than \$1,000/t in 2050." As a logical consequence, the increase in global mean temperature that would accompany the "optimal" carbon price recommended by the Nordhaus model is 3.5°C (6.3°F) by the year 2100, and rising afterwards. The DICE model thus recommends a temperature higher by 1.5 to two degrees than what climate scientists recommend on the grounds of physics. Economics serves as an anesthetic minimizing real climate damages rather than providing reliable quantification of it.

But there is more. Nordhaus shared the 2018 prize with Paul Romer, who was honored "for integrating technological innovations into long-run macroeconomic analysis." It must be noted that there is no actual intersection between the work of Romer and Nordhaus: Romer has never used his insights of growth theory to study climate and Nordhaus has relied on another stream of growth theory than the one devised by Romer when building the DICE model. The official announcement of the Prize states that "William D. Nordhaus and Paul M. Romer have designed methods for addressing some of our time's most basic and pressing questions about how we create long-term sustained and sustainable economic growth." What is really meant is much more dubious: The message conveyed in oddly associating Nordhaus and Romer, climate and growth economics, is that economic growth is the solution to climate change. But growth will not solve the blind destruction of our biosphere, as the Chinese example clearly shows (see Box 9.2).

# 10

# Social-ecology: Connecting the inequality and ecological crises

"As a system approaches its ecological limits, inequality only increases": With these words written more than thirty years ago, the Brundtland Report (1987)[1] sealed the profound intertwining of unsustainability and inequality.

As this book attempts to make clear, it is impossible to grasp fully the issue of sustainability without grasping the justice issue it contains. Bridging the challenges of sustainability and justice leads inevitably to the need to think about the social question and the ecological question together. When this is done, it appears that it makes environmental sense to mitigate our social crisis and social sense to mitigate our environmental crises. This is the basic statement of the social-ecological approach.

The social-ecological approach consists more precisely of considering the reciprocal relationship between social issues and ecological issues, demonstrating how social logics determine environmental degradation and crises, and in turn exploring the social consequences of these degradations of the human environment. Sustainability is a matter of not only inter-generational justice but also intra-generational justice.

Consider the "yellow vests" revolt that erupted in France in the Fall of 2018. It is the first social-ecological crisis of contemporary France and one of the first in Europe. It was triggered by the major issue – too long eluded in the country of pristine republican equality – of fossil fuels trapping millions of workers daily. Many other crises will follow or are already here, some blazing, others nagging. All ecological challenges are social issues and the environment is the new frontier of inequality. And yet, there is nothing inevitable about the social injustice of environmental taxation: The original French carbon tax of 2009 redistributed money to the 30% of the poorest French (today's *gilets jaunes*) on the basis of income and spatial location, while the most efficient ecological-tax systems on the planet (especially in the Nordic countries) are all built on a principle of social compensation. In other words, social-ecological analysis calls for social-ecological policy.

The social-ecological relationship is thus, on the question of inequalities, a two-way street: Social inequalities feed ecological crises, ecological crises in turn aggravate social inequalities.

The first arrow of causality, which runs from inequality to environmental degradation, can be labelled "integrative social-ecology," as it shows that the gap between the rich and the poor and the interaction of the two groups leads to the worsening of environmental degradations and ecological crises that affect every member of a given community (for example, greater inequality leads to a lesser adaptation capacity).

The reciprocal arrow of causality that goes from ecological crises to social injustice can be labelled "differential social-ecology," as it shows that the social impact of ecological crises is not the same for different individuals and groups, given their socio-economic status (the most vulnerable socially are "ecological sentinels" in the sense that they are first and foremost affected by current ecological crises).

Environmental risk is certainly a collective and global horizon but it is socially differentiated. Who is responsible for what and with what consequences for whom? Such is the social-ecological approach and it calls for social-ecological policy.

Sustainable development assembles three dimensions: economic, social, and ecological. While the economic-social and economic-ecological links have been explored in great detail in recent years (resulting in, respectively, the "inclusive development" and "green economy" paradigms, see figure), the social-ecological link is more obscure, although it is becoming the focus of growing academic and policy attention.[2] This chapter intends to shed some light on this missing link in sustainable development (Figure 10.1).

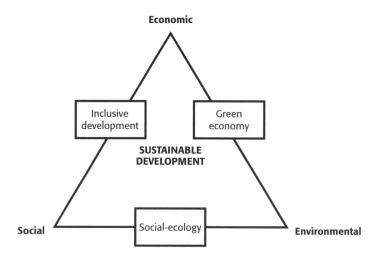

Figure 10.1 The three linkages of sustainable development

Empirically, it is hardly debatable that inequality on the one hand and environmental degradations and natural resources consumption on the other have been going up simultaneously in the last three decades. As this book made clear (especially in Chapter 6 and Chapter 7), environmental degradations and natural resources consumption are on the rise. What about trends in inequality?

Two fundamental results have been established in this respect. First, Piketty and his co-authors have documented the rise of domestic inequality (or "within countries" inequality): In the last three decades, income and wealth inequality has grown in all regions of the world, albeit at different speeds and from different initial situations (World Inequality Report 2018). Second, Branko Milanovic[3] has shown that if domestic inequality has increased, international inequality (or "between countries" inequality) has on the contrary started to decrease since 2000 but at a very slow pace: The Gini index of unweighted international inequality stands today close to 0.55. In short, the world is more equal than thirty years ago (but still at a very high level of inequality) but countries are a bit more unequal. The most remarkable evolution is the fact that weighted international inequality has started to decrease under the influence of the development of Global Asia, especially China and India.

It remains that when all trends are conflated to measure inequality between global citizens (considering all people in the world regardless of where they live), inequality has increased: The top one percent income share has grown significantly, while the bottom 50% has stagnated (World Inequality Report 2018) and the world's Gini index stands close to 0.63. Our task is thus to make sense theoretically of what is a documented empirical reality: the twin crises of inequality and the biosphere.

According to Andrew Dobson,[4] there are three ways to relate the theories of justice and environmental issues: Considering that the environmental quality (good and bad) is unevenly distributed among the members of a society; making justice into a condition of possibility of sustainability, and, finally, by doing justice to the environment or by doing justice in the name of the environment (that is, recognizing a right to Nature and creatures who inhabit it in one form or another).

When considering the second link, Dobson denies that inequalities contribute to environmental unsustainability. He recognizes that environmental amenities and damages are distributed according to the level of income. But, according to him, the fact that greater social justice (for example, through a better distribution of environmental ills) improves environmental sustainability has not received empirical evidence. On the contrary, Dobson argues, there are many cases in which social justice and sustainability will contradict one another: Improving the distribution of income and power could aggravate and not correct environmental unsustainability. This part argues against this view and highlights five channels through which inequality harms sustainability.

Because environmental damage results from the progress toward development, some in fact argue that eradication of poverty, rather than poverty itself, is the major obstacle to sustainability. Such a perspective, however, ignores the micro-ecological and macro-ecological dimensions of rising inequality. Let us first consider the micro-ecological level, that is, the behavior of rich and poor in isolation. With respect to the rich, Thorstein Veblen showed that the middle-class desire to imitate the lifestyles of the upper class can lead to a cultural epidemic of environmental degradation. Veblen called this phenomenon "conspicuous consumption," and the bigger cars, larger houses, more luxurious goods, that the rich buy and the middle class desire have a heavy environmental toll. With regard to the poor, Indira Gandhi explained in her speech at the first international environmental summit in Stockholm in 1972 that "poverty and need are the biggest polluters." In the developing world, poverty is indeed leading to unsustainable environmental degradation, such as the dramatic depletion of forest cover in Haiti or Madagascar, the product of a losing trade-off between present and future welfare.[5] Since the wealth of the world's poor lies in natural capital, because of lack of access to other forms of capital, the depletion of such natural resources leads to further impoverishment. The eradication of poverty, thus, is not only a social cause but also an environmental one, provided that it takes the form not of a game of consumerist catch-up, but of a redefinition of comprehensive wealth, its components, and its indicators.[6]

On the macro-ecological level – where the interaction of rich and poor and its environmental outcome is considered – it can be shown that a political economy lies behind environmental degradation (Boyce, 2002 and 2013). "Winners" of environmental degradations are able to impose the costs onto the losers because the losers are either not yet born, ignorant of the consequences of the degradation, or lacking in the power to limit them. Five macro-ecological channels through which rich and poor interact in environmental degradations, crises, and policies stand out in particular.

*(1) Inequality increases the need for environmentally harmful and socially unnecessary economic growth.*

Inequality inflates the need for economic growth. If wealth accumulation in a given country is increasingly captured by a small fraction of the population, the rest of the population will need to compensate with additional economic development. Paul Krugman summed this up well: "Here's a radical thought: if the rich get more, that leaves less for everyone else."[7] Since virtually no country in the world has managed to decouple (in absolute or net terms) economic growth from its negative environmental impact, e.g. carbon emissions or waste, more economic growth currently means more of such "bads," whether locally or globally.[8] In the United States, between 1993 and 2011, one percent of the population managed to capture 75% of economic growth. A more even distribution of income (i.e. a growth of income of two percent for the top ten percent and bottom 90% of the income distribution alike) would have reduced the total growth necessary to meet the needs of the vast majority of Americans and led to a small decline in $CO_2$ emissions (author's calculation based on Piketty and Saez, 2013). A more comprehensive empirical work has shown that if the US were to reduce inequality to the level of Sweden (halving their Gini index), emissions would go up by only 1.5%, suggesting that a very substantial but lower reduction in inequality would in fact decrease emissions.

But the equalization of economic conditions could, in fact, increase the ecological challenge since the marginal increase of environmental degradation is higher at the bottom of the income distribution than at the top.

Yet, first, by definition there are two ways to reduce inequality: from the bottom-up and from the top-down. Reducing the income of the richest segments of the world's population (the 10% that emits roughly 50% of $CO_2$) via adequate taxation will logically result in important cuts in emissions. Second, assuming higher emission intensity of consumption per expenditure by poorer households (based on the classical Keynesian argument of marginal propensity to consume) omits two important facts. The first one is that "luxuries" yields much more carbon emissions than "necessities" (to borrow the very relevant distinction introduced by Gough, 2017). This is the case in any given developed or developing country (as we have seen for emissions in the UK), this is also the case internationally:[9] A typical "super-rich" household of two people produces a carbon footprint of 129.3 $tCO_2e$ per year, with motor vehicle use generating 9.6 $tCO_2e$ per year, household energy emitting 18.9 $tCO_2e$ per year, secondary consumption 34.3 $tCO_2e$ per year, and 66.5 $tCO_2e$ per year generated by the leading emission contributor: air travel). Second, savings as well as consumption result in environmental degradations given the short-termism and inclination toward investments in fossil fuels of prominent financial institutions fueled by the global savings surplus (such as Goldman Sachs).

Moreover, such conclusions assume that the reduction of inequality would entail spreading the lifestyles, wasteful consumption, and ecological footprint of the richest. If so, then the ecological pressure would indeed become unbearable: Ecological footprint data clearly show that high income countries drive the global "ecological deficit." But an alternative view holds that shifting from captured development to shared development while redefining development itself can in fact create the necessary room for sustainable social progress (see previous chapter on alternative indicators to growth and GDP).

*(2) Inequality increases the ecological irresponsibility of the richest, within each country and among nations.*

Widening inequality exacerbates the fundamental tendency of capitalist enterprises to maximize profits by externalizing cost and turning socially deprived areas into "pollution havens" within countries and across their borders. The financialization of the economy over the past three decades has exacerbated this tendency by shortening time horizons and increasing indifference to unsustainable natural assets management. As the gap between rich and poor grows, governments and businesses find it easier to transfer the environmental damage of the activities of the rich to the neighborhoods of the poor. Income and power inequality, that tends to dissociate polluters from payers, thus act as a disincentive for ecological responsibility or as an accelerator of ecological irresponsibility.

On the consumption side, the richest consumers present a paradox. They declare in surveys that they care more about the environment than the poor do, and they are indeed, according to the same surveys, more likely to adopt the best environmental practices or to favor more ambitious environmental policy (see OECD, 2008). However, at the same time, they pollute more than the poor in volume because of their higher incomes and more expensive lifestyles. They are also more able to protect themselves from the negative impacts of their behavior as they become richer.

Widening inequality therefore increases not only the demand for a better environment among the richest but also their ability to acquire this good at a lower cost by transferring all corresponding environmental damages to the poorest. For example, in Spain, water has increasingly been diverted from small agricultural enterprises to large coastal tourist facilities. Wealthy tourists enjoy water as a natural amenity and are able to transfer the cost of its abduction and stress to growingly impoverished farmers who now face structural droughts.

On the production side, a company faces two essential options to reduce the environmental cost of its production. On the one hand, it can try to adopt the best available technology and to reduce the environmentally harmful impact of its production, a decision that can entail a high economic cost in the short run. On the other hand, it can seek to minimize the economic cost of the social compensation public authorities might demand from it. Income and power inequality will lead the company to relocate to a socially deprived area where people have low incomes and weak political mobilization capacities. The residents of that area would be, presumably, less willing to pay for environmental quality and therefore would demand lesser compensation for environmental damage. Likewise, the feeble political capability of the residents would limit the risk of the emergence of collective action to resist the damaging production (see below about the effect of inequality on collective action capability).

These dynamics also apply internationally and explain why inequality between countries can result in tragic but avoidable environmental disasters like the chemical pollution in Bhopal in December 1984 or the current degradation of the Niger Delta. Climate change is another case in point: Western societies are less likely to reduce their greenhouse gas emissions because they have little economic incentives to do so as long as they are able to adapt to the most devastating effects of climate change. The reverse is of course true for low-income countries, which contribute little to global emissions but will pay the highest human price for the coming destructive climate. The most striking example of this global injustice may be Africa. The continent accounts for less than three percent of global emissions, but water stress in Africa due to climate change could threaten the well-being of up to 600 million people in the coming decades.

These mechanisms could also account for the striking disparity in biodiversity preservation around the world, as measured by the World Wildlife Fund's Living Planet Index (see Chapter 6). The decline of the index has been uneven. From 1990 to 2008, the index increased in developed countries by seven percent, but it plummeted by 31% in middle-income countries and by 60% in low-income countries. According to the WWF, geographic factors explain only a fraction of the difference. International inequality likely plays an important role, for richer countries are able to preserve their biodiversity while simultaneously exploiting that of countries rich in natural capital but poor in income. For this very reason, evaluations of the ecological impact of a region like the EU, which imports much of its energy and raw materials, should take into account the damage done outside the region, in the original source of production and extraction.[10]

*(3) Inequality, which affects the health of individuals and groups, diminishes the social-ecological resilience of communities and societies and weakens their collective ability to adapt to accelerating environmental change.*

A substantial body of research, initiated by Richard Wilkinson and Michael Marmot, has confirmed the negative impact of social inequality on physical and mental health at the local and national level (via stress, violence, less access to health care).[11] Inequality also acts as an underlying driver of many diseases perceived as natural or biological in the developing world. Paul Farmer, for instance, has asserted that "inequality itself constitutes our modern plague."[12] Myriad governmental and international institutions have already begun to embrace this avenue of research in crafting policy agendas (the WHO to name only one).

The concepts of social-ecological resilience and vulnerability are in fact now common in the discourse of environmental science. Environmental scientists have begun to describe vulnerability to "natural" disasters as a function of exposure and sensitivity to a given shock, on the one hand, and adaptive capacity and resilience, on the other. Considered within this framework, inequality increases exposure and sensitivity and weakens adaptive capacity and resilience: It acts as a multiplier of the social damage caused by environmental shocks for developed and developing countries alike.

*(4) Inequality hinders collective action aimed at preserving natural resources.*

According to the "logic of collective action" (the classic theoretical framework formulated in Olson, 1965), a small group of wealthy individuals, convinced that they are the ones who will receive the greatest benefit from environmental protection, would be ready to pay the high cost of ambitious environmental policies. The few (richest), the argument goes, have a logistic comparative advantage over the many (poor). Accordingly, a larger group of people, with more heterogeneous revenues, would not be able to find ways to effectively organize to protect the environment.

This line of reasoning, which suggests that inequality is actually favorable to the preservation of natural resources, has been proven wrong both theoretically and empirically.[13] A number of studies has shown that inequality is, in fact, adverse to the sustainable management of common resources as it disrupts, demoralizes, and disorganizes human communities.[14] The work of Elinor Ostrom, already mentioned, in particular demonstrated that institutions that allow communities to preserve resources essential to their long-term well-being are based on principles of reciprocity and fairness, the very opposite of inequality. Adding to the evidence mentioned in point 3, Ostrom[15] links equality and the ability of communities around the world to organize efficiently in order to exploit sustainably natural resources and to resist ecological shocks such as climate change. Her critics however make one important point: the difficulty of extrapolating from a purely local context.

In order to account for scale, an analysis of the negative impacts of inequality on environmental decision-making must look toward national and international examples as well. The contemporary United States provides a useful illustration in this respect. Since the 1980s, the US has retreated from the ecological world stage, gradually transferring its prior role of global environmental leader to the European Union. Rapidly increasing income inequality and the corresponding political repercussions might provide an illuminating explanation for this turn of events.

Environmental policy-making requires a broad consensus transcending party boundaries, and the simultaneous rise of income inequality and political polarization (understood as growing distance between parties) has reduced the possibility of such bipartisan cooperation. It is now almost impossible in the US to enact ambitious legislation of the caliber of that passed in the 1970s, which later became a model for other nations. While the EPA was formed in 1970, at the beginning of the golden decade for environmental legislation, it is now much more difficult even to confirm a director for the agency. The EPA is also, internally, the subject of political pressure motivated by industrial lobbying, especially from fossil fuel companies that have been empowered by growing economic inequality.

As studies have identified a correlation between income inequality and political polarization in the US, we can think of environmental policy as one of the many policy casualties of the "dance" between these two trends.[16] Political polarization and economic inequality both deepened over the past decade. Correspondingly, inertia in the face of environmental degradation has worsened, with the devastation of the Appalachian region and the sabotage of climate negotiations. In this latter case, as with other domestic and global environmental challenges, polarization is combined with an overall shift to the right of the political spectrum, so that the status quo caused by polarization results in a more pro-business and anti-environmental policy.

This polarization dynamic at the local and national level replicates itself on the global scene. Recent research, for instance, has shown that "support is higher for global climate agreements that distribute costs according to prominent fairness principles."[17] Equality and fairness among parties to international environmental negotiations appears to be a key feature of successful global ecological governance (like the Montreal Protocol on ozone layer depleting substances). On the contrary, inequality in the negotiation process (procedural inequality) and/or distribution of costs (distributive inequality) among Nation States can alter the progress of ecological sovereignty pooling, as with UNFCCC conferences.

Finally, recent research (Motesharrei et al., 2014) goes a step further by arguing that inequality could play a key role in bringing about a global ecological collapse. The study investigates the possibility of civilizational collapse, drawing on a rich literature and relying on a new model named "HANDY" (Human And Nature Dynamical) which particularity is to add to already existing features of Earth models a social stratification variable. Humans, in the model, are divided between "Elites" and "Commoners" and their consumption of natural resources is differentiated according to their economic and political power.

The model's key insight is that ecological collapse can not only come about because of "the stretching of resources due to the strain placed on the ecological carrying capacity" but also due to "the economic stratification of society into Elites [rich] and Masses (or "Commoners") [poor]." The grim conclusion of the authors regarding one of their key scenarios goes as follows: "the Elites eventually consume too much, resulting in a famine among Commoners that eventually causes the collapse of society." Yet, the study also shows that this seemingly irresistible collapse by inequality can be prevented through a reduction of current levels of social stratification, a more equal distribution in the consumption of natural resources and a higher efficiency in this consumption (although technological progress alone can not, in the model, prevent the collapse).

*(5) Inequality reduces the political acceptability of environmental preoccupations and the ability to offset the potential socially regressive effects of environmental policies.*

Surveys on the political economy of environmental policies have shown that people generally view such policies as socially regressive, which they can, in fact, be.[18] Growing relative and absolute inequality can thus translate into a reduced acceptability of short-term social (real or perceived) "sacrifices" for long-term (social-ecological) benefits. The failure of France to adopt a carbon tax in 2009/2010 illustrates this argument.[19] The socially regressive effect of the tax was obvious, as the bottom 20% of French households spend 2.5 times as much of their income on energy as the top 20% of households do (Laurent, 2011). Unsurprisingly, polls reported that as much as 66% of the French population opposed the carbon tax, mostly on economic grounds, with a sharp division between lower-income and higher-income social categories. The government eventually decided to abandon the project in March 2010 after a gruelling political defeat amid rising unemployment and poverty in the context of the "great recession." In 2018, this time facing a full-blown social revolt in a context of severe tax injustice, the French government decided again to suspend the carbon tax.

The public budget constraints produced by growing inequality, which translates at the macroeconomic level into lower aggregate demand and lower tax revenues (Stiglitz, 2012) further exacerbate the problem of political acceptability. Inequality makes it more complex and costly, if not impossible, to implement effective compensation mechanisms to counteract possible regressive effects of certain environmental policies, because there are too many people to compensate with too little resource (Nordic countries have been able to successfully implement carbon taxation precisely because they have very low-income inequality levels, dynamic economies, and efficient welfare states which foster social consensus). However, social compensation for policies like carbon taxes is a key factor to their political acceptability and even their economic efficiency. In fact, all countries and localities that have adopted carbon taxes over the last two decades have also adopted compensation mechanisms for households and firms which overcame the initial resistance from citizens and businesses (such as in Nordic countries).

## The rise of environmental inequality

While the impact of inequality on environmental crises that has been detailed in the previous section may be harder to grasp, the reverse relation is easier to understand and to explain. Environmental conditions determine well-being, most prominently through health-related factors. Therefore, environmental degradation leads to significant and socially differentiated well-being impact.

Recent reports by the World Bank show that extreme climate shocks disproportionately affect the world's poorest and threaten to tip hundreds of millions of hungry people into poverty. But climate change is just as much a challenge for solidarity in European countries, as the European Environment Agency shows, detailing in a new study the many climate vulnerabilities that threaten our prosperity: Fluvial and coastal floods have affected millions of people in Europe in the last decade; health consequences include injuries, infections, exposure to chemical hazards, and mental health impacts; heat waves have become more frequent and intense, causing tens of thousands of premature deaths in Europe.

We have already seen in Chapter 4, in relation to the different approaches of environmental justice, a definition and a typology of environmental inequality and reviewed some facts about environmental inequality with regard to air pollution. We can now be a bit more specific about the various types of environmental inequality.

## Risk, Noise, and Chemical Pollution

With regard to chemical pollution of the environment, a first issue is the fairness of the distribution of hazardous or toxic sites in the country (the harmful nature of these facilities to health is not to be proven since it is their harmful nature that justifies their classification as toxic sites). Recent studies show that environmental exposure is far from being socially homogenous in the US,[20] China,[21] or Europe.[22]

Noise, considered by many experts to be the second biggest environmental risk behind air pollution in terms of its health impact (measured in lost years of disability adjusted life) must also be treated as a form of environmental pollution. A new report by the European Environmental Agency (2019),[23] reviewing a number of environmental inequalities faced by European citizens (related to air pollution or exposure to extreme temperatures) documents the importance and unequal distribution of noise pollution in the EU. The EEA estimates that environmental noise causes at least 16,600 cases of premature death in Europe each year, with almost 32 million adults annoyed by it and a further thirteen million suffering from sleep disturbance. In addition, cities with poorer populations have higher noise levels. The relationship between social inequalities and exposure to noise was highlighted by a study published in early 2013 by the Regional Health Agency of the Île-de-France region on the Paris major airport hubs (Bruiparif, 2013). The results reveal that the share of population exposed increases with the level of socio-economic disadvantage and that districts where there is a significant proportion of those exposed are those of the most disadvantaged. Other studies on noise, conducted for example in the Marseille region, arrive at less clear-cut conclusions and show in particular that it is rather the intermediate social groups that are most vulnerable to noise.

Chemical pollutions are also unevenly distributed across the country as a growing body of research in France has shown in recent years. The PLAINE model built by INERIS allows for example to map the presence of nickel, cadmium, chromium and lead in certain parts of the country (Caudeville, 2013 and INERIS, 2014). The results for the Nord-Pas-de-Calais region for cadmium document that two areas find themselves over-exposed (Metaleurop and the periphery of the Lille metropolitan area). This issue of chemical pollution and over-exposure of certain populations is related to the proliferation of "environmental cancer" that is to say cancers attributable to environmental factors, which are now estimated at around ten percent of all cancers in France.[24]

The occupational dimension of environmental inequalities becomes also more and more transparent. For the first time in 2011, the number of deaths from occupational diseases exceeded the number of deaths by accident in France. Suffice it to recall in this regard the considerable difference in life expectancy between occupational groups (seven years between managers and workers and six years between managers and employees), with a gap that increases rather than shrinks in the last thirty years.

At a more detailed level, exposure to endocrine disruptors (chemicals that may interfere with the body's hormonal system) is not homogeneous among occupations: Industry, agriculture, cleaning, and plastic sectors exhibit the greatest degree of exposure. As in the case of particulate matters pollution, prenatal and perinatal exposure to such pollutants may have lasting adverse consequences. For instance, some studies link exposure to arsenic in utero and increased infant mortality, low birth weight and reduced resistance to childhood infections. It is this type of study that led to the ban of bisphenol A in France, but much remains to be done on the many other endocrine disruptors.

## Access to natural resources (food, energy, water)

Another facet of environmental inequality is the unequal access to environmental amenities among which are natural resources instrumental in daily well-being such as (good) food, water and energy. We have reviewed these aspects in Chapter 6.

## Exposure to social-ecological disasters

Exposure to so-called "natural" hazards constitutes a major source of social inequality that is expected to worsen over the coming decades as ecological crises such as climate change become more severe. To put it in the phraseology of the United Nations (Disaster Risk Reduction or DRR), "There is no such thing as a 'natural' disaster, only natural hazards": The impact of a given disaster depends on the choices we make for our lives and our environment. Every decision and every action makes us more vulnerable or more resilient.[25]

There are two possible ways to look at natural risks. The first hypothesizes that "natural" disasters occur randomly and that humans can hardly do anything about them (that is the etymology of the word "dis-aster" which essentially points to bad luck or adverse fate). The second way is to think that human responsibility lies at the heart of these events, which rather deserve the name of "catastrophes" which etymologically orients toward the idea of a happy or unhappy ending depending on human behavior. Those two world-views have been respectively defended by French philosophers Voltaire and Rousseau during the controversy on the causes of the Lisbon earthquake in 1755 (Box 10.1).

## Box 10.1 Rousseau vs. Voltaire after the Lisbon earthquake of 1755

Modern seismology was born from the "Lisbon disaster": This devastating earthquake (followed by a tsunami and a giant fire), which, on November 1, 1755, caused some 50,000 casualties. It is also the beginning of a philosophical reflection on human responsibility in "natural" disasters. We remember the sarcasm of Voltaire in his Candide mocking the optimistic philosophers and in particular Leibniz, painted in the guise of a Pangloss who perishes in a Lisbon in ruins while Candide dies under his eyes. In his poem on the disaster of Lisbon (1756), Voltaire returns to charge in an elegiac fashion to accuse the "deceived philosophers" who shout "All is well" but also men who believe they can challenge Providence. This is precisely what will put Rousseau in a rage. In his Letter on Providence (August 18, 1756), he contrasts Voltaire's fatalism with human responsibility:

"I do not see how one can search for the source of moral evil anywhere but in man's freedom and perfection – which are also his corruption. As for our physical pains: If sensate and impassible matter is, as I think, a contradiction in terms, then pains are inevitable in any world of which man forms a part – and the question then becomes not 'why is man not perfectly happy' but 'why does he exist at all?' Moreover, I think I have shown that most of our physical pains, except for death – which is hardly painful, except for the preparations that precede it – are also our own work. Without leaving your Lisbon subject, concede, for example, that it was hardly nature who assembled there twenty-thousand houses of six or seven stories. If the residents of this large city had been more evenly dispersed and less densely housed, the losses would have been fewer or perhaps none at all. Everyone would have fled at the first shock, and would have been seen two days later, twenty leagues away and as happy as if nothing had happened. But we have to stay and expose ourselves to further tremors, many obstinately insisted, because what we would have to leave behind is worth more than what we could carry away. How many unfortunates perished in this disaster for wanting to take – one his clothing, another his papers, a third his money? They know so well that a person has become the least part of himself, and that he is hardly worth saving if all the rest is lost." [26]

According to the Centre for Research on the Epidemiology of Disasters (CRED), over the 1998–2017 period, 90% of 7,255 listed natural disasters have been linked to climatic factors (rainfall, droughts, storms), with floods and storms representing 70% of the total. In 2017, 335 natural disasters affected over 95.6 million people, killing an additional 9,697 and costing a total of US

$335 billion. But this burden was not shared equally, as Asia seemed to be the most vulnerable continent for floods and storms, with 44% of all disaster events, 58% of the total deaths, and 70% of the total people affected.[27]

The EM-DAT database maintained by the CRED distinguishes between two generic categories for disasters: natural and technological. The natural disaster category is divided into five sub-groups, which in turn cover fifteen disaster types and more than thirty sub-types. The technological disaster category is divided into three sub-groups which in turn cover fifteen disaster types.

This distinction between natural and human disasters is of course necessary and based on a completely understandable logic: The industrial accident that occurred in the Total refinery in Toulouse in September 2001 is not equivalent to the tragic earthquake that devastated Haiti in January 2010. But the contemporary ecological crises (climate, biodiversity, ecosystems) having a human origin, the resulting disasters (floods, droughts, fires) can hardly be considered as natural.[28] Even more importantly, existing empirical studies clearly show that major contemporary ecological crises (climate change, destruction of biodiversity, degradation of ecosystems) do not have the same social impact around the world: everywhere they reveal social inequalities (that was the case when hurricane Katrina hit the city of New Orleans in 2005, hardly affecting high-ground rich districts) and worsen them (many African-Americans were not able to recover from the disaster and had to leave the city).[29] The role of social capital for instance is crucial in social-ecological disasters.

In other words, current developments give increasing weight to Rousseau's view: Social factors do play a crucial role in so-called "natural" disasters, which are more appropriately "social-ecological" because their causes and impacts are more and more the results of actions taken by human societies.

An expression circulates in the humanitarian community that says that "natural" disasters rarely result from fatality: "Earthquakes do not kill people, buildings do." Three researchers have recently tried to give substance to this idea by measuring since 1900 the intensity of the earthquakes that hit the planet, taking into account the population density of the regions affected and the level of wealth of their inhabitants. There have been 2.5 million deaths since 1900 due to earthquakes, half of them in China and 200,000 in Iran. The author's first attempt to quantify the annual risk in the different countries of death by earthquake (per million inhabitants). While this figure reaches 92 in Armenia, 41 in Turkmenistan and 29 in Iran, it is only 0.6 in California and 0.008 in France.

But the study goes further in the analysis of data: Taking into account the number of earthquakes of magnitude greater than six, often considered as the destruction threshold, they obtain a ratio of 2300 deaths/million/magnitude six in Armenia, 1300 in Turkmenistan, 300 in Tajikistan, but only two in California and 0.8 in France.[30] Countries like Japan have learned throughout the twentieth century to literally immune themselves from earthquakes' human impact, but not all countries have had the means to do so, an obvious observation when one considers the consequence of the two similarly powerful earthquakes that devastated Haiti in 2010 and barely affected Japan in 2011.

How to explain this striking difference? Rich countries have simply "learned to protect themselves from earthquakes": There is a decrease in the number of victims over time.

This protection, which for some territories borders on seismic immunity, has been acquired through institutional progress.[31] One of the authors of the study, the French geophysicist Denis Hatzfeld, explains that rich countries have mobilized the means of research to identify areas at risk, assess the movement of the soil during earthquake or the behavior of structures.

At the heart of the question of so-called "natural" disasters, we find, once again, the issue of international and intra-national inequalities. One can thus make two points that both call for action: Human impact exacerbates natural disasters and makes some of them more frequent; much of the damage from all natural disasters occurs because of insufficient and unsustainable planning and a lack of foresight (e.g. the devastation associated with Typhoon Hayian in November 2013). Local and national policy-makers must thus anticipate announced and virtually certain future disasters – especially heat waves and floods in rich countries and severe hurricanes in poor countries – if they wish to spare their citizens implacable future injustice. In particular, the role played by structural environmental inequalities but also the lack of social capital in certain communities exposed to social-ecological disasters such as heat waves or hurricanes warrants deeper analysis. For example, minorities face more exposure to the risks connected to urban heat island effect because their neighborhoods often lack tree cover or contain too much impervious surfaces, such as asphalt and concrete.[32]

These various environmental inequalities can morph into persistent social inequalities through institutions. Environmental inequalities can produce lasting and severe damage on the socially disadvantaged, perpetuating and exacerbating injustice. Studies on the effects of air pollution in Los Angeles have shown how exposure to atmospheric pollution affects school performance through the impact of respiratory diseases developed by exposed children. It has been also shown that children from poor families are more likely to be born with poor health because of the polluted environment experienced by their mothers during pregnancy (Currie, 2011). This, in turn, results in poor educational attainment and eventually lower income and lower social status. How should this reality of the unequal impact of ecological crises inform public policy?

## From the welfare state to the social-ecological state

The modern welfare state was devised in the 1880s in unified Germany to forge a new alliance between labor and capital, and was built upon the idea that human beings are entitled to receive protection against the hazards of nature and social life. "Social security" – currently guaranteed to fewer than 30% of the world's population in about half of the planet's countries – is already a considerable extension of the "civil security" that Hobbes entrusted to the Leviathan in the mid 1600s.

The next stage consists in moving on from social security to social-ecological security by acknowledging that the nature of social risk underwent a fundamental change at the end of the twentieth century. A state fit for the twenty-first century should aim at forging a new alliance between social issues and environmental challenge. Because social risk today includes a major environmental dimension (floods, heat waves, hurricanes, storms, pollutions), citizens are entitled to expect public authorities to develop and put in place adequate means of protection. Because the well-being of individuals and groups is increasingly determined by environmental conditions, it is legitimate for social policy to include the environmental dimension. Environmental crises should be considered as social risks and therefore call for insurance.

How to begin the metamorphosis of our welfare state, thought in the nineteenth century to overcome the conflict between labor and capital, into a social-ecological state calibrated for the twenty-first century, that is to say designed to reconcile the social question and the environmental challenge? How to build institutions capable of guaranteeing social-ecological progress that can be defined as the progress of human development in a democratic framework in the Anthropocene age?

Two different paths can be taken to establish a philosophical continuity between the welfare state and the social-ecological state: that of social risk and that of individual well-being.

If we take the first approach (remaining true to the notion of welfare state), it appears that social risk today includes an important environmental dimension (floods, heat waves, storms …). Citizens have the right to expect the public power to develop the means to protect themselves. The other path refers to the Anglo-Saxon name of social protection, the Welfare State – "state of well-being," more precisely "state for well-being." We then consider not the risk that the individual faces, but the sources of his well-being (and his malaise). From the point of view of the welfare state, it is income, family life, health. In the social-ecological approach, it is recognized that the well-being of an individual or a group is partly determined by environmental conditions.

What is in this context a social-ecological policy? The development of a social-ecological policy requires prior identification and analysis of the associated and sometimes inextricable character of the social and the environmental dimensions: There is a need to recognize the ecological stakes within social issues, as well as to reveal the social stakes of ecological issues, at the national as well as European level (the social-ecological dimension of carbon taxation for instance is a national and European policy matter). This approach can be formalized using a social-ecological matrix (see Figure 10.2). Gough (2017) has very compelling arguments as to the respective merits (or comparative advantages) of social-ecological policies, in particular he argues for social investment (such as subsidies for home retrofitting) rather than social compensations (such as transfers in cash).

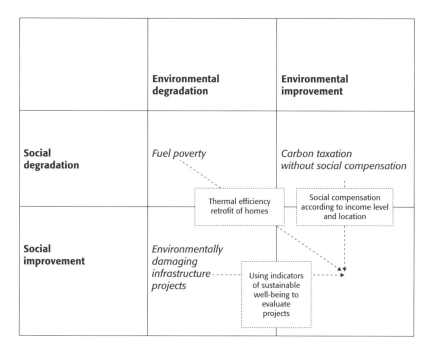

Figure 10.2   Social-ecological trade-offs and synergies

*Reading of Figure 10.2*

Each quadrant represents a combined assessment of the social and environmental outcome of a given situation or policy. In the top left quadrant, fuel poverty results both in monetary poverty and energy over-consumption. Thermal insulation (home weatherization) allows for a reduction in energy consumption (and thus lower related greenhouse gas emissions, triggering environmental improvement), which translates into lower expenditure devoted to energy by fuel-poor households, allowing for social progress.

In the top right quadrant, carbon taxation without social compensation is both socially regressive, as it hurts the poorest more because of their higher income share devoted to energy consumption, and environmentally efficient, because it reduces greenhouse emissions by pricing carbon. Introducing social compensation based on income level but also location (rural areas versus urban areas, suburban areas vs. urban centers) maintains the environmental efficiency of the policy measure (compensation should not be understood as exoneration), but eases its social impact and therefore its political acceptability.

Many countries (such as Indonesia) and localities have successfully introduced such compensations, in particular the province of British Columbia, which carbon tax was rejected by 43% of its residents when it was introduced without social compensations in 2008 and is now opposed by only 32% (support grew when compensations were introduced).[33]

Finally, the bottom left quadrant takes the example of cost-benefit analysis (CBA) applied to infrastructure projects, for instance housing. When biodiversity and ecosystems are not or only partially taken into consideration, building a residential complex on a wetland increases human well-being while at the same time destroying ecosystems and biodiversity. The social-ecological policy in this case is conceptual: It consists in changing indicators used to decide or not to implement the policy by integrating the social value of ecosystems and biodiversity. When a correct assessment based on comprehensive wealth analysis including benefits derived from natural capital is carried out, the infrastructure project will be moved to a better/less harmful location, resulting in both environmental and social progress.

Implementation of a social-ecological policy requires active awareness of the interplay of social issues and environmental challenges so as to enable progress in both of these dimensions simultaneously (as in the case of housing insulation). Yet there are numerous cases in which to envisage and devise a social-ecological policy is to recognize the need for arbitration between the social question and the environmental question as a prerequisite for finding appropriate solutions (e.g. carbon taxation which, if one is not careful, can entail harmful social consequences).

Going further, what could be the purpose of a social-ecological state? It would be no different from that fulfilled by the welfare state through its functions of allocation, redistribution, and stabilization, but these functions would be applied to environmental issues. In this respect, there is no fundamental difference between social and environmental policy: Both aim at correcting market economy failures such as imperfect information, incomplete markets, externalities, that justify public intervention. As a matter of fact, climate change has been called "the biggest market failure the world has seen" (Stern, 2008).

The allocation function of the social-ecological state means revealing the hidden social costs of ecological crises – such as respiratory diseases, strokes, and so on, caused by air pollution in European urban centers – in order to reduce them and the inequality that they compound. Numerous reports indeed stress the beneficial effect of environmental regulations on health and well-being (such as the Clean Air Act in the United States or the Montreal Protocol on the ozone layer at the global level). The social cost of ecological crises must be made visible in order to reveal the misguided allocation of resources to which the current economic systems lead.

Let us now consider the function of stabilization. In its traditional meaning, this consists of governments' bringing into play automatic stabilizers and discretionary policy in order to cushion an economic shock and prevent a recession from degenerating into a depression. The stabilization function thus increases resilience. The social-ecological stabilization function is, by the same logic, aimed at enabling individuals to deal with ecological shocks (e.g. the heat wave of 2003) by preserving their well-being. Of the 158 billion the cost of so-called natural disasters estimated by the Swiss group of Reinsurance Swiss Re for the year 2016 worldwide (compared to $94 billion of 2015 dollars) approximately $49 billion in damages were covered by insurance companies.

Finally, when it comes to redistribution, tax systems should be reformed to penalize the excessive use of natural resources, starting with fossil fuels. Countries of the world, starting with the most developed, should embark on a third tax revolution, after the taxation of income at the beginning of the twentieth century and of consumption in the 1950s. Currently, on average, environmental taxation in the European Union for instance, the most advanced region of the world on the matter, only represents six percent of total taxation and has declined since 2002 (when it represented 7%). In the rest of the developed world, it remains much too low to influence behaviors and shift production and consumption systems toward greater sustainability (see Table 10.1), with only a few countries being an exception such as Denmark.

| Table 10.1 Environmentally related tax revenue for some OECD countries, 1994–2016 (in % of GDP) | | | |
|---|---|---|---|
| | 1994 | 2005 | 2016 |
| Austria | 2.2 | 3.2 | 2.7 |
| Denmark | 4.1 | 5.1 | 4.0 |
| Netherlands | 3.4 | 3.7 | 3.5 |
| Poland | 1.9 | 2.4 | 2.0 |
| Switzerland | 1.6 | 2.0 | 1.6 |
| Turkey | 1.1 | 4.0 | 3.3 |
| United States | 1.0 | 0.8 | 0.7 |
| OECD Asia Oceania | 1.8 | 1.9 | 1.7 |
| OECD – Europe | 2.6 | 2.6 | 2.5 |
| OECD – Total | 1.8 | 1.7 | 1.6 |

Source: OECD

In short, a social-ecological state should organize the social-ecological transition to respond to environmental change with social progress.[34]

# 11

# The social-ecological transition in context: Capitalism, democracy, globalization, and digitalization

The history of transitions points to the role of institutions as drivers of social change. Industrial revolutions are not merely technological revolutions but first of all institutional revolutions that rely on new ways to do work, business, and government. Empirical studies indicate that beyond geography and trade, institutions are in fact the essential vectors of human development and human change, whether in behaviors (that depend on the price system), attitudes (that depend on the value system) or both. History suggests that both can change for the better, sometimes suddenly and dramatically, as in the case of responses to an oil shock or a natural disaster. Institutions are thus the key elements of the dynamics of any transition because their vocation is to pass the test of time in order to facilitate social cooperation.

The current global effort to shift social and natural systems toward a more sustainable path does not take place in a vacuum but in an institutional context characterized by at least four features: Capitalism, democracy, globalization, and digitalization. This chapter examines some central debates around these institutional features and their bearings on the social-ecological transition.

## Anthropocene or Capitalocene?

According to the International Union of Geological Sciences (IUGS), the professional organization that defines Earth's time scale, the current time belongs to an epoch named the Holocene (the "new whole"), which began 11,500 years ago after the last ice age.

But in 2000,[1] Crutzen and Stoermer, wanting to "emphasize the central role of mankind in geology and ecology" proposed "to use the term 'Anthropocene' for the current geological epoch." "To assign a more specific date to the onset of the 'Anthropocene,'" they say "seems somewhat arbitrary," but they proposed "the latter part of the 18th century." They explain their choice: "we choose this date because, during the past two centuries, the global effects of human activities have become clearly noticeable." Even more precisely, they chose 1784, the year James Watt invented the steam engine. The choice of this new era is thus technologic: The waves of innovation and economic growth triggered by the first industrial revolution has unleashed the power of domination and destruction of human economies.

The Working Group on the Anthropocene voted to formally designate the epoch Anthropocene and presented the recommendation at the International Geological Congress in August 2016. But these experts recommended that the new epoch should begin much more recently, about 1950, defined by the radioactive elements dispersed across the planet by nuclear bomb tests. Again, technology is, according to this view, the key to the beginning of human domination of Earth's ecosystems.[2] But what about social dynamics?

In 2013, Jason Moore[3] contested the idea of the Anthropocene that considers "humanity as an undifferentiated whole" and instead argued for the adoption of the term "Capitalocene," "understood as a system of power, profit, and re/production in the web of life." As was mentioned in Chapter 10, it is obvious from the perspective of this book that the currently prevalent models used to represent ecological knowledge have in common a relative lack of attention to the social dimension. The Anthropocene theory, indeed, presents us with a unified human species that, on account of its overweening collective intelligence, has set in motion a geological revolution, to the perverse effects of which the human species as a whole now finds itself subject. The "planetary boundaries" approach puts forward, along similar lines, the notion of global thresholds (for example the two degrees of average planetary warming) beyond which the environment – without any social distinction – would no longer be safe for human beings. Both representations, which undoubtedly have their uses are flawed by the same shortcoming and point up the same need, namely, for a socially differentiated ecological analysis both in terms of cause and consequence (see Chapter 10).

Yet should we point, as Moore advocates, at capitalism as the engine of environmental degradation rather than inequality? The conversation about capitalism and the need to overcome or even destroy it, brought about by genuinely concerned and frustrated citizens and scholars, is too often fixated on abstractions while specific and situated institutions and policies such as taxation, redistribution, and regulation should instead be at the center of the discussion. Let us consider a series of counter-arguments to the theory of "Capitalocene." First, it is useful and indeed necessary to distinguish between economic liberalism, market economy, and capitalism. Economic liberalism means the freedom to perform economic actions such as innovating, producing, and consuming. It is actually a condition of sustainability rather than its impediment. Market economy means private property rights, competition for profit, culture of consumption, relatively free markets (in terms of prices and volumes). Some of these elements obviously lead to environmental degradations (such as the culture of consumption), others to sustainability (such as the establishment of private property rights for non-renewable resources). Finally, capitalism today means the regime of "salariat" (wage earning via employment contract), the reign of finance and, to borrow from the Marxist repertoire, an exploitation of workers by shareholders, this latter feature being the key contemporary driver of both human well-being and environmental degradations. The problem is that capitalism, which encompasses economic liberalism and market economy, can and does take countless forms in time and space, as the literature on "varieties of capitalism" makes clear. Capitalism, as such, does not exist. The most sustainable countries on the planet (from an economic, social and environmental standpoint), the Nordic countries, are capitalist. While, as we have seen in Chapter 9, the most unsustainable country in all economic history happens to be communist (China, another historical example being the former USSR).[4]

Hence the importance of considering the role of the State in capitalism, which can act as a regulatory power, a counter-force or an accelerator of the potential detrimental effects of certain forms of capitalism. The reason why Danish capitalism is not as destructive as the US current capitalist regime is precisely because of the role of its State in implementing environmental legislation that counters the inclination of the economic system to treat environmental resources (such as biodiversity and ecosystems) from the pure standpoint of short-term profitability. It also reigns in the destructive power of inequality (see Chapter 10) through significantly higher taxes and transfers than any other country. This calls for a broader reflection on the relation between democracy and sustainability.

## Democracy or "green" dictatorship?

A fundamental critique directed at democracy is that, while endowed with the good institutions allowing it to face the issue of sustainability, it will in any event prove incapable of making good use of it: It cannot in fact counter the influence of capitalist political economy which forces it to over-exploit natural resources in the name of greater profit. In the best case, democracy will have a second-rate on environmental degradation: It can eventually repair the damage of capitalism, but in any case it will not be able to counter its ecologically destructive logic, which aims at the outsourcing of costs, privatization of gains, and mutualization of cost of environmental damage. The only real solution to ecological crises would therefore be to abolish capitalism. As York et al. write, "Political and social variables may diminish and perhaps even counter the anthropogenic environmental impact, but they can not overcome it."[5] Is democracy ecologically doomed and why? At least two powerful anti-democratic criticisms have been put forward in recent decades.

Hans Jonas in Chapter V of *The Imperative of Responsibility* (1979) develops an ethical critique of democracy: In a liberal democracy, citizens are left to their own devices to learn temperance and moderation. They simply won't: It will have to be imposed on them, if necessary by force. An enlightened elite, deciding for the people and in the name of their good, must take charge of human destinies to avoid the ecological catastrophe. This ecological autocracy or green dictatorship has, according to Jonas, its "advantages" in the name of which it is important to dispense with the prior consent of the base to install a "benevolent tyranny," well informed and animated by the right understanding of things that borrows from communism its "ascetic morality" to counter a "democratic and liberal" capitalism.

The institutional criticism of democracy, bordering on ethical criticism, does not rest on the liberal foundation of the democratic regime, but on its inability to promote effective collective action for environmental preservation. Two opposing critics have been addressed to democracy: its myopia and its slowness. Democracy is accused of being both paralyzed by its heaviness and frantically obsessed by the short term.

This criticism of democratic slowness and myopia is a triple detente: Democracy may not perceive the ecological problem; it may be aware of it, but unable to do anything meaningful about it; it can finally recognize its gravity, pretend to engage rhetorically in action but not bring any real solution beyond the discourse of sustainability.

The denunciation of the myopia of democracy deserves clarification. There is the classic argument that the political cycle that obeys the majority principle does not fit the long-term stakes (future generations do not vote). Even the citizens themselves, regardless of the obsession of their rulers to be re-elected, may not perceive their own long-term interest. This is true of the construction of houses in flood zones: It is at the time of the disaster that their owners realize the consequences of their improvidence. Democracy would therefore be by nature, because of the governors as well as the governed, short-termist. In economic language, it will be said that it suffers from a problem of temporal inconsistency.

This criticism is old and profound. Democracies have long been described as temporally dysfunctional with marked preference for the present that constrain their political horizon. This last argument echoes the work of the philosopher Jon Elster.[6]

The first Elster in fact justifies the existence of institutional mechanisms aimed at compelling collective action by taking as a model an individual who, like Ulysses, would be interested in limiting a will that could prove to be "self-defeating." But the second Elster recognizes that to extrapolate in this way from the individual to the social is not self-evident: There is a world between private constitutions and public constitutions. To constrain oneself, explains the philosopher, is acceptable because it is "the individual today" who constrains "the individual tomorrow." A public constitution is of a totally different order: The individuals elected today compel their fellow citizens today and others tomorrow. However, since no group can pretend to embody the general interest, there is a truly democratic reason for democracy to be tied to the choices of the present.

This can be turned into a critique of the process of representative democracy, as do Dominique Bourg and Kerry Whiteside.[7] The fundamental incentives regulating the functioning of representative institutions the authors argue have the effect of postponing confrontation with environmental problems that are distant in time or developing slowly.

Faced with this strong criticism, let us first try to adopt an operative definition of democracy. There are indeed many varieties of democracy, some that may fall under the ethical and institutional criticism, others which could escape them. Let us stick to a contemporary definition: Democracy is an effective representative electoral system based on the law of the majority, it contrasts with authoritarian regimes based on the tyranny of a party or clan (in any case a small group of individuals) perceiving themselves as an elite.

To the ethical criticism, one can first answer that democracy is the regime of freedoms and that it therefore allows the environmental demand to express itself, which the dictatorship does not allow. Even if they affect the well-being of citizens, environmental degradation can simply not be made public without recourse to the civil liberties and political rights guaranteed by democracy. It is thanks to the freedom of speech inscribed at the heart of the democratic regime that the scale of ecological crises and the risks associated with them is now known and that NGOs can (often appropriately) denounce … the slowness of democracy.

To the criticism of myopia and short-termism, we can respond that democracy is precisely able to take the time to organize in-depth and "open-air" debates on collective choices under the control of citizens which can include a wide range of interests, much wider than in authoritarian regimes. Democracy can therefore, if it wants to, see both from afar and closely and even weigh these two points of view. Democracy also makes it possible legally to distinguish between the short term (political life) and the long term (the constitutional order), which can, provided that it is put to good use, prove to be of prime importance when it is a question of differentiating the horizons of the public action.

To answer the Institutional criticism, we can show that democracy is flexible and can correct its mistakes, a cardinal virtue in a world as complex and uncertain as ours, that the political scientist Rodger Payne has called "the reactivity of the democratic regime."[8] Jonah himself noted that the autocracy had at least two risks attached to a centralized bureaucracy: the propensity to make mistakes for lack of adequate information and the propensity to exaggerate the mistakes made in the past. On the contrary, democracy has the capacity to learn from its mistakes, which might be its greatest strength.

The analysis developed by the economist and philosopher Amartya Sen about the relationship between famine and democracy is particularly illuminating here to understand the link between the distribution of resources and democracy. As he writes, "a famine is a sign that people do not have enough to eat, not that there is not enough to eat." The central notion of his reasoning is that of "access rights" granted or not to the most fragile populations. Sen's well-known conclusion is absolutely topical: "Never has a famine occurred in a country that respects democratic rules and multiparty politics." Due to the existence of elections, opposition parties, public expression channels open to public criticism, "the shock wave of famine is shaking up political leaders and the ruling elite" in a democracy, unlike what happens in a dictatorship. According to Sen, democracy has a "protective" role against the effects of natural disasters.

## Globalization and its environmental discontent

One simple metric of how far globalization has gone in the last decades is the degree of openness of the world's economies:[9] It has more than doubled on average over the last fifty years, from 25% in 1960 to 55% in 2017 (Graph 11.1). It is true for low and middle countries as well as high-income countries.

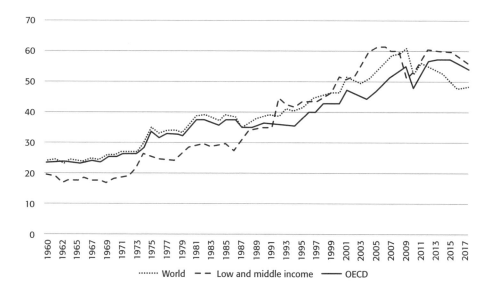

Graph 11.1   Globalization in the last 50 years (openness ratio, i.e. trade in % of GDP)

*Source:* World Bank

There are at least two different questions regarding this important dynamic of contemporary economies of the environment: The first has to do with the increase of natural resource consumption and environmental damage triggered by the intensification of international trade of goods and services that globalization triggered. The second has to do with the effect of trade agreements on the possibility of pursuing and implementing ambitious environmental policy and the opportunity of a globalized world to develop global environmental governance. Let us take a look at each issue in turn.

Globalization has obviously fed a "physical trade" that is today at a peak, reaching 11.6 billion tonnes in 2017 (see Chapter 7). Three other material flows are not taken into account in this already impressive figure: carbon flows, water flows, and transports flux.

In fact, because of the extent of globalization, the transfer of carbon between regions, either physically or embodied in production, represents a substantial fraction of global carbon emissions.[10] Approximately 25% of all $CO_2$ emissions from human activities "flow" (i.e. are imported or exported) from one country to another. Some studies find that as high as 10.2 billion tonnes $CO_2$ or 37% of global emissions are from fossil fuels traded internationally and an additional 6.4 billion tonnes $CO_2$ or 23% of global emissions are embodied in traded goods.[11] In other words, when apparent and hidden flows of carbon are accounted for, they represent a substantial majority of global emissions (60%).

Water flows can be measured using the "water footprint" metric that measures the amount of water used to produce each of the goods and services we use. As is the case for carbon, a nation's water footprint can be viewed from two perspectives: production and consumption.[12] Data for some countries in the world reveal some striking differences between countries with respect to these indicators, regardless of income level or population size (see Table 11.1).

| Table 11.1 Internal and external water footprint (2011) | | | | |
|---|---|---|---|---|
| | Population in milllions | Total water footprint million m3/year | Water footprint per capita/litre/day | Internal % | External % |
| France | 59.4 | 110,000 | 4,900 | 53 | 47 |
| USA | 289 | 820,000 | 7,800 | 80 | 20 |
| China | 1,280 | 1 400,000 | 2,900 | 90 | 10 |
| South Africa | 45.2 | 57,000 | 3,400 | 78 | 22 |
| Brazil | 175 | 360,000 | 5,600 | 91 | 9 |
| UK | 59.3 | 75,000 | 3,400 | 25 | 75 |
| Germany | 82.1 | 120,000 | 3,900 | 31 | 69 |
| Norway | 4.5 | 6,400 | 3,900 | 32 | 68 |

Source: Water Footprint Network

Transports of goods flux have considerably increased in just the last fifteen years, from 40% to 70% depending on the mode of transportation, generating considerable greenhouse gas emissions (Table 11.2).

Finally, globalization also offers the possibility for rich countries to easily outsource pollutions to so-called "pollution havens." For instance, more than

| Table 11.2. Goods transportation, 2000–2016 | | | | |
|---|---|---|---|---|
| | Air transport, freight (billion tonne-km) | Container port traffic (TEU: 20 foot equivalent units, millions) | World Seaborne Trade (total goods unloaded, millions of tonnes) | Freight transport Road, billion tonne-kilometres |
| 2000 | 118 | 224 | 6,273 | 6,877 |
| 2010 | 182 | 560 | 8,444 | 12,148 |
| 2016 | 187 | 695 | 10,282 | 14,130 |
| Increase in % | 37 | 68 | 39 | 51 |

*Source:* World Bank, UNCTAD, OECD, and author's calculations

90% of deaths related to air pollution occur in low-income countries where high-income countries have outsourced their more damaging pollution.

The second issue regards the legal constraints put on environmental policy by trade agreements and the opportunity of global environmental governance. It is not just that trade agreements increase the flow of goods and services traded and carbon and water flows that go with them, it is also that they can put in place new rules constraining environmental policy of parties. The example of CETA is a case in point (Box 11.1).

## Box 11.1 The CETA and environmental policy

On September 21, 2017, a very controversial free trade agreement came into effect: CETA. This is a trade agreement signed in October 2016 by Canada and the European Union. The agreement aims to facilitate trade in manufactured food products with the aim of increasing European and Canadian GDP over the long term.

The investor-state dispute settlement mechanism guarantees investors the opportunity to claim compensation for injury caused by the host State if it breaches its commitments under the Agreement. Its objective is to ensure a stable and predictable investor environment, to protect foreign investors from discriminatory or unfair treatment by governments, particularly in sectors that involve large capital inflows and that bind investors to the host State for long periods.

Several large pending cases directly involve the environmental or health policies of some states. The Swedish energy company Vattenfall requires under the Energy Charter treaty 4.7 billion euros compensation to Germany, whose decision to exit the nuclear power has led to the shutdown of two nuclear power plants. Similarly, the rejection of the "Keystone XL" 12 pipeline project by the Obama administration, citing the climate argument, prompted NAFTA's ISDS referral by its Canadian manufacturer, TransCanada. The latter requires US $15 billion in compensation from the US state.

The initial ISDS involved a panel of three arbitrarily appointed private arbitrators, sometimes alternately acting as arbitrators and lawyers and paid by the parties to the conflict. The modalities of these tribunals have been strongly criticized for the proven risk of conflicts of interest, the transparency of judgments, and the lengthy and costly procedures. Instead, (Article 8.27) a more stable and transparent system called ICS (Investment Court System) was preferred. This system, originally proposed by France, involves a permanent court composed of fifteen judges appointed by the Canadian and European authorities for terms of five or ten years. Cases will be randomly assigned to them on a rotational basis, and will be paid directly by a mutual fund funded by Ottawa and Brussels to limit the potential for conflicts of interest.

Its operation may present the risk of constraining the ability of states to adopt new environmental legislation and thus to call into question certain democratic decisions. Asymmetric by construction, it can only be seized by foreign investors, actually introducing a privilege over domestic companies, unjustified when national jurisdictions already provide an effective degree of protection.

There is no guarantee in the Treaty that the future environmental provisions necessary to achieve France's energy transition and sustainable development objectives will not be challenged before this jurisdiction. It is also impossible to pronounce on the possibility of a possible conviction of France for its environmental protection.

But can globalization produce a global environmental governance? It has not done so yet, at least not on the scale of current and future environmental challenges. The first United Nations conference on the environment, held in Stockholm from June 15–16, 1972 was held in the almost general indifference of the Heads of State and Government. From the first steps of what would become global environmental governance, the question of its real scope and its effectiveness was raised.

In fact, the number of multilateral environmental agreements (MEAs) has increased considerably since 1972, especially after the Rio Conference (which commemorated the twentieth anniversary of Stockholm in 1992). The only decade of 1990 will see the signing of more than one hundred different agreements (less than 40 agreements existed before Stockholm. Today, there are 500 agreements and institutions on the environment, leading to thousands of decisions whose overall logic and legal scope are questionable. However, all signed texts are not ratified and even less applied, far from it. Thus, among the twenty or so major agreements governing the atmosphere, maritime areas, biodiversity or toxic substances, the level of ratification varies today from 94 UN member states to almost universality (almost all UN member states are parties to the agreement), with strong regional disparities.

If one looks at environmental degradations since 1972 and 1992, which marks the entry and resolve of nation-states into a general process of international environmental cooperation, the situation on almost all fronts has steadily deteriorated except for the ozone layer.[13]

As shown by the success of the Montreal Protocol already alluded to in previous chapters, global environmental governance is not destined to fail, as it is too often concluded, but it must be reformed in depth in order to be truly effective. Environmental governance is thus taken, at the global level, in a contradiction:

It presupposes, to be fully effective, a geometrically variable cooperation between the sovereign states according to the different environmental issues concerned (water, toxic substances); but it also requires an integrated institutional architecture to avoid overlap, duplication, and contradiction, all the more so since the interrelationships between the major contemporary environmental problems (climate, biodiversity, ecosystems) are more and more strong and apparent. Global environmental governance must therefore be both deep and specialized, in order to be closer to the ideal of an informed government of global public goods, but also general and integrated, in order to make the best use of scarce financial resources, and limited human capital.

## Digital and ecological transition: Friends or foes?

California is home to two unique types of ecosystems: natural ecosystems and digital ecosystems. The first have entered a structural crisis since the beginning of 2010: drought, fires, floods, air pollution. The second are flourishing: Apple has become in 2018 the first company in history to reach $1,000 billion of market capitalization. The Californian allegory of the two ecosystems tells us how much the digital transition is a success and how much the ecological transition is a failure.

But is there any relation between the two transitions? Can we reasonably say that one is conducted at the detriment of the other? A number of elements support this hypothesis: the high volumes of energy (80% fossil today) required by the data processing and storage centers,[14] the growing quantities of waste produced by the metamorphosis of our society of consumption in society of delivery,[15] the important ecological damage associated, upstream, with the extraction of the components of digital devices[16] and, downstream, with their minimal recycling, when it exists.

More importantly, natural resource extraction and consumption growing patterns suggest that the promised de-materialization of the digital transition is morphing into an economic re-coupling (see Chapter 7). If the digital transition makes work more efficient, it is at the price (most of the time invisible on the market) of increased consumption of energy and natural resources. It is therefore relying on an extensive (and extractive) growth much more than an intensive one (digital growth is much more materialistic than immaterial, in fact more Marxian than Smithian).

Since the fruits of labor productivity have been increasingly unevenly distributed over the last thirty years, this increased consumption of natural resources and energy is in fact mainly used to finance the lifestyle of the wealthiest segments of the population to the detriment of the more vulnerable socially who suffer in addition to the ecological backlash of this accelerated extraction and consumption. We are thus faced with a double social inequality, upstream and downstream of the production process.

One could think that the developed countries, where the digital transition is the most advanced, are experiencing an economic dematerialization. But this is not the case: The consumption of natural resources per capita in Europe increases between 2000 and 2010 from 13 to 15 tonnes per inhabitant (counting exports and imports) and again between 2010 and 2017 to reach 16 tonnes per inhabitant (it follows more or less the same evolution in North America). For OECD countries, this indicator increases from 14 to 16 tonnes between 2000 and 2017. The "material footprint" data (taking into account the overall ecological impact of economies) confirm this dynamic: GDP and material footprint are almost aligned with each other between 2000 and 2010 for OECD countries, with the material footprint exceeding GDP over the period.

Even more fundamentally, the two transitions, ecological and digital, lead our economies toward opposite horizons: Where the digital transition pretends to dematerialize, the ecological transition intends at re-materializing. When the digital transition gives the illusion of a weightless economy suspended in the "cloud," the ecological transition is meant to remind us how much economies are weighing on terrestrial ecosystems and invites humans, for their own good, to reduce this footprint before economies do not give in under its weight.

Moreover, where the ecology is futuristic, the digital is, in spite of appearances, presentist and often backward-looking. The digital transition engages humans in a war against time that shortens all their horizons and prevents them from serenely thinking about the future in the name of perpetual agitation, which constantly entertains attention and swears by the "new news" innovation designed to make the previous obsolete. Hence the great convergence, this one quite real, between the world of innovation and that of finance (Silicon Valley is now as much a financial center than it is a "tech hub").

A recent book pushes even further this temporal paradox of the digital transition. Cathy O'Neil[17] shows not only that the arbitrary use of algorithms leads to a further decline in social justice in the United States, but also how they lock individuals in their past choices, assigning them to an immutable future extrapolated by machines. If the destiny of humanity is now to educate the robots to govern humans,[18] it seems that we educate robots to unfair government.

Also disturbing, the digital transition is occupied by the hypertrophy of the virtual world (video games, digital photographs, social networks) in proportion to the atrophy of the real world. As if the digital was intended to archive the reality before it is swept away by ecological crises. The digital transition, much more focused on the past than the future, would be fundamentally a gigantic diversion and conservation endeavor that masks and softens the destruction of the biosphere. In archiving a world we are destroying, the digital transition becomes the memory of our failure.

Can we not say at least that the digital transition is a formidable accelerator of knowledge and action essential to the resolution of ecological crises? This is all but obvious: There is nothing to indicate that humanity is tremendously more intelligent now than twenty years ago. The increasing intensity of ecological crises is rather a sign that the great race between understanding our environment and destroying it is being lost. To take only the example of climate science, its broad lines, incredibly robust, were determined in the late 1980s, exactly before the dawn of the digital transition. By the same token, low-tech civic movements of the 1960s and 1970s have done considerably more for the ecological transition than social networks.

But would it not be easy to put the digital transition at the service of the ecological transition? It is the contrary that is more and more apparent: The digital transition hurts the ecological transition materially, symbolically, and psychologically. Because it gives the comfortable illusion of a dematerialization of the economy at a time when we must measure and reduce its destructive footprint of our well-being. Because it accelerates endlessly time to make it profitable and shortens our collective horizons at the precise moment when we need to think about the future and focus on the long-run. Because it locks us into societies of intermittency and diversion, of high frequency but of low intensity, whereas the social and ecological challenges that we face require maximum and continuous social energy.

The young twenty-first century seems to be characterized by two crises and two transitions. The two crises, that this book has explored at length, are the crisis of inequality and the biosphere. Apparently conflicting, they can actually be thought about and mitigated jointly. The two transitions, the digital transition and the ecological transition, on the other hand, appear more and more incompatible.

# 12

# Urban sustainability and polycentric transition

Under the combined impact of globalization and urbanization, cities (and larger metropolitan areas) have become key economic and ecological players along nation-states in our globalization: The 265 metropolitan areas of the OECD now concentrate more than half of the population and jobs. The combined effect of globalization and urbanization has thus resulted in a third revolution: agglomeration. Cities matter greatly in the opportunities given to their residents, starting with their well-being (geography influences history) but also have a critical impact on sustainability (they account for 66% of the energy consumed and 75% of $CO_2$ emissions). Put simply, cities are spaces of dynamic justice.

## What is a city?

So far, no standardized international criteria exist for determining what a city is, in particular what its boundaries are and what its functions should be. There are four possible definitions of a city related to four different disciplines leading to key concepts and metrics to analyze and reform urban systems from the perspective of the sustainability–justice nexus.

The first one is a geographic and political definition, related to functional and administrative dimensions. The French statistical agency INSEE defines an "urban unit" on the basis of two criteria: the continuity of buildings and the number of inhabitants. An urban unit is a municipality or group of municipalities with a continuous built area (no more than 200 meters between two buildings) with a population of at least 2,000 people. Living areas that do not fit those two criteria are considered rural areas. The administrative definition is combined with two density criteria. A "large urban area" is a set of urban areas, in one piece and without enclave, constituted by an urban pole of more than 10,000 jobs, and by rural areas or urban peripheral areas of which at least 40% of the resident population having a job works in the urban pole. We can add to those criteria the fact that people living in urban areas share its infrastructures (roads, bridges, schools).

Cities can thus be defined as non-rural, dense and inter-connected living areas. The term "urban systems" reflects this complexity. Already, the question of the hierarchy between spaces and the issue of mobility between them appear salient. This functional definition brings us naturally to the economic approach of cities, which is centered around the notion of agglomeration. A simple glance at a map of the geographical distribution of economic wealth in today's world reveals a striking contradiction: The "death of distance" induced by technological innovations, progress of means of transport, low cost of energy, decline in customs tariffs and administrative barriers to trade in recent decades is superimposed on a hyper-concentration of wealth on a global scale and within each country, dictated by the economic and social benefits of agglomeration. While economic location should no longer matter and in a sense matters less with globalization, it seems that it has never mattered so much within each country. The expected "end of geography" because of globalization has therefore engendered a triumph of space. How to understand this paradox of distance?

In simple terms, humans have never been more nomadic and sedentary at the same time. Globalization, which should have abolished distance and make localization indifferent, was accompanied by another revolution: For the first time in the long history of humanity (seven million years), more humans now live in cities than outside them (it is the case since 2007) while cities occupy only five percent of the planet's surface. This twin dynamic results in a considerable concentration of wealth and opportunities in localities open to global flows. This agglomeration presents itself in the developed world under the features of "metropolization," whereby large and complex globalized urban areas become driving economic forces for whole countries. It is the logic of agglomeration that holds together globalization and urbanization and makes it possible to understand the paradox of distance.

To grasp this new urban momentum, the "new economic geography" (Krugman, 1991)[1] has developed since the early 1990s models where distance is the key aspect of economic activity. Trade-off between transport cost and economies of scale (due to increasing returns in human interactions) determine in these models where the production should be localized. Urban economics, which basic intuition is to consider simultaneously and not separately housing and transport costs, has refined those intuitions at the household level showing that economic decisions beyond production are shaped by spatial factors. Space driven decisions – which main variables are employment concentration, the presence of social and cultural amenities, the price of land, cost and size of housing and travel costs – explain, in the words of Brueckner (2011),[2] "why cities exist" and how they evolve.

In this perspective, a city is a place of efficient agglomeration of jobs, goods, services, people, and ideas. When its size increases, the benefits of economic, social and non-market amenities that the city can provide also increase. But the price of housing and costs related to congestion also go up because of concentration, triggering social issues and potential inequality. Urban sprawl can somewhat respond to this costly dynamic by lowering housing prices (or increasing the size of available housing). This spread in turn increases the distance between home and employment (or place of study or leisure) and thus forced or voluntary movement (such as car commuting), that in turn generate environmental problems such as local and global pollution. The trade-off for individuals between the cost of housing and transportation, which results in the determination of their preferred location, is not just about private cost and benefits but fundamentally about social cost and benefits. The case of France illustrates how ecological issues arise alongside these economic dynamics, bringing with them justice and sustainability issues (Box 12.1).

## Box 12.1 The double penalty of urban sprawl: The case of France.

Urban space has risen by nearly 20% in mainland France in the last decade only (27% for the periphery of urban centers), cities now occupying a quarter of the national territory. In the urban area of Paris for instance, between 1968 and the mid 2000s, people live on average 5 km farther from the center of the city. This urban sprawl can be explained by the skyrocketing price of housing in city centers. While the real cost of housing[3] index was 60 in 1990 in France, it reached 102 in 2017 (for OECD countries on average, the index was 80 in 1990 and 107 in 2017). Yet, urban sprawl is also an ecological matter.

In 2015, each French citizen emitted an average of 5.1 metric tons of $CO_2$, based solely on activities within the country (production or territorial emissions), while British and German citizens emitted 6.2 and 9.6 metric tons each and the EU average was 6.8 metric tons. This is reasonably close to the world average (4.9 metric tons) and is due to the importance of nuclear energy in electricity generation in France (75%). Moreover, greenhouse gas emissions have significantly fallen between 1990 and 2017, by some 15%. But France has not managed to contain its road transportation emissions during the last 25 years because of its urban sprawl. Transport (95% of it by road) accounts for 30% of all French emissions, by far the largest contribution. While emissions in all sectors have fallen between 1990 and 2017, sometimes very significantly, emissions from road transportation have on the contrary increased (see table).

| MtCO$_2$e and % | | | | |
|---|---|---|---|---|
| | 1990 | 2017 | Difference in volume | Difference in % |
| Total | 546.4 | 466.1 | -80.3 | -15 |
| Transports | 122.3 | 137.9 | 15.6 | 13 |
| Buildings | 91.4 | 91 | -0.4 | - 0,4 |
| Agriculture | 93.8 | 88.4 | -5.4 | -6 |
| Industry | 143.9 | 79 | -64.9 | -45 |
| Energy production | 78.1 | 54.5 | -23.6 | -30 |
| Waste | 17 | 15 | -2 | -12 |

Source: CITEPA

The combination of increasing road transport and prevalence of diesel engines among vehicles (close to 70%) results in urban pollution harming the well-being of the French: Close to 60,000 people die prematurely in France each year because of urban pollution and among the top twenty largest cities in France all but three exceed WHO sanitary thresholds (see graph).

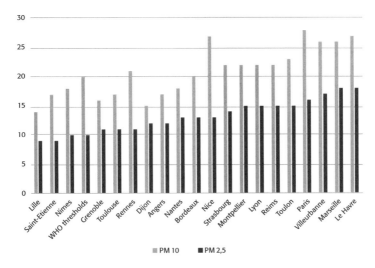

Air pollution in the twenty largest cities in France (annual exposure in µg/m3)

But there is more to cities than economic dynamics. The third definition comes from sociology and defines cities of spaces of cooperation (sociology). Indeed, contemporary research indicates that urban spaces are the theater of social interactions that go beyond economic benefits and trade-offs. People find in cities multiple sources of well-being: security, mobility, and social networks, but also culture, knowledge, emotions. The urban planner and American activist Jane Jacobs has superbly described and defended this cooperative diversity of urban spaces.

In *The Death and Life of Great American Cities*, she shows how neighborhoods are not just collections of buildings but webs of relationships and social networks. The key notion here is that of urban diversity, meaning that urban spaces should have different use for different people with streets being kept busy through day and night by different kinds of people using them for different purposes: "Streets and opportunities to turn corners must be frequent"; "The district must mingle buildings that vary in age and condition"; and finally a city should provide in its districts a "dense concentration of people, for whatever purposes they may be there." In other words, the urban space must be shared to achieve its essential purpose.

Finally, the city is a human settlement submitted to environmental conditions and affecting in return its local and global environment. The key concepts here are that of urban metabolism and urban adaptation. Urban metabolism[4] considers the city as a living organism or ecosystem and focuses on the amount of resources that it needs to function (water, energy). Urban adaptation is especially important with respect to climate change and refers to the process of adjustment to actual or expected climate and its effects on urban systems (e.g. heat wave, floods).

## The rise of cities

It might be difficult to believe, but in 1700, only two percent of the world's inhabitants lived in cities, a century later only three percent of humans lived there. This proportion rises to 15% in 1900 under the combined effect of urbanization, industrialization and globalization and then doubles to 30% in just fifty years, the 50% threshold is reached in 2007. In 2018, 55% of the world's population lived in urban settlements. The growth of urban spaces has been twice as fast as that of the world's population and it is predicted that the physical expansion of cities during the first three decades of the twenty-first century will be greater than the cumulative expansion of all cities in the course of human history as a whole. According to the World Bank, today's urban population of about 3.5 billion people is projected to reach five billion by 2030 (or two-thirds of the global population, see graph). The growth of the urban population since 1950 has been extremely rapid, from 751 million to 4.2 billion in 2018 (an increase by a factor 5.5 in 70 years, see Graph 12.1).

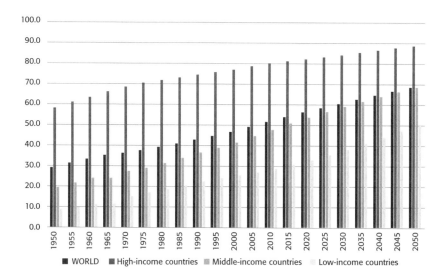

Graph 12.1   Percentage of population residing in urban areas by country, 1950–2050

*Source:* United Nations, Department of Economic and Social Affairs, Population Division (2018). World Urbanization Prospects: The 2018 Revision, online edition

Half of the urban population now lives in cities larger than 500,000 people and mega-cities of more than ten million, already home to seven percent of the global population, are expected to grow further in numbers by 2030 (Table 12.1).

| Table 12.1 The global urban population, 2018 and 2030 | | | | | | |
|---|---|---|---|---|---|---|
| | 2018 | | | 2030 | | |
| | Nb | Population | % | Nb | Population | % |
| Urban | | 4,220 | 55.3 | | 5,167 | 60.4 |
| 10 million or more | 33 | 529 | 6.9 | 43 | 752 | 8.8 |
| 5 to 10 million | 48 | 325 | 4.3 | 66 | 448 | 5.2 |
| 1 to 5 million | 467 | 926 | 12.1 | 597 | 1,183 | 13.8 |
| 500,000 to 1 million | 598 | 415 | 5.4 | 710 | 494 | 5.8 |
| Rural | | 3,413 | 44.7 | | 3,384 | 39.6 |

Source: United Nations, Department of Economic and Social Affairs, Population Division (2018). World Urbanization Prospects: 2018 Revision, online edition

International inequality in urbanization is obvious at the regional level: While Northern America (with 82% of its population living in urban areas in 2018), Latin America and the Caribbean (81%), Europe (74%) and Oceania (68%) display high rates of urbanization, India has the largest rural population (893 million), followed by China (578 million) and Africa remains mostly rural, with 43% of its population living in urban areas (but these two continents will account for 90% of the future growth in urban population).

## Justice and the city

A city is by definition a politicized space, a domain defined by the legal authority under which it is placed by a human community. It is therefore by nature a place of justice between people, a territory governed by the law. If Latin defines on the one hand *urbs* (the physical space) and on the other *civitas* (the community of citizens), Greek's *polis* means at once city and political community. Actually, cities are institutions, in the sense of economist Douglas North: "humanly devised constraints that structure political, economic, and social interactions."

Space is not only, in the words of Henri Lefèbvre, "the projection on the ground of social relations." It also helps to structure their projection in time, their dynamics. Space, in short, has a lasting impact for the people who occupy it. Social injustice is reflected in space (through spatial inscription of social inequality like the striking racial segregation of the city of Detroit); spatial organization produces injustice (spatial creation of social inequalities, like the outsourcing of pollution in poorer neighborhoods); and social relations, especially inequalities, produce space (social creation of space, like when public spaces are reclaimed by citizens in New York City). Citizens are "people in places."

Social sciences took hold of the question of spatial and urban justice in the 1920s and 1930s, with the "urban ecology" approach developed by the socio-logical school of Chicago, which was particularly concerned with the influence of spatial factors on social phenomena. The first occurrence of the concept of "spatial justice" in the academic literature goes back to the work of David Harvey.[5]

There are schematically four contemporary theories of justice that can all be translated into theories of spatial justice. The first one is the libertarian school, which recognizes as just or unjust the procedures for allocating resources and not the results of these procedures (putting procedural justice ahead of distrib-utive justice). A spatial policy based on such a conception of justice could tolerate spatial inequalities so strong that they would result in a considerable economic inefficiency (this is the case of the vertiginous costs engendered today by congestion and pollution in major Chinese cities). The utilitarian model, originally designed by Jeremy Bentham, is more demanding, as it aims at maximizing the collective well-being considered on average. Spatial inequality is acceptable according to this view as long as the average standard of living is increasing by physical agglomeration of economic resources (and possible redistribution from the most dynamic urban centers to the least well-off localities). To get a clearer idea of the spatial translation of these two approaches, it should be noted that the position defended by the World Bank in a report[6] devoted to geographical issues oscillates more or less between the libertarian and utilitarian conceptions of spatial justice.

The approaches developed in the 1970s and 1980s by John Rawls and Amartya Sen have in common to be much more refined. They are based respectively on the rights of individuals and the real inequalities they suffer. The Rawlsian model aims to equip human societies with just institutions that recognize each person's basic freedoms (in the form of "primary goods"). In a given urban space, one could thus identify the Rawlsian precepts to the combination of a universal right to mobility and a priority given to the most disadvantaged districts (in the form of specific housing and education policies for instance). Amartya Sen, unlike Rawls, is interested in the concrete situa-tions of inequality, situated injustices, and not just the conditions of possibility and the properties of just institutions. In the perspective of Sen, cities must therefore become vectors of the human development and capabilities of their inhabitants that is to say of their right to a substantial freedom to be and to act (urban spaces should therefore for instance be equally conducive in terms of access to employment).

In this latter perspective, urban inequality can take many forms, from income disparities of neighborhoods, segregation, and unequal access to mobility. A recent report of the OECD[7] shows that in US cities, the "lack of public transport connections between minority neighborhoods and employment centers hinders job opportunities for residents of these neighborhoods." A difference of just one percentage point higher in the share of white residents can translate into eighteen more jobs available within a thirty-minute commute on public transport. This can widen gaps in unemployment and therefore opportunities given to residents. A typical illustration of urban inequality in capabilities, with cities acting as multipliers or dividers (vectors or obstacles) of people's capabilities.

## The ecological impact of cities

For the last thirty years, cities have been growing in perimeter, whereas for centuries they had tended to become denser. On average, the world's urban areas are growing today twice as fast as their population, with considerable ecological consequences.[8]

Cities thus find themselves at the heart of climate change mitigation policies needed in coming years and decades as they account for around two-thirds of global energy use, three-quarters of global energy-related greenhouse gas (GHG) emissions and up to half of global overall GHG emissions.

The form of cities (density and functionality) has obviously important impacts on its resource use: first, on resources used for constructing the built environment (including infrastructure and buildings), and second, on resources used for operating urban systems. Both impacts relate to the notion of urban metabolism. A "compact city" will have much less environmental impact than a city.

More precisely, according to the International Energy Agency (IEA), buildings are the biggest source of energy consumption globally: Buildings and buildings construction sectors combined are responsible for 36% of global final energy consumption and nearly 40% of total direct and indirect $CO_2$ emissions (final energy consumption by buildings doubled between 1971 and 2010 to reach 2,794 Mtoe). Under current policies, the global energy demand of buildings is projected by the IEA to grow by an additional 838 Mtoe by 2035 compared to 2010.

These simple facts mean that the way cities regulate buildings will be critical to mitigate climate change. A recent analysis by the Global Commission on the Economy and Climate has identified four priorities regarding the building sector (Table 12.2) that could, if implemented, represent 57% of all needed cuts in emissions in coming decades.

**Table 12.2 Priority actions for a low carbon building strategy**

| | |
|---|---|
| New building heating efficiency | New buildings are constructed at passive heating levels: <30 kWh/m2 from 2020–2030 and 15 kWh/m2 from 2031–2050 |
| Heating retrofits | Old buildings are upgraded at a rate of 1.4–3% of the building stock per year, such that all existing buildings are upgraded by 2040. The retrofit reduces building energy intensity by 30–40% compared with the baseline scenario and includes heat pumps in mid-latitude countries |
| Appliances and lighting | Efficient lighting and appliances are aggressively deployed, based on the IEA's 2DS scenario |
| Solar PV | Building-mounted solar PV is ambitiously installed, based on the assumption that half of the solar PV in IEA's 2DS scenario is distributed PV deployed in cities, in proportion to the regional urban population. |

*Source:* Gouldson et al., "Accelerating Low-Carbon Development in the World's Cities," 2015

Along similar lines, the IEA estimates that improvements in space heating, water heating, and space cooling combined could increase energy efficiency in buildings by 70% up until 2040. As a key part of this overall strategy, the need for new energy efficiency standards is directly related to the reform of building codes that have been found to be one of the most effective and cost-effective policies in reducing greenhouse gas emissions from both existing and new buildings (IEA, 2013).[9] In the scenario outlined by Global Commission on the Economy and Climate, the implementation of new building heating efficiency in the residential sector alone actually represents 15% of all cuts in emissions, more than any other policy (including transport and waste).

LEED (Leadership in Energy and Environmental Design), the most widely used green building rating system in the world, through its certification system, allows best practices to be adopted globally with respect to sustainable construction sites, energy efficiency, water efficiency, materials and resource use, indoor environmental quality, emissions, operations, and maintenance.[10]

The design of urban space and buildings thus has a global impact. This is why cities have been gradually integrated in climate negotiations in recent years. In fact, the contribution of cities is crucial in making up for nation-states shortcomings when it comes to climate mitigation. A recent study has showed that ambitious climate change mitigation policies by cities could generate an annual GHG savings of 3.7 Gt $CO_2$e in 2030 and 8.0 Gt $CO_2$e in 2050.[11] These emission reductions, additional to the national pledges, could represent close to 20–30% of the gap between COP 21 national pledges and a sustainable climate future (see Chapter 8).

What is most encouraging is that the COP 21 has seen for the first time in climate negotiations history cities become full actors of the process, although they were not directly involved in the negotiations themselves. Cities networks such as Cities Climate Leadership Group (C40), Local Governments for Sustainability (ICLEI), and the United Cities and Local Governments (UCLG) have been very active all through the two weeks of the COP 21 and the newly formed "Compact of Mayors," bringing together these networks, has gained momentum. The final declaration of the Climate Summit for local leaders states that the willingness to "Advance and exceed the expected goals of the 2015 Paris Agreement to be reached at COP 21."[12] The UN hosted Lima-Paris Action Agenda (LPAA) and NAZCA (Non State Actors Zone for Climate Action) platforms have registered climate actions and pledges covering over 7,000 cities, including the most vulnerable to climate change, from over 100 countries with a combined population with one and a quarter billion people.

Yet cities are not really acknowledged in the text of the Paris Agreement. They were mentioned just once in the pre-agreement text published before the COP 21 (in the "III. DECISIONS TO GIVE EFFECT TO THE AGREEMENT" section, where the parties welcome "the efforts of all actors to address climate change, including those of civil society, the private sector, financial institutions, cities and other subnational authorities, local communities and indigenous peoples" and invite all the actors "above to scale up their efforts and support further undertaken by Parties to reduce [and/or avoid] emissions and/or to build resilience and decrease vulnerability to the adverse effects of climate change").

In the final version of the text, while this statement is reaffirmed, the specific contribution of local governments and cities to climate change mitigation and adaptation is not even mentioned.[13] The need for an efficient cooperation mechanism between nation-states (that remain at the center of climate negotiations) and cities is even clearer after the COP 21.

Beyond the strategic issue of climate change mitigation, urban metabolism can take many forms as a new UN report[14] shows. In terms of method, authors identify and carefully consider different "layers" of the problem: "Layer 1" relates to spatial boundaries, constituent cities, population, and economy; "Layer 2" to biophysical characteristics such as land area, urbanized area, climate and building gross floor area; "Layer 3" relates to urban energy metabolism with consumption of parameters materials, water, food, energy – all types; electricity sources; and sectors related to energy consumption (water, waste water, food, transport, housing), waste generated from consumption; "Layer 4" should examine the role of utilities, the number and ownership of distributors and suppliers of resources: water, energy (electricity, natural gas, access to basic services), food, waste; "Layer 5" finally looks at policy frameworks, existing policies that shape the direction of resource flows. To support this analytical approach, a wide-ranging dataset[15] has been recently put together.

## The ecological impact on cities

Cities are vulnerable to existing and future ecological crises. An obvious example of current environmental crisis is air quality. Air pollution is actually the first environmental cause of death in the European Union, responsible for more than 400,000 premature deaths per year. Urban areas residents are especially exposed to this pollution: A total of 16% of the EU-28 urban population was exposed to PM10 levels above the daily limit value and approximately 50% was exposed to concentrations exceeding the stricter WHO AQG value for PM10 in 2014 (Table 12.3).

**Table 12.3 Urban population in the EU-20 exposed to air pollutant concentrations above certain EU and WHO reference concentrations (2012–2014), in %**

| | |
|---|---|
| PM2.5 | 8–12 |
| PM10 | 16–21 |
| O3 (Ozone) | 8–17 |
| NO2 | 7–9 |
| Benzo(a)pyrene (BaP) | 20–24 |

*Source:* European Environmental Agency

At the global level, according to WHO's most recent survey of close to 4,500 cities worldwide, only 20% of the urban population surveyed live in areas that comply with WHO air quality guideline levels for PM2.5, with average particulate air pollution levels in many developing cities can be 4 to 15 times higher than WHO air quality guideline levels (almost all of cities in low- and middle-income countries with more than 100,000 inhabitants do not meet WHO air quality guidelines). Of the ten most polluted cities in the world, nine are in India. Highlighting how sustainability is connected to justice in urban centers, the WHO notes that "health inequities may be more pronounced in poor neighborhoods, which are more often sited near environmental hazards, such as highways, power plants, and industrial complexes."

Regarding future crises, "natural" disasters loom large on the urban horizon. According to the UN, of the 1,146 cities with at least 500,000 inhabitants in 2018, 679 (59%) were at high risk of exposure to at least one of six types of natural disaster, namely cyclones, floods, droughts, earthquakes, landslides, and volcanic eruptions. Taken together, cities of 500,000 inhabitants or more facing high risk of exposure to at least one type of natural disaster were home to 1.4 billion people in 2018. One hundred and eighty-nine cities – most located along coastlines – were at high risk of exposure to two or more types of natural disaster; 26 cities – including megacities Manila, Osaka and Tokyo – faced high risk of exposure to three or more types of disaster.

According to the 2018 Verisk Maplecroft Report, out of the one hundred fastest growing cities by population, 84 are rated 'extreme risk', with a further fourteen in the 'high risk' category regarding climate change (the top five of cities at risk include Jakarta, Indonesia, Manila, Philippines Lagos, Nigeria, Baghdad, Iraq, and Addis Ababa, Ethiopia).

Inequalities between individuals and groups in the face of urban social-ecological disasters will depend on a combination of their respective exposure (socio-economic context, geographical context, individual behaviors) and their respective sensitivity (age, state of health). The significance of this distinction is clear: Different people are at various risk resulting from extreme natural phenomena.

A number of studies has shown that the human impact of Hurricane Katrina (that hit the city of New Orleans in September 2005) was determined by racial and social inequality. Brown University sociologist John Logan[16] demonstrated that the neighborhoods of the social groups with the least resources were the hardest hit. Specifically, almost half of the population in the most damaged areas was black, poorer, and less employed than non-affected areas. Logan concludes that most vulnerable residents have also been shown to be at higher risk, emphasizing the cumulative nature of social and environmental inequalities. The least favored were the least prepared to deal with the hurricane, the least able to escape it, the least likely to be rescued by the government and the least able to return to a normal life after the disaster.[17]

## Toward sustainable urban systems

### Re-inventing the city

The Habitat III Conference in October 2016 saw the adoption of the "New Urban Agenda" setting new objectives for urban governance. The documents' social-ecological ambition is clear: "By readdressing the way cities and human settlements are planned, designed, financed, developed, governed and managed, the New Urban Agenda will help to end poverty and hunger in all its forms and dimensions; reduce inequalities; promote sustained, inclusive and sustainable economic growth; achieve gender equality and the empowerment of all women and girls in order to fully harness their vital contribution to sustainable development; improve human health and well-being; foster resilience; and protect the environment."

Further, the text offers a new vision of "cities for all" a new approach combining equity and sustainability demands: "referring to the equal use and enjoyment of cities and human settlements, seeking to promote inclusivity and ensure that all inhabitants, of present and future generations, without discrimination of any kind, are able to inhabit and produce just, safe, healthy, accessible, affordable, resilient, and sustainable cities and human settlements to foster prosperity and quality of life for all."

The Lancet Commission (2015) has also called for an urban "transition" that supports and promotes lifestyles that are healthy for the individual and for the planet. Steps to achieve this transition include development of a highly energy efficient building stock, ease of low-cost active transportation and increased access to green spaces. Such measures could at once ease the environmental pressure from cities while enhancing the health of their residents.

## Measuring and advancing urban well-being

This quest for "urban co-benefits" calls for new metrics to guide urban policy. Cities, like nations, need to reform the indicators with which they are managed and governed (see Chapter 9). An illustration of this reform is the notion of urban well-being in a city like Paris (Box 12.2).

### Box 12.2 Urban well-being: The case of Paris

In Paris, urban well-being has passed through three main historical phases in the last two centuries: the first was that of hygiene, the second that of auto-mobility, the third, that of social-ecology.

The hygienist movement made progress as early as the eighteenth century and culminated at the beginning of the twentieth century, advocating a logic of separation and sanitation of urban elements (soils, water, air). Nuisances were outsourced outside the urban space (the essential problem being to evict from the heart of cities "inconvenient" and "unhealthy" activities). The fundamental question that lies at the heart of both the imperial decree of October 15, 1810 and the law of December 19, 1917 can be understood as a form of industrial-ecological arbitration: While recognizing the economic necessity of industrial establishments at the beginning and the peak of the first industrial revolution, both laws attempt to neutralize their nuisances to residents. Both laws establish the unhealthy and/or inconvenient nature of certain production activities that can be toxic for health and offensive for the sense of smell. These activities are thus subject to a control of the public power and possibly displaced far from residential areas.

As early as the eighteenth century, most Parisian cemeteries were "outsourced" at the same time as the fortifications were cut down to plant vegetation. Water purification in Paris (as well as in other European cities) between the end of the nineteenth century and the first third of the twentieth century is a good illustration of the way cities have concentrated then reduced environmental problems. The development of clean water and sanitation systems that have accompanied urbanization have constituted a major advance in environmental health, resulting in lower urban mortality and morbidity.

In the 1950s and 1960s, with the reign of auto-mobility, nuisances and pollutions are re-introduced in the heart of cities in the name of fluidity and accessibility that become the priority objectives of urban spaces.

Finally, in the 1990s, Paris, like many other global cities, has rediscovered the ecological challenge related to health in the light of the observation of excess urban mortality (heat waves, fine particle pollution).

The major challenge for Paris in the early twenty-first century is no longer the problematic proximity of housing and production sites, it is the problematic distance between employment and residential areas leading to congestion and local and global pollution. Paris, like London and New York must articulate the city's vocation for mobility with its environmental quality, without one degrading the other. The issue of justice among Parisians with respect to environmental quality has recently given birth to the first ever environmental health program (Paris Santé Environnement) that recognizes the notion of environmental inequality in terms close to the approach of this book.

In fact, 90% of Parisians live in a polluted environment and 2,500 people die each year in Paris because of pollution, this nuisance being ranked as the third most concerning Parisians. A first restricted traffic zone was set up in Paris on September 1, 2015. It prohibited access for trucks, buses, and coaches registered before October 1, 2001. Since July 2016, cars and light commercial vehicles registered before January 1, 1997 are also banned in the capital. Results are encouraging, although Paris remains one of the most polluted cities in France (graphs).

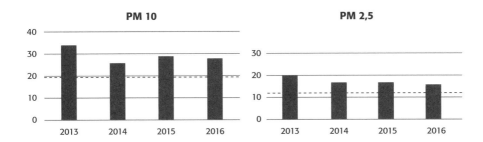

Air pollution in Paris, 2013–2016

Source: WHO

## Fostering the "polycentric transition"

In one of her last papers,[18] Elinor Ostrom advocated, yet again, for polycentricity and more precisely for a polycentric transition in addressing ecological crises. "A polycentric approach has the main advantage of encouraging experimental efforts at multiple levels, leading to the development of methods for assessing the benefits and costs of particular strategies adopted in one type of ecosystem and compared to results obtained in other ecosystems." The central idea is that cities, contrary to nations, face similar challenges and thus can produce positive emulation by looking at best practices and success stories (while the UK Prime Minister would have a hard time governing Germany, the Mayor of London would be more at ease governing Berlin). Cities around the world must all manage and find sustainable solutions for food, energy, water, shelter, transportation-communication, sanitation and waste, and green spaces (although developing and developed cities face specific challenges: the Mayor of Beijing might find it difficult to govern London).

The C40 and the Global Covenant of Mayors for Climate and Energy Networks advocate a cooperative dynamic based on these common challenges, stressing that underlying drivers of emissions in cities are largely the same (inefficient buildings in terms of heating, cooling, and lighting, solid waste landfills, traffic congestion, inefficient water systems, outdoors lighting becoming waste heat). While some cities all over the planet have managed significant progress in key areas, moving toward sustainable urban systems and, in very tangible ways, inventing new ways to reconcile human well-being with its sustainability by advancing the polycentric transition, they can serve as inspirations for others (Box 12.3).

## Box 12.3 Urban success stories

**Kalundborg** (Denmark) is a small town of about twenty thousand inhabitants that has built in 1998 a unique model of circular energy system. Kalundborg's "industrial symbiosis" comprises private partners (including a refinery, a power plant, a plasterboard factory) and the municipality itself which have set up 26 exchange contracts for materials, water or energy use. The circular flows avoid pumping three million liters of water every year and save 20,000 tonnes of oil and 200,000 tonnes of gypsum (savings are worth around fifteen million dollars each year).

The nearby city of **Copenhagen** (Denmark) has ambitions to achieve carbon neutrality in 2025. It aims for 50% of bicycle trips by 2025. For this, the Danish capital has planned to invest 134 million euros in ten years, especially in a plan for bicycles "super-highways" which will extend to the nearby suburbs. The first of the 28 planned routes opened in 2014, eleven more were completed by the end of 2018. Intermodality is encouraged: the transport of bicycles is free on regional trains.

**Curitiba** (Brazil) has grown from 150,000 inhabitants in 1950 to close to two million today and needed to find sustainable solutions for urban mobility. The master plan of urbanism of 1968 transformed the city by creating five arteries on which the public transport circulate, which radiate from the city center. On either side of a two-lane central bus corridor is a lane for one-way automobiles. In 1974, the municipality took the first initiative to develop public transit, with the creation of bus lines and in 1991 it opted for a full-blown and clean bus system instead of the subway system. 1.9 million passengers are transported each day, air pollution having been reduced by 30%.

In 2006, 73,000 acres of land were sold by Syd Kitson to the state of Florida for the creation of the Babcock Ranch Preserve with the project of creating a new model town on 18,000 acres, **Babcock Ranch** (United States). 50% of the town's footprint is set aside for green spaces and the city's development is built on green building, solar energy, water efficiency, native plants and materials, sustainable local materials, and tree preservation and relocation. The first residents officially moved in to Babcock Ranch's first neighborhood, Lake Timber, in January 2018.

In 2008, **Berlin** (Germany) created a low-emission urban area of 88 km² in the center, which concerns about a third of its inhabitants. All gasoline and diesel vehicles that do not meet environmental norms of pollution control are prohibited in the area. Between 2009 and 2015, Particulate matter (PM2.5) have been reduced from 1834 tonnes per year to 1216 and Particulate matter (PM10) have been reduced from 3135 to 2526 (see graph).

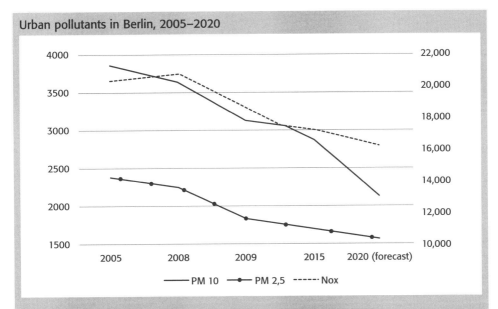

Urban pollutants in Berlin, 2005–2020

Legend: —— PM 10   —•— PM 2,5   ------ Nox

*Source:* City of Berlin

In order to avoid further shortages after the big drought in 2008, **Barcelona** (Spain) authorities opted to build the largest desalination plant in Europe, which opened in July 2009. The plant filters 200,000 cubic meters of drinking water a day, supplying nearly 20% of the region's inhabitants (the desalinated water is only used for urban consumption of drinking water and is used exclusively for the region).

In 2003, **San Francisco** (United States) set itself the goal to recycle or compost 100% of its detritus by 2020. In 2018, it reached the threshold of 80% thanks to an innovative system of selective sorting.

In preparing to face climate change impact in coming decades, **New York City** (United States) has issued Climate Resiliency Design Guidelines in April 2018, to incorporate forward-looking climate change data in the design of all City capital projects. The blueprint provided a consistent methodology for engineers, architects, landscape architects and planners to design facilities that are resilient to changing climate conditions.

Finally, new forms of rural–urban cooperation should be pursued to face social-ecological challenges such as food and water provision, energy use and climate change adaptation. The "Milano Metropoli Rurale Agreement" in the city of **Milan** (Italy) is an example of such cooperation.

# Conclusion: Open economics

In almost every standard economics textbook, two types of economies are drawn apart: closed and open. A closed economy is a self-sufficient system, which is by definition shut to foreign influence (trade and external flows of capital). An open economy, on the contrary, finds outside of its borders in part the means of its prosperity. The enormity of twenty-first century challenges reviewed in this book coupled with the severity of the shortcomings of mainstream economics converge toward the need to shift from closed to open economics.

Since the beginning of the twentieth century, mainstream economics has indeed postured as a cold and rational science, expurgated from all ethical "sentimentalism," translating universal social laws into mathematical language and endowed with robust empirical tools to usefully inform public policies.

Yet mainstream economics, like humanity on Earth, is suffering from a paradox of domination and dependence. It is dominant in social science but largely shut to other disciplines, omnipresent in the public debate and policy-making but practiced by a small minority that knows its secret codes. And yet, as this book made clear since its opening pages, economics cannot, alone, properly address the two major twin crises of the early twenty-first century – that of inequality and the biosphere – both challenging its relevance.

On this ground, this book has tried to advocate for a new approach of economics, more lucid on its inner failures and limitations and more open to the insights of other forms of knowledge. If economics is the discipline (not science) that attempts to measure and value human well-being and present citizens and policy-makers with alternatives to improve it, then environmental economics is economics guided by ethical principles and bounded by the limits of the biosphere.

How to go further in updating economics for the twenty-first century? First, by avoiding two deceptive reforms: Imitating other disciplines is not the same as engaging with them; absorbing other disciplines does not equate to being challenged by them.

As was mentioned in the introduction, economics has first wanted to imitate physics while gradually forgetting all physics laws. More recently, economists have postured as doctors[1] and engineers,[2] with little regard still for human biology or natural constraints. By the same token, humbly reducing economics to a set of "neutral" formal methods and empirical techniques that can be applied to any problem in all human domains is a step *away* from inter-disciplinarity and toward intra-disciplinarity, a step *away* from modesty and toward arrogance.

But, if it can stay clear of these two mirages, economics – the type for which this book advocates – *could* play an important role in the plural and dynamic approach of justice that must become the social-ecological inter-discipline of the twenty-first century. For the fundamental goal of humanity in coming decades is not to "save the planet" but to save the hospitality of the planet for humans and to preserve the most vulnerable among us from the worst consequences of the ecological crises for which we are, in the fullest sense, responsible.

# Notes

## Introduction: Economics for the twenty-first century

1 Milton Friedman made this analogy clear: "Positive economics is, or can be, an 'objective' science, in precisely the same sense as any of the physical sciences," Friedman (1953).

2 The "People's Agreement of Cochabamba" or "Cochabamba Declaration," agreed upon at the World People's Conference on Climate Change and the Rights of Mother Earth on April 22, 2010 in Bolivia states: "It is imperative that we forge a new system that restores harmony with nature and among human beings" (see Chapter 4).

3 H.Res.109 – Recognizing the duty of the Federal Government to create a Green New Deal. 116th Congress (2019–2020).

4 *Sustainable Equality – Report of the Independent Commission for Sustainable Equality*, 2018.

5 Speech at the COP 24, December 15, 2018.

6 Agyeman, Bullard and Evans (2002) have first mentioned the idea of a nexus between "sustainability, environmental justice and equity."

7 See for instance Laurent (2011 and 2018); Dasgupta and Ramanathan (2014); Motesharrei et al. (2014); and Gough (2017).

8 Boyce (1994).

9 To illustrate this point, consider the fact that while human population has increased by 87% between 1970 and 2010, the exposure of people to tropical cyclones increased by 192% in the same period (more than twice), most of them living in the poorest countries of the planet (source: UN). Typhoon Haiyan that hit the Philippines on November 8, 2013 caused the death of 6,000 people and the forced displacement of three and a half million others.

10 It has been estimated by the Union of Concerned Scientists in 2017 that emissions from 90 fossil-fuel and cement industries, including Exxon Mobil, Chevron, Royal Dutch Shell, BP, Peabody Energy, ConocoPhillips, and Total, contributed nearly half of the increase in global average temperature, and 30% of the rise of the oceans between 1880 and 2010. See Ekwurzel, Boneham, Dalton et al. (2017).

11 Report of the Brundtland Commission, "Our Common Future," 1987.

## 1  What the classics know about our world; what twentieth-century economics forgot

1 Physiocratic ideas first emerged in the *Journal d'agriculture, du commerce et des finances*, which started its publication in July 1765.
2 Analyse de la formule arithmétique du Tableau économique de la distribution des dépenses annuelles d'une nation agricole  (*Journal de l'agriculture, du commerce et des finances*, June 1766).
3 The term is here used in its classical sense, which in America today is much closer to "libertarians."
4 Jean-Baptiste Colbert (1619–1683) was the controller general of finance under King Louis XIV of France and carried out a vast program of economic reconstruction that consolidated France's dominance in Europe.
5 According to the mercantilist doctrine, what is won by one country is lost by the other (zero sum game) in international trade, so it is wise to conquer (if necessary by force) new outlets and close as much as possible his own market to maximize the gain resulting from trade.
6 Among them French historian Emmanuel Le Roy Ladurie.
7 Steffen et al. (2015).
8 Absolute advantage in trade is based on the lower unit cost of production compared to another country in the production of the same good and implies a specialization in the production of goods in which this advantage exists. Comparative advantage, as formulated by David Ricardo, implies that even if a country is the most efficient in all productive activities, it is necessarily relatively more productive in some than in others. Trade is thus no longer based on an absolute comparison with the productive efficiency of the exchange partner, but on a relative comparison, within the country itself, between the different productive aptitudes. It is this comparison that will decide international specialization. The country will specialize in the production of the good for which it is relatively or comparatively the best.
9 Mill (1848).
10 Rodrik (2016).
11 "Without unequal priorities and capacities, there would be no trade, no specialization, no gain from cooperation. In fact, there would be no economics and [all economists] would be busy selling insurance policies. In fact, not even, because there would be nothing to ensure!" in Welch (1999).
12 Available at http://wir2018.wid.world/.
13 Wilkinson and Pickett (2009).
14 They expand their argument in a new book, Wilkinson and Pickett (2018).
15 Stiglitz (2012).
16 For a synthesis, see Ostrom (2010).
17 See Laurent (2014).

## 2  Humans within the biosphere: The paradox of domination and dependence

1 For more on the identification of the Anthropocene, see Chapter 11.
2 Ernst Haeckel went as far as, like Darwin before him, talking about the economy of nature.
3 "Anthropos" is Greek for human and "kainos" means recent.
4 Vitousek et al. (1997).
5 Ecosystems are "natural units that include living and non-living parts interacting to produce a stable system in which the exchange of materials between the living and non-living parts follows circular paths," Odum (1953).
6 Ellis et al. (2010).
7 Not just plants but also animals. For instance, bears enter dormant state when food is scarce (hibernation), which is of tremendous value for medicine to investigate and possibly find a cure to osteoporosis and type-2 diabetes (see Chivian and Bernstein, 2008).
8 See Hamilton (1964) and (1970) and Bourke (2011).
9 There is a fundamental difference between the human species and the others in the capacity we have not only to reproduce cooperative behaviors observed among our elders, but to build sustainable and flexible institutions that allow cooperation of every human with every other, beyond the bonds of blood. The lionesses teach their offspring very early, through play, to hunt in packs. But it's still the same way that lion cubs learn and that, becoming lions, they will hunt. And they will never hunt with strangers. Humans can change the rules of the social game for each generation.
10 Domestic material consumption (DMC) represents the total amount of materials directly used by an economy (the annual quantity of raw materials extracted from the domestic territory, plus all physical imports minus all physical exports) and metabolic rates of the economy stands for the amount of natural resources consumed per capita per year (or DMC per capita). See Chapter 7 for additional considerations and data on material flow accounting.
11 IRP (2017).
12 Kathiresan and Rajendran (2005).


## 3  Governing the commons fairly

1 Nash (1972).
2 Worster (1979).
3 Cronon (1992).
4 Cronon (1991).
5 Muir (1938).
6 The Roosevelt Arch has become the formal North Entrance to Yellowstone National Park at Gardiner, Montana.
7 The motto of the National Trust is "For ever, for everyone." It takes care of

778 miles of coastline and over 248,000 hectares of land which are inalienable (they cannot be sold or developed against the wishes of the Trust without the consent of Parliament).

8 "... we sow cereals and plant trees; we irrigate our lands to fertilize them. We fortify river-banks, and straighten or divert the courses of rivers. In short, by the work of our hands we strive to create a sort of second nature within the world of nature." Cicero, *De Natura Deorum* (The Nature of the Gods, c. 45 BC).

9 Mumford (1931).

10 Pinchot (1909).

11 Hard or strong sustainability implies that renewable resources must not be drawn down faster than they can be renewed – i.e. that (critical) natural capital must not be spent: We must live off the income produced by the capital. Soft or weak sustainability accepts that certain resources can be depleted as long as they can be substituted by others over time. Natural capital can be used up as long as it is converted into manufactured capital of equal value.

12 After a heated public argument between Muir and Pinchot among others, the City of San Francisco was authorized by the US Congress to build a dam and reservoir in Hetch Hetchy Valley in 1913.

13 "Every individual ... neither intends to promote the public interest, nor knows how much he is promoting it ... he intends only his own security; and by directing that industry in such a manner as its produce may be of the greatest value, he intends only his own gain, and he is in this, as in many other cases, led by an invisible hand to promote an end which was no part of his intention." Adam Smith, *The Wealth Of Nations*, Book IV, Chapter II, p. 456, para. 9.

14 Ostrom (1990).

15 See for instance Dasgupta (2005).

16 Finus (2008).

## 4   Spheres of environmental justice

1 Agyeman, Bullard, and Evans (2002).

2 Executive Order (E.O.) 12898 – Federal Actions to Address Environmental Justice in Minority Populations and Low-Income Populations – was issued by President William J. Clinton in 1994. Its purpose is to focus federal attention on the environmental and human health effects of federal actions on minority and low-income populations with the goal of achieving environmental protection for all communities.

3 The Scottish Executive, *Choosing our Future: Scotland's Sustainable Development Strategy*, Edinburgh, 2005.

4 Yet, the racial dimension of environmental justice is as obvious in European countries, such as France, as it is in the US. A 2008 study (Laurian, 2008) showed that French towns are not equally affected by the risks inherent to storage sites of hazardous waste, the cities whose inhabitants have the lowest incomes and who display the highest proportion of immigrants (both foreign and nationals

of foreign origin) are much more likely than other municipalities to bear this risk. A more recent study (Laurian and Funderburg, 2014) reinforces these first results: Not only is the presence of incinerators positively correlated with the presence of low-income people and immigrants but authors are able to prove that incinerators are installed near vulnerable groups and not the other way around. This question of chronological precedence is the topic of an essential debate in the American literature on environmental justice: It is indeed always possible to assume that disadvantaged and vulnerable populations settled near toxic sites for financial reasons. In the French case, this study shows that an increase of one percent in foreign-born population leads to an increase by almost 30% of the probability of having an incinerator installed in the corresponding municipality.

5 Karl Marx, *Capital*, vol. 1. London: Penguin, 1976.
6 Moore (2015).
7 Bookchin (1993).
8 King (1983).
9 Shiva (1988).
10 Agarwal (2016).
11 Alier (2002).
12 Srinivasan et al. (2008).
13 Schlosberg and Carruthers (2010).
14 For more on the capabilities approach applied to environmental justice, see Schlosberg (2007).
15 Laurent (2017).
16 Currie (2011).
17 See Laurent (2011), (2014), and (2018).
18 Lelieveld et al. (2019).
19 Aphekom (Improving Knowledge and Communication for Decision Making on Air Pollution and Health in Europe).
20 For results, maps and papers, see http://www.equitarea.org/index.php/fr/.
21 See Boyce, Zwickl, and Ash (2016).

## 5  Natural resources, externalities, and sustainability: A critical toolbox

1 Hotelling (1931).
2 Pigou (1920).
3 Victor (1972) opened this line of work.
4 In September 1982, a group of scholars met in Stockholm to create what would become the International Society for Ecological Economics. Around the same time, neoclassical economists founded the Association of Environmental and Resource Economists. In the first issue of Ecological Economics, the founding president of the International Society for Ecological Economics, writes: "Environmental and resource economies as it is currently practiced,

covers only the application of neo-classical economies to environmental and resource problems. Ecology, as it is currently practiced, sometimes deals with human impacts on ecosystems, but the more common tendency is to stick to 'natural' systems. Ecological Economies aims to extend these modest areas of overlap. It will include neo-classical environmental economies and ecological impact studies as sub-sets, but will also encourage new ways of thinking about the linkages between ecological and economic systems."

5 James Boyce, "Political Economy of the Environment," Econ4 – Economics for people, for the planet and for the future and the University of Massachusetts Amherst department of economics, 2018 http://econ4.org/uncategorized/political-economy-of-the-environment-new-video-series-from-econ4. See also Boyce (2019).

6 Distributive justice, whose concern is to know how goods and bads or nuisances are distributed among the different groups and to determine the fairness of this distribution; procedural justice, the concern of which is the fairness of access to the decision-making process on environmental policy and the existence of a right to recourse; effective justice, which looks at the results of public decisions in environmental matters and how they affect different social groups.

7 The accumulation of greenhouse gas emissions in the atmosphere has the effect of gradually depriving all individuals of a preserved climate. But at present, an Indian cement plant that emits one ton of $CO_2$ does not prevent a Chinese coal-fired plant from also emitting one ton of $CO_2$. The climate would become rival if a fixed amount of emissions was accepted beforehand by both countries – which is one of the goals of international negotiations.

8 IPBES, The Assessment Report on Pollinators, Pollination, and Food Production, 2017.

9 The Congestion Charge is an £11.50 daily charge for driving a vehicle within the charging zone between 07:00 and 18:00, Monday to Friday.

10 *The Cost of Air Pollution – Health Impacts of Road Transport*, OECD, 2014.

11 Drupp et al. (2018).

12 OECD (2018).

13 The World Bank estimates that 73 Countries and over 1,000 companies support a price on carbon while China has started regional experimentation of cap-and-trade that could lead to the establishment of a national carbon price in years to come. This carbon pricing agenda is also being pursued by local jurisdiction (such as British Columbia in Canada) and corporations (such as Phillips and Unilever), preparing for a possible increase of fossil-fuel prices under the constraint of climate change and making financial provisions for such an outcome.

14 Methods to calculate environmental social cost include aggregate or marginal social cost, cost of damage and cost of abatement.

15 Such tool can be powerful. An international campaign for fossil fuel divestment launched by American pioneer climate activist Bill McKibben in February 2013

in Rolling Stones Magazine, has been gaining momentum in the United States and in Europe. The idea of the promoters is to use divestment against the fossil fuel industry the way it was used to isolate South Africa in the 1980s. The goal is not just to attempt to financially starve fossil fuel companies but to instil in public opinions worldwide and especially in the developed world the idea that the use of fossil fuel is immoral (the campaign's website defines divestment as "getting rid of stocks, bonds, or investment funds that are unethical or morally ambiguous").

16 "America's Light Bulb Revolution," *The New York Times*, March 8, 2019.

17 The Nagoya agreement also contains the Nagoya Protocol on biological and genetic resources (biopiracy) that created an International Regime on Access and Benefit Sharing of Genetic Resources in order to insure the control and compensation of genetic material and "traditional knowledge" taken from developing nations that has been used to create patented drugs or other products in developed countries.

18 Carbon taxation can happen within the borders of a country or at the border of a country, serving as a trade policy tool.

19 The European Commission was the first international institution to propose a carbon tax in 1992 in a directive proposal (COM (92) 226 final) whereby the different forms of energy would be taxed according to their energy content and to the $CO_2$ emissions emitted in their use.

20 This is known as the "abatement cost function" of the firm.

21 This goes back to the two different meanings of efficiency: Reducing costs or determining ends (note that when neoclassical environmental economics conflated these two types of efficiency, analyzing the respective merits of environmental policy instruments becomes impossible).

22 The idea can be traced further back to Peter Barnes.

23 Economists' Statement on Carbon Dividends, Climate Leadership Council, January 17, 2019 https://www.clcouncil.org/economists-statement/.

24 Ramsey (1928).

25 Kahneman and Tversky have shown that 84% of individuals faced with equal expected monetary value will choose certain gains over risky bets, see Kahneman and Tversky (1979).

26 Chivian and Bernstein (2008).

27 "Shadow price" reflects the social value and relative importance among various types of capital for human well-being but while they take into account some form of environmental valuation, they don't account for its distribution.

28 See the EPA technical document accessible at https://www.epa.gov/sites/production/files/2018-08/documents/utilities_ria_proposed_ace_2018-08.pdf.

## 6   Biodiversity and ecosystems under growing and unequal pressure

1 Bar-On, Phillips, and Milo (2018).

2 The fifth extinction happened 65 million years ago with the extinction of

Dinosaurs, the fourth so-called "Permian Great dying" occurred 250m ago, when 95% of marine life was wiped out. Almost all of these past waves of life destruction occurred because of climate events.

3  The Living Planet index calculated by the WWF tracks the evolution of 3,038 vertebrate species (fish, birds, mammals, reptiles, amphibians) on the globe serving as a control sample of global terrestrial biodiversity.

4  Sukhdev (2011).

5  According to the World Resource Institute, 2.6 billion people worldwide depend on agriculture (1.3 billion for direct employment), including more than 500 million in sub-Saharan Africa (90% of agricultural production in Africa comes from small family or tribal farms) and 1.6 billion people depend in one form or another on forests.

6  Conde and Christensen (2008).

7  At the heart of this problem lies the time horizon of individuals: Poverty increases the urgency of survival, even at the cost of unsustainable environmental degradations. Poverty dictates consuming natural capital instead of maintaining it, in the same way that liquidity needs compel an individual subject to the reduction of his income to consume savings which could bring him future cash flows. The eradication of poverty is therefore an end in itself but also an essential means to achieve sustainable development.

8  *Source:* UNEP.

9  *Source:* World Bank.

10  Ellis et al. (2010).

11  IPBES, Land Degradation and Restoration Assessment (2018).

12  Erisman et al. (2008). The authors further estimate that "nitrogen fertilizer has supported approximately 27% of the world's population over the past century, equivalent to around four billion people born (or 42% of the estimated total births) since 1908."

13  Motta, Raymann, and Moran (2018).

14  The State of the World's Biodiversity for Food and Agriculture, FAO, 2019.

15  The five scenarios are the following: the "Metropolization" scenario, characterized by growth at any cost, with a transition to more highly-processed and animal food products; the "Communities" scenario, which envisions a world subject to recurring crises and increased regional fragmentation, leading to slower growth and stagnation – or even the collapse – of crop yields, in turn creating uncertainty for the global food supply; the "Healthy" scenario imagines healthy food diets in terms of nutrition and quantity, based on diversified agricultural production. The "Regionalization" scenario has each region of the world developing its own "food sovereignty" strategy by reducing trade with outside regions to a minimum. Changes in regional agriculture will be necessary to return to the traditional food diets implicit in this scenario. The last scenario, "Households," carves out a major role for cooperatives and family farming. It couples strong mobility between rural and urban areas with hybrid food diets combining traditional and modern foods (INRA/CIRAD). See http://

institut.inra.fr/en/Objectives/Informing-public-policy/Foresight/All-the-news/
Agrimonde-Terra-foresight-study.

16 "Food insecurity" can be defined as the reduced or culturally unacceptable access to adequate food (in terms of quality, quantity, and safety), or as an abnormal risk of losing access.

17 Between February 2016 and October 2018, the price of fuel has increased in France by 26% and that of diesel by 50% (fuels returning to the peak reached in 2012). Because the tax component of the price of fuels is close to 60% in France, the protest against fuel prices has turned into a protest against taxes. The movement, which brought violence and destruction right in the center of Paris, led to the suppression of the carbon tax that was supposed to increase in January of 2019.

## 7   Beyond EXPOWA (extraction, pollution, and waste)

1 Bourg and Arnsperger (2016).

2 If Domestic material consumption (DMC) is the total amount of materials directly used by an economy (the annual quantity of raw materials extracted from the domestic territory, plus all physical imports minus all physical exports), then the metabolic rate of the economy is equivalent to the tonnes of natural resources consumed per capita per year or DMC per capita.

3 Between 1970 to 2010, the annual global use of materials grew from 26.7 billion tonnes to 75.6 billion tonnes (the last three decades of the twentieth century saw yearly average growth in global material use of 2.3%, which accelerated to 3.5% in the first decade of the twenty-first century).

4 Krausmann, Weisz, and Eisenmenger (2016).

5 Following the example of other environmental footprints (such as the carbon footprint), the material footprint is an indicator that allows us to take into account the full amount of raw materials used to satisfy a given country's level of domestic consumption. The results provide a better representation of the true impact of resource use, including both materials extracted within the country and those mobilized indirectly outside our borders in order to produce and transport imported products.

6 Murali Krishna and Valli Manickam (2017).

7 Towards a pollution-free planet, UN, 2017.

8 Towards a pollution-free planet, UN, 2017.

9 About 41.8 million metric tons of e-waste were generated in 2014, almost 25% more than in 2010 and no less than a third of the food produced worldwide is lost or wasted every year.

10 Municipal waste is defined as household and similar waste collected by or on behalf of municipalities, and originating from households, offices and small businesses. Material recovery includes recovery for recycling and composting.

11 Krausmann et al. (2009).

12 Schaffartzik et al. (2014).

13  Grossman and Krueger (1995).
14  Chakravarty, Dasgupta, and Roy (2013).
15  Korhonen, Honkasalo, and Seppälä (2018).


## 8   Energy, climate, and justice

1  *Source:* Climate Action Tracker.
2  Global Warming of 1.5°C. An IPCC Special Report, IPCC, 2018.
3  Nathaniel Rich, "Losing Earth: The Decade We Almost Stopped Climate Change," *The New York Times Magazine*, August 1, 2018.
4  Coady et al. (2017).
5  According to the Global Carbon Project http://www.globalcarbonproject.org/, which records emissions from fossil fuel consumption and cement production.
6  WMO Statement on the State of the Global Climate in 2017, World Meteorological Organization, 2018 https://library.wmo.int/doc_num.php?explnum_id=4453.
7  Author's calculation based on Piketty and Saez (2013).
8  The Kyoto Protocol reinforces the 1992 Convention by committing Annex 1 countries to individual, legally binding, greenhouse gas emission reduction or limitation objectives. The individual objectives of Annex 1 countries are listed in Annex B of the Kyoto Protocol, which explains why the term "Annex B countries" is sometimes used instead of "Annex 1 countries."
9  According to United Nations figures, if emissions of all Annex 1 countries fell by 10.6% between 1990 and 2012 (almost exactly double the 5.2% commitment made in 1997), the so-called transition economies (Russia and its then satellites) emissions were down over 38%, this reduction being acquired in 1995. Meanwhile, OECD–Annex 1 countries (EU 15, United States, Japan, Canada, Australia) have seen their emissions rise by 2%, this increase being as high as 10% before the great recession of 2009. In other words, two recessions explain that the Kyoto target was reached and even surpassed.
10  Intended Nationally Determined Contribution Submission, *Intended Nationally Determined Contribution of the EU and its Member States* (Riga, Latvia: Latvia and the European Commission on behalf of the European Union and its Member States, March 2015) http://ec.europa.eu/clima/news/docs/2015030601_eu_indc_en.pdf.
11  Intended Nationally Determined Contribution Submission, *Enhanced Actions on Climate Change: China's Intended Nationally Determined Contribution* (Beijing, China: Department of Climate Change, National Development and Reform Commission of China, June 2015) http://www4.unfccc.int/submissions/INDC/Published%20Documents/China/1/China%27s%20INDC%20-%20on%2030%20June%202015.pdf.
12  Report of the Ad Hoc Working Group on the Durban Platform for Enhanced Action, *Further Advancing the Durban Platform: Draft Decision -/CP.XX*, by the President (Lima, Peru: Conference of Parties, United Nations Framework Convention on Climate Change, December 2014), http://unfccc.int/resource/docs/2014/cop20/eng/l14.pdf.

13 When one considers historical responsibility, the same concentration of responsibility can be found among top emitters: 75% of cumulative emissions from fossil fuel and industry (1870–2016) are the responsibility of USA 26%, EU28 22%, China 13%, Russia 7%, Japan 4%, and India 3%.

## 9  Well-being and our environment: From trade-offs to synergies

1 Watts et al. (2017).
2 Between August 1 and 4, 2003, temperatures recorded by Météo France increased dramatically from around 25°C to 37°C, and remained as high as 36°C/37°C until August 13. The duration, intensity and geographical scope of the 2003 heat wave ("canicule") that struck most of France was unprecedented since temperatures were first recorded in Paris in the mid nineteenth century. According to Météo France, the summer of 2003 was overall 2°C over the previous records established in 1976, 1983, and 1994.
3 More precisely, emissions from fossil fuel combustion are often partitioned into $CO_2$ and "co-pollutants" like SO2, so reductions in fossil fuel use yield both climate benefits from less $CO_2$ and public health co-benefits from less co-pollutants.
4 By the same token, an earlier study by the US Environmental Protection Agency on the Clean Air Act, the major legislation to regulate air pollution in the United States passed in the 1970s, shows that the cost of upgrading the US production system and the human benefits (mainly in terms of health) allowed by this law are in a ratio of 1 to 30.
5 Aiming for the elimination of all ozone-depleting gases, particularly chloro-fluorocarbons (CFCs), The Montreal Protocol has gradually been extended to all states of the planet. It is the only agreement that can claim universal ratification (196 states) since the accession of East Timor on September 16, 2009.
6 *Source:* négaWatt and IRENA.
7 See the related collection of papers and studies at https://web.stanford.edu/group/efmh/jacobson/Articles/I/WWS-50-USState-plans.html.
8 Economic growth is the increase of Gross Domestic Product at constant prices (i.e. in volume). Gross domestic product can be defined as a composite indicator measuring only marketable and monetized economic activity. It was first developed in 1934 by Simon Kuznets at the demand of the US Congress, whose members wanted to have a clear and synthetic view of what had happened to the American economy after the 1929 stock market crash.
9 See Laurent (2018).
10 Proceedings of this conference can be found here: http://ec.europa.eu/environment/beyond_gdp/2007_conference_en.html.
11 A good place to keep track of this production is the news section of the Beyond GDP blog maintained by the European Union: http://ec.europa.eu/environment/beyond_gdp/news_en.html as well as the Wikiprogress website http://wikiprogress.org/.

12  See Laurent (2018).

13  While GDP partially measures some human development dimensions (such as public services like health and education), it does so based on their supply cost and not their outcomes or the actual benefits they provide citizens such as health status or educational attainments.

14  See World Inequality Database and Gallup.

15  There actually are some important differences, one of them being that the top CFC producer (DuPont) also happened to hold patent rights to its main substitutes.

16  See for instance Laurent (2018).

17  Nobel precisely wrote that his capital's interests be divided each year into five parts: "one part to the person who made the most important discovery or invention in the field of physics; one part to the person who made the most important chemical discovery or improvement; one part to the person who made the most important discovery within the domain of physiology or medicine; one part to the person who, in the field of literature, produced the most outstanding work in an idealistic direction; and one part to the person who has done the most or best to advance fellowship among nations, the abolition or reduction of standing armies, and the establishment and promotion of peace congresses.

18  Offer and Söderberg (2016).

19  Boyce (2017).

## 10   Social-ecology: Connecting the inequality and ecological crises

1  Report of the World Commission on Environment and Development: Our Common Future, 1987.

2  A number of international institutions has tried to bring the issue to the forefront of the global agenda, most notably the Human Development Report Office of the United Nations, the IPCC, and the World Bank. In 2010, the HDRO former released "Sustainability and Equity: A Better Future for All," arguing that "the urgent global challenges of sustainability and equity must be addressed together – and identifies policies on the national and global level that could spur mutually reinforcing progress toward these interlinked goals." The link between equity and sustainability has also emerged in the third instalment of the AR5 IPCC Report. In a book-long chapter, its authors note with "high confidence" that "equity is an integral part of sustainable development." More specifically, they argue that three dimensions should be considered in both mitigation and adaptation climate policy: "a moral justification that draws upon ethical principles; a legal justification that appeals to existing treaty commitments and soft law agreements to cooperate on the basis of stated equity principles; and an effectiveness justification that argues that a fair arrangement is more likely to be agreed internationally and successfully implemented domestically." The World Bank has recently published several

reports linking climate change, poverty and social vulnerability. The research on the link between social inequality and ecological crises and degradations is also spreading to policy-making circles, such as the European Parliament (see Sustainable Equality – Well-Being for Everyone in a Sustainable Europe, 2018).

3 Milanovic (2016).
4 Dobson (1998).
5 See TEEB (2010) and Barrett, Travis, and Dasgupta (2011).
6 Laurent (2018).
7 Paul Krugman, "For Richer," *The New York Times Magazine*, October 20, 2002.
8 Absolute decoupling of GDP growth and $CO_2$ emissions has actually been achieved in a number of countries over certain periods of time, but only on the basis of production or territorial emissions. Once the global ecological impact of their economic development is taken into account (i.e. "net decoupling"), only relative decoupling remains.
9 Otto et al. (2019).
10 See Davis, Peters, and Caldeira (2011) and Laurent (2011).
11 Richard Wilkinson and Michael Marmot can be credited for opening this avenue of research, now widely pursued in governmental and international institutions.
12 See studies from the WHO on "preventable burden" of diseases, especially Prüss-Üstün and Corvalán (2006) and Margai (2010).
13 Baland and Platteau (1997), Klooster (2000).
14 See for instance Andersson and Agrawal (2011).
15 For a synthesis, see Ostrom (2010).
16 McCarty, Poole, and Rosenthal (2008).
17 Bechtel and Scheve (2013).
18 Serret and Johnstone (2006).
19 Laurent (2010).
20 See, for example, Mohai and Saha (2015).
21 See Liu (2012).
22 European Environment Agency (2019).
23 European Environment Agency, Unequal exposure and unequal impacts: Social vulnerability to air pollution, noise and extreme temperatures in Europe, EEA, 2019.
24 For more on this see http://www.cancer-environnement.fr/.
25 UNISDR : http://www.unisdr.org/who-we-are/what-is-drr.
26 Rousseau to Voltaire, August 18, 1756, from J.A. Leigh, ed., *Correspondence complète de Jean Jacques Rousseau*, vol. 4 (Geneva, 1967), pp. 37–50; translated by R. Spang.
27 Despite this, the Americas reported the highest economic losses, representing 88% of the total cost from 93 disasters. China, US, and India were the hardest hit countries in terms of occurrence with 25, 20, and 15 events respectively.
28 Wisner, Blaikie et al. (2004) made the case for the need to set apart "natural events" and "natural disasters."

29 On those two points, see Pastor et al. (2006).

30 Hatzfeld, D., Jackson, J., Tucker, B., "Can we minimize earthquake disasters," mimeo, 2009.

31 The authors are able to determine that in Italy, three earthquakes prior to 1915 have claimed over 120,000 lives, and since then there have been fewer than 10,000 deaths. In California, since the 1906 San Francisco earthquake that killed 3,000 people, there have been only 350 deaths. In Japan, since the 1923 earthquake that left nearly 120,000 dead, there have been only 30,000 deaths despite a very high number of earthquakes (190 earthquakes of magnitude greater than six).

32 African-Americans are 52% more likely than whites to live in exposed neighbor-hoods, Asians 32%, and Hispanics 21%, see Jesdale, Morello-Frosch, and Cushing (2013).

33 *Source:* Focus Canada 2015, Canadian public opinion about climate change.

34 Bits of this social-ecological state are emerging around the world, for instance in the "Green New Deal" bill proposed in the House of Representatives in February 2019.

## 11   The social-ecological transition in context: Capitalism, democracy, globalization, and digitalization

1 Crutzen and Stoermer (2000).

2 Other proposals exist, "The evidence suggests that of the various proposed dates two do appear to conform to the criteria to mark the beginning of the Anthropocene: 1610 and 1964," see Lewis and Maslin (2015).

3 Moore (2013) and (2016).

4 The case of the USSR allows us to understand how an authoritarian regime, more precisely totalitarian, may have wanted to subject its environment to its ideological priorities in defiance of the ecological sustainability and health of its citizens. Regarding the extent of environmental depredations of soviet communism, one can refer to the vast literature on the subject and stick to a single emblematic tragic episode. The most striking example from the point of view of the prometheism of the Soviet regime is undoubtedly that of the Aral Sea, whose ecological equilibrium, probably lost forever, was wiped out by the blindness of a regime whose technicity had become a deadly religion. The two rivers that fed this stretch of water of nearly 70,000 km² were in fact diverted from the 1960s to develop the cotton crop, which led thirty years later to its near disappearance (its surface was divided by four). The USSR has given proof of the ecological danger of modern science when it is freed from the democratic framework. In other words, communist regimes can be as destructive as capitalist regimes for their environment and the biosphere.

5 York, Rosa, and Dietz (2003).

6 Elster (1979) and (2000).

7 Bourg and Whiteside (2009).

 8 Payne (1995).
 9 Measured as trade as a percentage of GDP.
10 Peters, Davis, and Andrew (2012).
11 Davis, Peters, and Caldeira (2011).
12 "The water footprint of production is the amount of local water resources that are used to produce goods and services within the country. This includes the water footprint of agriculture, industry and domestic water use and tells us the total volume of water and assimilation capacity consumed within the borders of the country. This can also be measured for any administrative unit such as a city, province, river basin, or even the whole world. We can also view the water footprint from the perspective of consumption. In this case, the water footprint is calculated for all the goods and services that are consumed by the people living in a country. This water footprint may be partly inside the country and partly outside of it, depending on whether the products are locally produced or imported. The water footprint of consumption can also be measured for any administrative unit." (*Source*: The Water footprint network.)
13 World Scientists' Warning to Humanity: A Second Notice, 2017.
14 The digital sector consumes nearly 10% of global electricity production in 2015, with data centers capturing 18% of this consumption.
15 In the US, cardboard use has jumped 8% in the period 2012–2017 but cardboard recycling has dropped: In 2017, 300,000 fewer tonnes of corrugated containers were recycled in the USA than in the year before.
16 China produces close to 90% of global supply of the seventeen chemically similar elements crucial to smartphone or camera lens called "rare earths." Processing one ton of rare earths produces 2,000 tonnes of toxic waste, the city of Baotou in China, which provides half of China production engenders 10m tonnes of waste water per year.
17 O'Neil (2017).
18 Through our duly recorded deeds and gestures, we are constantly optimizing probing algorithms that in return are ever more firmly governing societies and individual lives.

## 12   Urban sustainability and polycentric transition

 1 Krugman (1991).
 2 Brueckner (2011).
 3 The housing prices indicator shows indices of residential property prices over time. Included are rent prices, real and nominal house prices, and ratios of price to rent and price to income; the main elements of housing costs. The real house price is given by the ratio of nominal price to the consumers' expenditure deflator in each country, both seasonally adjusted, from the OECD national accounts database.
 4 In 1965, the American engineer Abel Wolman defined urban metabolism as

"all the materials and commodities needed to sustain the city's inhabitants at home, at work and at play" (Wolman, 1965).

5  Harvey (1973).

6  The *World Development Report 2009: Reshaping Economic Geography*, argued that "the most effective policies for promoting long-term growth are those that facilitate geographic concentration and economic integration, both within and across countries."

7  OECD (2018).

8  Setoa, Güneralpa, and Hutyrac (2012).

9  "Modernising Building Energy Codes," Policy Pathway Series, IEA, 2013.

10  Among the 110,000 LEED existing projects, only 6500 have achieved the (highest) LEED Platinum status.

11  Erickson and Tempest (2014).

12  Among existing initiatives, one can distinguish between network and individual initiatives. Among the former, the new Covenant of Mayors (drafted by the European Union in October 2015) commits its signatories to developing "Sustainable Energy and Climate Action Plan" aimed at reducing carbon emissions on their territory by at least 40% by 2030 through improved energy efficiency and greater use of renewable energy sources and states that "the building sector has the most potential for delivering significant and cost-effective GHG emission reductions."

13  The final has added a reference to "Agreeing to uphold and promote regional and international cooperation in order to mobilize stronger and more ambitious climate action by all Parties and non-Party stakeholders, including civil society, the private sector, financial institutions, cities and other subnational author-ities, local communities and indigenous peoples."

14  Musango, Currie, and Robinson (2017).

15  The database contains 202 unique processes (or 334 when the different capacities are counted). These processes all manage energy, water, and waste, encompassing 63 resource types, of which 25 are main resources. https://metabolismofcities.org/.

16  Logan (2006).

17  See Pastor et al. (2006).

18  Ostrom (2012).

## Conclusion: Open economics

1  See for instance Fisher (1933): "it would be as silly and immoral to 'let nature take her course' as for a physician to neglect a case of pneumonia. It would also be a libel on economic science, which has its therapeutics as truly as medical science."

2  Roth (2002) embraces the analogy: "Engineering is often less elegant than the simple underlying physics, but it allows bridges designed on the same basic model to be built longer and stronger over time, as the complexities and how to deal with them become better understood."

# References

Adger, W.N., Lorenzoni, I., and O'Brien, K. (eds.), 2009, *Adapting to Climate Change: Thresholds, Values, Governance*. Cambridge: Cambridge University Press.

Agarwal, Bina, 2016, *Gender Challenges*, 3 vols. Oxford: Oxford University Press.

Agyeman, J., Bullard, R., and Evans, B., 2002, Exploring the nexus: Bringing together sustainability, environmental justice and equity, *Space and Polity*, 6 (1): 70–90.

Alier, J.M., 2002, *The Environmentalism of the Poor: A Study of Ecological Conflicts and Valuation*. Cheltenham, UK: Edward Elgar.

Althor, G. et al., 2016, Global mismatch between greenhouse gas emissions and the burden of climate change, *Sci. Rep.* 6: 20281.

Ambec, Stefan, Cohen, Mark A., Elgie, Stewart, and Lanoie, Paul, 2013, The porter hypothesis at 20: Can environmental regulation enhance innovation and competitiveness? *Rev. Environ. Econ. Policy*, first published online January 4.

Andersson, K. and Agrawal, A., 2011, Inequalities, institutions, and forest commons, *Global Environmental Change* 21(3), 866–875.

Arrow, K. J., 1999, Discounting, morality, and gaming, in Portney, P. R. and Weyant, J. P. (eds.). *Discounting and Intergenerational Equity. Resources for the Future*, Washington DC.

Baland, J.-M. and Platteau, J.-P., 1997, Wealth inequality and efficiency in the Commons. Part I: The unregulated case, *Oxford Economic Papers*, n.s., 49 (4), October: 451–482.

Bar-On, Yinon M., Phillips, Rob, and Milo, Ron, 2018, The biomass distribution on Earth, *Proceedings of the National Academy of Sciences*, 115 (25), June: 6506–6511.

Barrett, Christopher B., Travis, Alexander J., and Dasgupta, Partha, 2011, On biodiversity conservation and poverty traps, *PNAS*, 108 (34): 13907–13912, Biodiversity Conservation and Poverty Traps Special Issue.

Bechtel, Michael M. and Scheve, Kenneth F., 2013, Mass support for global climate agreements depends on institutional design, *PNAS*, July 25.

Blaikie, Piers, Cannon, Terry, Davis, Ian, and Wisner, Ben, 2004, *At Risk: Natural Hazards, People's Vulnerability, and Disasters*. New York: Routledge, 2nd edn.

Bookchin, M., 1993, *Society and Ecology*, online.

Bourg, Dominique and Whiteside, Kerry, 2009, Pour une démocratie écologique, *La Vie des Idées*.

Bourg, Dominique and Arnsperger, Christian, 2016, Vers une économie authentiquement circulaire; Réflexions sur les fondements d'un indicateur de circularité, *Revue de l'OFCE* 2016/1 (145).

Bourke, Andrew F.G., 2011, *Principles of Social Evolution*, Oxford: Oxford University Press.

Boyce, J.K., 1994, Inequality as a cause of environmental degradation, *Ecological Economics*, 11 (3): 169–178.

___ 2002, *The Political Economy of the Environment*. Cheltenham: Edward Elgar.

___ 2013, *Economics, the Environment and Our Common Wealth*. Cheltenham: Edward Elgar.

___ 2017, The humble economist: What economics can – and can't – tell us about climate change, mimeo.

___ 2018, Carbon pricing: Effectiveness and equity, *Ecological Economics*, 150, August: 52–61.

___ 2019, *Economics for People and the Planet: Inequality in the Era of Climate Change*. London: Anthem Press.

Boyce, J. K., Zwickl, Klara, and Ash, Michael, 2016, Measuring environmental inequality, *Ecological Economics*, 124, issue C: 114–123.

Brueckner, Jan K., 2011, *Lectures on Urban Economics*. Cambridge, MA: MIT Press.

Bruiparif, 2013, Rapport d'étude SURVOL volet 1: Renforcement de la surveillance de l'exposition au bruit autour des plateformes aéroportuaires. Paris.

Brundtland Report, 1987, *Our Common Future: World Commission on Environment and Development*. Oxford and New York: Oxford University Press.

Case, A. and Deaton, A., 2015, Rising morbidity and mortality in midlife among white non-Hispanic Americans in the 21st century, *PNAS*, 112 (49): 15078–15083.

Caudeville, J., 2013, Caractériser des inégalités environnementales, in Éloi L., *Vers l'égalité des territoires*. La Documentation française.

Ceballos, G. et al., 2017, Biological annihilation via the ongoing sixth mass extinction signaled by vertebrate population losses and declines, PNAS (30) July 25: 114.

Chakravarty, D., Dasgupta, S., Roy, J., 2013, Rebound effect: How much to worry? *Curr. Opin. Environ. Sustain.* 5 (2): 216–228.

Chen, Yuyu, Ebenstein, Avraham, Greenstone, Michael, and Li, Hongbin, 2013, Evidence on the impact of sustained exposure to air pollution on life expectancy from China's Huai River policy, *PNAS*, 110 (32): 12936–12941.

Chivian, Eric and Bernstein, Aaron (eds.), 2008, *Sustaining Life. How Human Health Depends on Biodiversity*. New York: Oxford University Press.

Cicéron, 1935, *De la nature des dieux, traduction: Charles APPUHN*, Livre I. Paris: Garnier.

Climate Change Vulnerability Index (CCVI), 2018, Verisk Maplecroft.

Coady, David, Parry, Ian, Sears, Louis, and Shang, Baoping, 2017, How large are global fossil fuel subsidies?, *World Development*, 91 (C): 11–27.

Conde, D.A. and Christensen, N., 2008, Vicious cycle of poverty and environmental degradation: Haiti, in Sukhdev, P. (ed.), *The Economics of Ecosystems and Biodiversity: An Interim Report*. Publications Office, p. 24.

Costanza, R., Kubiszewski, I., and Giovannini, E. et al., 2014, Development: Time to leave GDP behind, *Nature*, 505 (7483): 283–285.

Cronon, W., 1991, *Nature's Metropolis: Chicago and the Great West*. New York: W.W. Norton.

___ 1992, A place for stories: Nature, history, and narrative, *Journal of American History*, 78 (4), March 1: 1347–1376.

Crutzen, Paul Josef and Stoermer, Eugene F., 2000, The Anthropocene, Global Change, *NewsLetter*, 41 [archive]: 17–18. IGBP.

Currie, J., 2011, Inequality at birth: Some causes and consequences, *American Economic Review*, American Economic Association, 101 (3), May: 1–22.

Dasgupta, P., 2005, Common property resources: Economic analytics, *Economic and Political Weekly*, 40 (16), April 16–22: 1610–1622.

Dasgupta, P. and Ramanathan, V., 2014, Pursuit of the common good, *Science*, 345 (6203): 1457–1458.

Davis, Steven J., Peters, Glen P., and Caldeira, Ken, 2011, The supply chain of $CO_2$ emissions, *Proceedings of the National Academy of Sciences*, 108 (45) November: 18554–18559.

Dobson, Andrew, 1998, *Justice and the Environment, Conceptions of Environmental Sustainability and Theories of Distributive Justice*. Oxford: Clarendon Press.

Drupp, Moritz A., Meya, Jasper N., Baumgärtner, Stefan, Quaas, Martin F., 2018, Economic inequality and the value of nature, *Ecological Economics*, 150: 340–345.

Dunbar, Charles F., 1876, Economic science in America, 1776–1876, *The North American Review*, 122 (250): 124–154.

Dupont de Nemours, Pierre-Samuel, 2017, De l'origine et des progrès d'une science nouvelle, 1768 (édition de 1910), *Collection des économistes et des réformateurs sociaux de la France*, Bibliothèque nationale de France.

Easterlin, R.A., Wang, F., and Wang, S., 2017, Growth and happiness in China, 1990–2015, in *World Happiness Report*. Sustainable Development Solutions Network.

Ekwurzel, B., Boneham, J., Dalton, M.W. et al., 2017, The rise in global atmospheric $CO_2$, surface temperature, and sea level from emissions traced to major carbon producers, *Climatic Change* 144: 57.

Ellis, E.C. et al., 2010, Anthropogenic transformation of the biomes, 1700 to 2000, *Global Ecology and Biogeography*, 19 (5), September: 589–606.

Elster, J., 1979, *Ulysses and the Sirens: Studies in Rationality and Irrationality*. New York, Cambridge University Press.

___ 2000, *Ulysses Unbound: Studies in Rationality, Pre-Commitment, and Constraints*. New York: Cambridge University Press.

Erickson, P. and Tempest, K., 2014. Advancing climate ambition: How city-scale actions can contribute to global climate goals. SEI Working Paper No. 2014–16. Seattle, WA, US: Stockholm Environment Institute.

Erisman, Jan Willem, Sutton, Mark A., Galloway, James, Klimont, Zbigniew, and Winiwarter, Wilfried, 2008, How a century of ammonia synthesis changed the world, *Nature Geoscience*, 1 (10), September 28: 636–639.

Esty, Aniel C. and Porter, Michael, 2005, National environmental performance: An empirical analysis of policy results and determinants, *Environment and Development Economics*: 391–434.

European Environment Agency, 2019, Unequal exposure and unequal impacts: Social vulnerability to air pollution, noise, and extreme temperatures in Europe, EEA.

Finus, M., 2008, Game theoretic research on the design of international environmental agreements: Insights, critical remarks, and future challenges, *International Review of Environmental and Resource Economics*, 2: 29–67.

Fisher, Irving, 1933, The debt-deflation theory of great depressions, *Econometrica*, 1 (4), October: 337–357.

Friedman, M., 1953, *Essays in Positive Economics*. Chicago: University of Chicago Press.

Gadrey, J. and Jany-Catrice, F., 2006, *The New Indicators of Well-Being and Development*. London: Palgrave Macmillan.

GBD, 2015, Tobacco collaborators. Smoking prevalence and attributable disease burden in 195 countries and territories, 1990–2015: A systematic analysis from the Global Burden of Disease Study 2015. *Lancet*; published online April 5 (2017).

Gouldson, A., Colenbrander, S., Sudmant, A., McAnulla, F., Kerr, N., Sakai, P., Kuylenstierna, J., 2015, Exploring the economic case for climate action in cities, *Glob Environ Chang*, 35: 93–105.

Gough, I., 2017, *Heat, Greed and Human Need: Climate Change, Capitalism and Sustainable Wellbeing*. London: Edward Elgar.

Grossman, Gene and Alan Krueger, 1995, Economic growth and the environment. *Quarterly Journal of Economics*, 110 (2): 353–377.

Hallegatte, Stephane, Vogt-Schilb, Adrien, Bangalore, Mook, Rozenberg, Julie, 2017, *Unbreakable: Building the Resilience of the Poor in the Face of Natural Disasters. Climate Change and Development*. Washington, DC: World Bank.

Hamilton, W.D. 1964, The genetical evolution of social behavior, I and II, *J. Theor. Biol.*, 7: 1–52.

___ 1970, Selfish and spiteful behaviour in an evolutionary model, *Nature*, 228: 1218–1220.

Harvey, David, 1973, *Social Justice and the City*. Baltimore: The Johns Hopkins Press.

Hatzfeld, D., Jackson, J., and Tucker, B., 2009, Can we minimize earthquake disasters? mimeo.

HDRO, Human Development Report 2010 – 20th Anniversary Edition, *The Real Wealth of Nations: Pathways to Human Development*. NY: United Nations.

Helliwell, J., Layard, R., and Sachs, J., 2017, *World Happiness Report*. New York: Sustainable Development Solutions Network.

Holland, Tim G., Peterson, Garry G., and Gonzalez, Andrew, 2010, A cross-national analysis of how economic inequality predicts biodiversity loss, *Conservation Biology*.

Hotelling, Harold, 1931, The economics of exhaustible resources, *Journal of Political Economy*, 39 (2), April 1931: 137–175.

Ineris, 2014, *Atlas Régional d'inégalités environnementales*. Paris.

IPBES, 2017, The Assessment Report on Pollinators, Pollination and Food Production.

IPBES, 2018, Land Degradation and Restoration Assessment.

IPBES, 2019, Global Assessment Report.

IPCC, 1992, First Assessment Report Overview and Policymaker Summaries and Supplement, WMO and UNEP.

___ 2014, Summary for policy-makers, In *Climate Change 2014: Impacts, Adaptation, and Vulnerability*. Part A: Global and Sectoral Aspects. Contribution of Working Group II to the Fifth Assessment Report of the Intergovernmental Panel on Climate Change [Field, C.B., Barros, V.R., Dokken, D.J., Mach, K.J., Mastrandrea, M.D., Bilir, T.E., Chatterjee, M., Ebi, K.L., Estrada, Y.O., Genova, R.C., Girma, B., Kissel, E.S., Levy, A.N., MacCracken, S., Mastrandrea, P.R., and White, L.L. (eds.). Cambridge and New York: Cambridge University Press.

IRP, 2017, *Assessing Global Resource Use: A Systems Approach to Resource Efficiency and Pollution Reduction*. Bringezu, S., Ramaswami, A., Schandl, H., O'Brien, M., Pelton, R., Acquatella, J., Ayuk, E., Chiu, A., Flanegin, R., Fry, J., Giljum, S., Hashimoto, S., Hellweg, S., Hosking, K., Hu, Y., Lenzen, M., Lieber, M., Lutter, S., Miatto, A., Singh Nagpure, A., Obersteiner, M., van Oers, L., Pfister, S., Pichler, P., Russell, A., Spini, L., Tanikawa, H., van der Voet, E., Weisz, H., West, J., Wijkman, A., Zhu, B., Zivy, R. A Report of the International Resource Panel. United Nations Environment Programme. Nairobi, Kenya.

Jesdale, Bill M., Morello-Frosch, Rachel, and Cushing, Lara, 2013, The racial/ethnic distribution of heat risk-related land cover in relation to residential segregation, *Environmental Health Perspectives*, May.

Jevons, William Stanley, 1866 [1865], *The Coal Question – An Inquiry Concerning the Progress of the Nation, and the Probable Exhaustion of Our Coal-Mines*. London: Macmillan, 2nd edn (revised).

Jonas, Hans, 1990 [1979], *Le principe responsabilité: Une éthique pour la civilisation technologique*. Paris: Le Cerf.

Kahneman, Daniel and Tversky, Amos, 1979, Prospect theory: An analysis of decisions under risk, *Econometrica*, 47 (2): 313–327.

Kathiresan, K. and Rajendran, N., 2005, Coastal mangrove forests mitigated tsunami, *Estuar. Coast. Shelf Sci.*, 65.

Kidder, Tracy, 2010, *Partner to the Poor: A Paul Farmer Reader*. Ed. by Haun Saussy, 1st edn. California: University of California Press. JSTOR, www.jstor.org/stable/10.1525/j.ctt1ppcmr.

King, Y., 1983, The ecology of feminism and the feminism of ecology, in Plant, J., *Healing the Wounds: The Promise of Ecofeminism*. Philadelphia, California: New Society Publishers, pp. 18–28.

Klooster, D., 2000, Institutional choice, community, and struggle: A case study of forest co-management in Mexico, *World Development*, 28: 1–20.

Korhonen, Jouni, Honkasalo, Antero, Seppälä, Jyri, 2018, Circular economy: The concept and its limitations, *Ecological Economics*, 143, January: 37–46.

Krausmann, Fridolin et al., 2017, Global in-use material stocks in the 20th century, *Proceedings of the National Academy of Sciences*, 114 (8) February: 1880–1885.

Krausmann, F., Gingrich, S., Eisenmenger, N., Erb, K.H., Haberl, H., and Fischer-Kowalski, M., 2009, Growth in global materials use, GDP and population during the 20th century, *Ecological Economics*, 68 (10): 2696–2705.

Krausmann, F., Weisz, H., Eisenmenger, N., 2016, Transitions in sociometabolic regimes throughout human history, in Haberl, H., Fischer-Kowalski, M., Krausmann, F., Winiwarter, V. (eds.) *Social Ecology: Society–Nature Relations across Time and Space*. Dordrecht: Springer. pp. 63–92.

Krugman Paul, 1991, Increasing returns and economic geography, *Journal of Political Economy*, 99 (3): 483–499.

___ 2002, For richer, *The New York Times Magazine*, October 20.

Ladurie, Emmanuel LeRoy, 2009, *Histoire du climat depuis l'an mil, deux tomes*. Champs Histoire: Editions Flammarion.

Laurent, É., 2011a, *Social-écologie*. Paris: Flammarion.

___ 2011b, Issues in environmental justice within the European Union, *Ecological Economics*, 70 (11), September 15: 1846–1853.

___ 2014a, *Le bel avenir de l'Etat Providence*. Paris, LLL.

___ 2014b, Environmental inequality in France: A theoretical, empirical and policy perspective, in Walker, G., Environmental justice: Empirical concerns and normative reasoning, *Analyse and Kritik*, February, Stuttgart: 251–262.

___ 2014c, Inequality as pollution, pollution as inequality. The social-ecological nexus, Stanford Center on Poverty and Inequality Working Paper.

___ 2017, From the Paris Agreement to the carbon convergence, in *Global Carbon Pricing – The Path to Climate Cooperation*, MacKay, David J.C., Ockenfels, Axel, and Stoft, Steven (eds.), Cambridge: MIT Press.

___ 2018, *Measuring Tomorrow: Accounting for Well-being, Resilience and Sustainability in the 21st Century*. Oxford and Princeton: Princeton University Press.

Laurian, L. A., 2008, Environmental justice in France, *Environmental Planning and Management*, 51(1): 55–79.

Laurian, Lucie and Funderburg, Richard, 2014, Environmental justice in France? A spatio-temporal analysis of incinerator location, *Journal of Environmental Planning Management*, 57 (3): 424–446.

Lefebvre, H., 1972 [1968], *Le Droit à la ville suivi de Espace et politique*. Paris: Anthropos.

Leigh, J.A. (ed.), 1967, *Correspondence complète de Jean Jacques Rousseau*, vol. 4; translated by R. Spang. Geneva, pp. 37–50.

Lelieveld, Jos, Klingmüller, Klaus, Pozzer, Andrea, Pöschl, Ulrich, Fnais, Mohammed, Daiber, Andreas, Münzel, Thomas, 2019, Cardiovascular disease burden from ambient air pollution in Europe reassessed using novel hazard ratio functions, *European Heart Journal*, ehz135.

Lewis, S.L., Maslin, M.A., 2015, Defining the Anthropocene, *Nature*, 519 (7542): 171–180.

Liu, L., 2012, Environmental poverty, a decomposed environmental Kuznets curve, and alternatives: Sustainability lessons from China, *Ecol. Econ.*, 73: 86–92.

Logan, John R., 2006, *The impact of Katrina: Race and Class in Storm-Damaged Neighborhoods*. Brown University, mimeo.

McCarty, Nolan, Poole, Keith T., and Rosenthal, Howard, 2008, *Polarized America: The Dance of Ideology and Unequal Riches*. London: MIT Press.

Malthus, Thomas Robert, 1798 [1826], *An Essay on the Principle of Population*, London: John Murray.

Margai, Florence, 2010, Environmental health hazards and social justice, geographical perspectives on race and class disparities, *Earthscan*.

Marmot, Sir Michael, 2010, *Fair Society, Healthy Lives: A Strategic Review of Health Inequalities in England Post-2010*. The Marmot Review final report. London: University College.

Mersch, Marcel (ed.), 2018, Report of the Independent Commission for Sustainable Equality, Progressive Society, Brussels.

Milanovic, Branko, 2016, *Global Inequality. A New Approach for the Age of Globalization*. Cambridge, Harvard University Press.

Mill, John Stuart, 1848, *Principles of Political Economy with Some of Their Applications to Social Philosophy*, Book 4, Chapter 6, Of the Stationary State. London: J.W. Parker.

Mohai, Paul and Saha, Robin, 2015, Which came first, people or pollution? A review of theory and evidence from longitudinal environmental justice studies, *Environmental Research Letters*, 10.

Moore, J.W. 2013, Anthropocene, capitalocene, and the myth of industrialization, Part I, *World-Ecological Imaginations* (May 13).

___ 2015, *Capitalism in the Web of Life: Ecology and the Accumulation of Capital*. New York, Verso.

___ 2016, *Anthropocene or Capitalocene? Nature, History, and the Crisis of Capitalism*. Oakland: PM Press.

Motesharrei, Safa, Rivas, Jorges, Kalnay, Eugenia, 2014, Human and nature dynamics (HANDY): Modeling inequality and use of resources in the collapse or sustainability of societies, *Ecological Economics*, 101, May: 90–102.

Motta, Eric V.S., Raymann, Kasie, Moran, Nancy A., 2018, Glyphosate perturbs the gut microbiota of honey bees, *Proceedings of the National Academy of Sciences*, 115 (41), October: 10305–10310.

Muir, John, 1938, John of the Mountains: The Unpublished Journals of John Muir, p. 313.

Mumford, Lewis, 1931, *The Brown Decades: A Study of the Arts in America, 1865–1895*. New York: Harcourt, Brace, p. 78.

Murali, I.V. and Manickam, Krishna Valli, 2017, Environmental Management Science and Engineering for Industry, *Elsevier*: 1–4.

Musango, J.K., Currie, P., and Robinson, B., 2017, *Urban Metabolism for Resource Efficient Cities: From Theory to Implementation*. Paris: UN Environment.

Mutter, J.C., 2010, Disasters widen the rich–poor gap, *Nature*, 466: 104, published online August 25.

___ 2015, *Disaster Profiteers: How Natural Disasters Make the Rich Richer and the Poor Even Poorer*. London: Palgrave Macmillan through Saint Martin's Press.

Nash, Roderick, 1972, American environmental history: A new teaching frontier, *Pacific Historical Review*, 41 (3), August: 362–372.

Nobel, 2019, Alfred Nobel's will. NobelPrize.org. Nobel Media AB. https://www.nobelprize.org/alfred-nobel/alfred-nobels-will-2/.

Nordhaus, William, 2008. *A Question of Balance: Weighing the Options on Global Warming Policies*. New Haven, CT: Yale University Press.

Nordhaus, W. and Tobin, J., 1973, Is Growth Obsolete? in *The Measurement of Economic and Social Performance*, ed. Milton Moss. New York: National Bureau of Economic Research.

Ocasio-Cortez, H., 2019/2020, Res.109 – Recognizing the duty of the Federal Government to create a Green New Deal. 116th Congress.

Odum, E.P., 1953, *Fundamentals of Ecology*. Philadelphia: W.B. Saunders Company.

OECD, 2008, *Household Behaviour and the Environment: Reviewing the Evidence*. Paris.

OECD, 2018, *Effective Carbon Rates 2018, Pricing Carbon Emissions Through Taxes and Emissions Trading*.

Offer, Avner and Söderberg, Gabriel, 2016, *The Nobel Factor. The Prize in Economics, Social Democracy and the Market Turn*. Princeton: Princeton University Press.

Okun, Arthur M. and Summers, Lawrence H., 2015, *Equality and Efficiency: The Big Tradeoff*. Brookings Institution Press. JSTOR, www.jstor.org/stable/10.7864/j.ctt13wztjk.

Olson, M., 1965, *The Logic of Collective Action: Public Goods and the Theory of Groups*. Cambridge and London: Harvard University Press.

O'Neil, Cathy, 2017, *Weapons of Math Destruction: How Big Data Increases Inequality and Threatens Democracy*. New York: Crown Publishers.

Ostrom, E., 1990, *Governing the Commons: The Evolution of Institutions for Collective Actions*. Cambridge: Cambridge University Press.

___ 2009, A general framework for analyzing sustainability of social-ecological systems, *Science*, 325: 419.

___ 2010, Beyond markets and states: Polycentric governance of complex economic systems, *American Economic Review*, 100 (3): 641–672.

___ 2012, Nested externalities and polycentric institutions: Must we wait for global solutions to climate change before taking actions at other scales? *Economic Theory*, 49: 353–369.

Otto, Ilona M., Kim, Kyoung Mi, Dubrovsky, Nika, and Lucht, Wolfgang, 2019, Shift the focus from the super-poor to the super-rich, *Nature Climate Change*, 9: 82–84.

Pareto, Wilfredo, 1982, *Œuvres complètes*, 26 vols. Paris: Genève-Paris, 1964–1982.

Pascal, M. and Medina, S., 2012, *Résumé des résultats du projet Aphekom 2008–2011. Des clefs pour mieux comprendre les impacts de la pollution atmosphérique urbaine sur la santé en Europe*. Saint-Maurice: Institut de veille sanitaire.

Pastor, M., Morello-Frosch, R., and Sadd, J., 2006, Breathless: Air quality, schools, and environmental justice in California, *Policy Studies Journal*, 34 (3): 337–362.

Pastor, Manuel et al., 2006, *In the Wake of the Storm: Environment, Disaster and Race after Katrina*. New York: Russell Sage Foundation.

Payne, Rodger A., 1995, Freedom and the environment, *Journal of Democracy*, 6 (3), July: 41–55.

Peters, G. P., Davis, S. J., and Andrew, R., 2012, A synthesis of carbon in international trade, *Biogeosciences*, 9: 3247–3276.

Pigou, Arthur C., 1932 [1920], *The Economics of Welfare*, 4th edn. London: Macmillan.

Piketty, Thomas and Saez, Emmanuel, 2013, Income Inequality in the United States, 1913–1998, *Quarterly Journal of Economics*, 118 (1): 1–39. (Tables and Figures Updated to 2012, September 2013).

Pinchot, Gifford, 1909, Conservation, in addresses and proceedings of the first National Conservation Congress, August 26–28, Seattle, Washington: The executive committee of the National Conservation Congress, p. 72.

Prüss-Üstün, A. and Corvalán, C., 2006, Preventing disease through healthy environments. Toward an estimate of the environmental burden of disease, World Health Organization.

Quesnay, F., 2005, Œuvres économiques complètes et autres textes, éditées par C. Théré, Charles, L. and Perrot, J.-C., 2 vols. Paris: Institut national d'études démographiques.

Ramsey, F.P., 1928, A mathematical theory of saving, *The Economic Journal*, 38 (152): 543–559.

Rawls, John, 1999, *A Theory of Justice*, revd edn. Cambridge, MA: Harvard University Press.

Ricardo, David, 1821 [1817], *On the Principles of Political Economy and Taxation*. London: John Murray, Albemarle-Street.

Rich, Nathaniel, 2018, Losing earth: The decade we almost stopped climate change, *The New York Times Magazine*, August, 1.

Rodrik, D., 2016, *Economics Rules: The Rights and Wrongs of the Dismal Science*. New York: W.W. Norton.

Roth, Alvin E., 2002, The economist as engineer: Game theory, experimentation, and computation as tools for design economics, *Econometrica*, 70 (4), July: 1341–1378.

Schaffartzik, A., Mayer, A., Gingrich, S., Eisenmenger, N., Loy, C., and Krausmann, F., 2014, The global metabolic transition: Regional patterns and trends of global material flows, 1950–2010, *Global Environmental Change* 26: 87–97.

Schlosberg, D., 2007, *Defining Environmental Justice: Theories, Movements, and Nature.* Oxford: Oxford University Press.

Schlosberg, D. and Carruthers, D., 2010, Indigenous struggles, environmental justice, and community capabilities, *Global Environmental Politics*, 10 (4): 12–35.

Sen, Amartya K., 2009, *The Idea of Justice*. Cambridge, MA: The Belknap Press of Harvard University Press.

Serret, Ysé and Johnstone, Nick, 2006, Distributional effects of environmental policy: Conclusions and policy implications, in *The Distributional Effects of Environmental Policy*. London: Edward Elgar Publishing.

Setoa, Karen C., Güneralpa, Burak, and Hutyrac, Lucy R., 2012, Global forecasts of urban expansion to 2030 and direct impacts on biodiversity and carbon pools, *PNAS*, September.

Shiva, V., 1988, *Staying Alive: Women, Ecology and Survival in India*. New Delhi: Kali for Women.

Srinivasan, U. Thara, Carey, Susan P., Hallstein, Eric, Higgins, Paul A.T., Kerr, Amber C., Koteen, Laura E., Smith, Adam B., Watson, Reg, Harte, John, and Norgaard, Richard B., 2008, The debt of nations and the distribution of ecological impacts from human activities, *Proceedings of the National Academy of Sciences*, 105 (5), February: 1768–1773.

Steffen, Will et al., 2015, Planetary boundaries, *Science*, 347 (6223), February.

Stern, Nicholas, 2008, The economics of climate change, *American Economic Review*, 98 (2): 1–37.

Stiglitz, Joseph, 2012, *The Price of Inequality: How Today's Divided Society Endangers Our Future*. New York: W.W. Norton.

Sukhdev, Pavan, 2011, Putting a price on nature: The economics of ecosystems and biodiversity, *Solutions*, 1 (6), January 6: 34–43.

TEEB, 2010, *The Economics of Ecosystems and Biodiversity: Mainstreaming the Economics of Nature: A Synthesis of the Approach, Conclusions and Recommendations of TEEB*.

Victor, A.P., 1972, *Pollution: Economy and Environment*. London: Georges Allen and Unwin Ltd.

Vitousek, Peter M., Mooney, Harold A., Lubchenco, Jane, and Melillo, Jerry M., 1997, Human domination of earth's ecosystems, *Science*, n.s., 277 (5325), July 25: 494–499.

Voltaire, 1756, *Poèmes sur le désastre de Lisbonne, et sur la loi naturelle*, Geneva: Cramer, Bibliothèque nationale de France.

Walker et al., 2018, Formal ratification of the subdivision of the Holocene Series/Epoch

(Quaternary System/Period): Two new Global Boundary Stratotype Sections and Points (GSSPs) and three new stages/subseries, Episodes, IUGS.

Walras, Léon, 1988, Éléments d'économie politique pure, Lausanne, 2 fasc., 1874–1877, in C. Mouchot dir., Œuvres économiques complètes d'Auguste et de Léon Walras, vol. VIII, Paris: Economica.

Watts, Nick et al., 2015, The Lancet Countdown: Tracking progress on health and climate change, *Lancet*, Volume 389, Issue 10074, 1151–1164.

___ 2017, The Lancet Countdown on Health and climate change: From 25 years of inaction to a global transformation for public health. *Lancet*, October 30, 2017.

Weitzman, M.L., Prices vs. Quantities. *Review of Economic Studies* [Internet]. 1974; October, 41 (4): 477–491.

Welch, Finis, 1999, In defense of inequality, *American Economic Review*, 89 (2): 1–17.

Wiedmann, Thomas O., Schandl, Heinz, Lenzen, Manfred, Moran, Daniel, Suh, Sangwon, West, James, and Kanemoto, Keiichiro, 2015, The material footprint of nations, *Proceedings of the National Academy of Sciences*, 112 (20), May: 6271–6276.

Wilkinson, Richard and Pickett, Kate, 2009, *The Spirit Level: Why More Equal Societies Almost Always Do Better*. London: Allen Lane.

___ 2018, *The Inner Level: How More Equal Societies Reduce Stress, Restore Sanity and Improve Everyone's Wellbeing*. London: Penguin.

Wisner, Ben, Blaikie, Piers, Cannon, Terry, and Davis, Ian, 2004, *At Risk: Natural Hazards, People's Vulnerability and Disasters*. 2nd edn. London and New York: Routledge.

Wolman, Abel, 1965, The metabolism of cities, *Scientific American*, 213: 179–190.

Worster, D., 1979, *Dust Bowl: The Southern Plains in the 1930s*. New York: Oxford University Press.

World Bank, *The World Development Report 2009: Reshaping Economic Geography*. Washington.

World People's Conference on Climate Change and the Rights of Mother Earth, 2010, Cochabamba, Bolivia. April 22, People's Agreement, available at https://pwccc.wordpress.com/2010/04/24/peoples-agreement/.

World Scientists' Warning to Humanity: A Second Notice, William J. Ripple, Christopher Wolf, Thomas M. Newsome, Mauro Galetti, Mohammed Alamgir, Eileen Crist, Mahmoud I. Mahmoud, William F. Laurance, 15,364 scientist signatories from 184 countries, *BioScience*, 67 (12), December 1, 2017: 1026–1028.

WWF, 2014, The Living Planet Report.

York, R., Rosa, E.A., and T. Dietz, T., 2003, Footprints on the earth: The environmental consequences of modernity, *American Sociological Review*, 68: 279–300.

# Index